THE FIRST WALL STREET

THE FIRST ❦
WALL STREET

CHESTNUT STREET,

PHILADELPHIA, *and*

the BIRTH *of*

AMERICAN FINANCE

ROBERT E. WRIGHT

THE UNIVERSITY OF CHICAGO PRESS ✺ CHICAGO AND LONDON

ROBERT E. WRIGHT is clinical associate professor of economics at the Leonard N. Stern School of Business, New York University. He is the author of *Origins of Commercial Banking in America, 1750–1800; Hamilton Unbound: Finance and the Creation of the American Republic;* and *The Wealth of Nations Rediscovered: Integration and Expansion in American Financial Markets, 1780–1850.*

The University of Chicago Press, Chicago 60637
The University of Chicago Press, Ltd., London
© 2005 by The University of Chicago
All rights reserved. Published 2005
Printed in the United States of America

14 13 12 11 10 09 08 07 06 05   1 2 3 4 5

ISBN: 0-226-91026-1

Library of Congress Cataloging-in-Publication Data

Wright, Robert E. (Robert Eric), 1969–
   The first Wall Street : Chestnut Street, Philadelphia, and the birth of American finance / Robert E. Wright.
      p.   cm.
   Includes bibliographical references and index.
   ISBN 0-226-91026-1 (alk. paper)
   1. Stock exchanges—Pennsylvania—Philadelphia—History.   2. Stock exchanges—New York (State)—New York—History.   3. Stock exchanges—United States—History.   I. Title.
   HG5131.P5W75   2005
   332.64′273′09034—dc22   2005009428

JUN 1 4 2006

CONTENTS

ACKNOWLEDGMENTS

No book every really has a single author. (Though, of course, I alone take all responsibility for any errors of fact or interpretation—as well as all the royalties.) Most generally, this book would not have been possible without the loving affections of my parents and brother Tom or my own family: Deborah, Stephanie, Madison, Alexander, and TJ. Nor would it have been possible without the years of "postgraduate" education I received in the classrooms, libraries, and seminar rooms of Temple University, the University of Virginia, New York University, and the sundry other schools that provided me temporary succor. The most helpful of my colleagues and friends have been David Jack Cowen, John James, Ron Michener, Sharon Murphy, George D. Smith, Richard E. Sylla, and Jack Wilson. I also have to thank some of my MBA students at New York University, especially Aimee Fusco, who suggested that I place more emphasis on modern Wall Street early in the book, and Victor Cohen and Jake Sigmund, who always kept the faith. Finally, special thanks goes to editor Alex Schwartz and the excellent anonymous reviewers that he found to comment on earlier versions of the manuscript.

1

OF FINANCIAL MARKETS
AND MARKETPLACES

"I got that Wall Street job I wanted!" one of my best students announced.

"Wonderful," I replied, "as I will be consulting for a Wall Street firm next year. We should have lunch together at least once a week."

"Definitely," he stated, enthusiastically.

The student and I never met for lunch, though we continued to maintain a close professional relationship via e-mail and telephone. No, we were not too busy to eat or to meet. As it turns out, we both conflated a concept with a physical place. Admittedly, I was closer, consulting for a company in Hanover Square, near Delmonico's, just a few blocks south of Wall Street. My erstwhile student, though, worked for a financial services company in a business park off Route 1, in the wilds of New Jersey, a good hour away by train. Our mistakes were honest ones. Wall Street *is* a physical place, about a quarter-mile-long thoroughfare that runs uphill from the East River to Manhattan's Trinity Church. But, of course, for most people the phrase "Wall Street" connotes much more.

In the same way that "Washington" has become synonymous with "the federal government," Wall Street symbolizes not just New York City's financial district but the entire nation's financial system. It doesn't matter that most financial firms are, in fact, not located on Wall Street or even in downtown New York, or that some of our most important financial exchanges are found in Chicago. Both those who admire and revile the financial system find "Wall Street" a convenient, if often technically incorrect, shorthand.

Financial systems often find themselves inexorably linked to physical places, like Boston's Boylston Street, London's Lombard Street, Paris's rue Quincampoix, or Bangkok's Asoke Street. Many people, it appears, have difficulty comprehending *markets,* wall-less institutions where the abstract forces of supply and demand interact to determine prices and quantities traded. So they personalize those forces, conflating the abstract market with the many *marketplaces* where supply and demand play out in day-to-day life. This propensity is particularly pronounced when it comes to the financial system, a series of interrelated markets for various types of promises to pay (hereafter IOUs). For the uninitiated, IOUs and their markets are bewildering, to say the least. It is little wonder, then, that people make the complexity more manageable by equating the financial system with something tangible and easily identifiable, like a city street.

People do not identify the financial system with any old random street. They choose the thoroughfare that appears to contain the largest density of important financial firms, businesses employed in some aspect of the IOU trade. Financial companies, after all, tend to cluster geographically. Close proximity lowers transaction costs between firms, serves as a customer and employee magnet, and creates other side benefits (aka "positive externalities"). Of course, there are limits to those benefits, and too much clustering leads to adverse consequences, like high rents and easy corporate espionage, so financial firms are usually found peppered around districts rather than densely congregated on individual city blocks. Although clustering is always incomplete, an area relatively densely populated with financial firms—the metaphorical if not the physical center of the financial district—almost invariably arises.

Why a particular street within a given financial district takes a leadership role is a difficult question. Chance and history probably play the largest roles. Once established, the positive external benefits that the street or district creates become the justification of its continued existence. Financial districts tend to enjoy lives so long that to successive generations they look like permanent features of the financial landscape. But like everything else in life, they are transitory. This book is the story of a financial district eventually shorn of its luster, dethroned from its financial kingship, if you will. Many people, including some eminent historians, assume that Wall Street has always been the focal point of the U.S. financial system. But we all know what happens when we assume, or rather when we "ass-u-me." As it turns out, America's first "Wall Street"—to wit, its first leading financial district—was in Philadelphia, not Manhattan. Centered on Chestnut Street, Philadelphia's financial district ruled the nation's financial system until 1836.

Chestnut Street was one of early Philadelphia's "tree" streets, straight, broad thoroughfares like Walnut, Pine, and Spruce that ran westward from the Delaware to the Schuylkill River. One block south of High Street (later Market), the city's central east–west avenue, Chestnut Street by 1794 lay in the center of the most densely populated, highest rent section of the city. It was also home to the State House (aka Independence Hall), the Library, the War Office, the president's mansion, and the New Playhouse, as well as the Bank of the United States, the Bank of North America, and the Bank of Pennsylvania, three important early commercial banks. Chestnut Street was, in short, the place to be, at least until Andrew Jackson came to power in 1829.[1]

Chestnut Street's rise and fall forms the narrative core of this book. But in the broadest terms, *The First Wall Street* is about economic growth, increased real per capita aggregate output. In simpler terms, it is about wealth creation and the reasons why a few nations produce much more wealth per person than most other countries manage to do. A brief overview of the major components of the financial system and their importance to U.S. economic growth is therefore in order.[2]

✺ Between 1770 and 1900, the English-speaking settlements along the East Coast of North America transformed themselves from a series of agricultural colonies into the most powerful industrial nation in the world. How did the American colonies do so, where so many other former colonies have stumbled? The answer is at the same time both simple and complex: competitive financial markets and institutions. But what does that phrase mean? And how does finance lead to growth?[3]

Early Americans could not simply extract precious metals or liquids from the ground and live off the proceeds. They had to work hard felling timber, plowing fields, and bringing their wares to market. But hard work alone was not the key to wealth creation. Early Americans had to work "smart," to discover ways of working more *efficiently*. They struggled to get another bushel of wheat out of each acre, another hogshead of tobacco out of each field, another bale of cotton out of each plantation, another ton of iron out of each furnace blast.[4]

Such is the nature of human beings, to strive to get more output from a given amount of input. All peoples want to be productive so that they can enjoy more wealth and more leisure. Not all people, however, have access to institutions that make increased levels of productivity possible. The mere desire to be more efficient is insufficient to drive productivity to higher levels because efficiency comes with start-up costs. Those costs will eventually be repaid many times over, but the initial cost of increased productivity is often a barrier that thwarts the introduction of innovations or reforms. The farmer knows that fertilizer would increase his crop yields more than enough to pay the cost of the fertilizer, but he cannot afford the initial outlay months before his crops will be harvested and sold. The planter knows more slaves would pay for themselves many times over with increased tobacco or cotton production, but alas he cannot afford to buy or raise them. The ironmaster realizes that he could produce more iron if only he could purchase a new, improved bellows. In each of those cases, the desire and the knowledge to increase productivity is present but yet the improvement goes unrealized.[5]

The missing component is the financial sector, firms and markets that help entrepreneurs to borrow to make productive investments in their businesses. If the farmer could borrow, he could buy the fertilizer, produce more wheat, and repay the loan plus the interest. The planter could use a loan to buy or rent slaves, who would grow more staples and again leave the borrower *and* the lender better off (everyone but the poor slave). If a financial sector exists, the ironmaster could borrow to purchase the bellows that would help him to create more iron and more profits. With finance, fertilizer and tool suppliers enjoy higher incomes. And, of course, the world is blessed with more wheat, tobacco, cotton, iron, and higher employment.[6]

At its most basic level, financial history is the story of the competition between different means of linking the savings of investors to the spending of entrepreneurs. Investors (savers, lenders) are economic entities—households, business firms, or governments—that run a budget surplus, earning more in a given time period than they consume. Entrepreneurs (spenders, borrowers), by contrast, run a budget deficit, expending more than they earn.[7]

Investors possess the excess funds that entrepreneurs need to fund their enterprises. Ergo, trade potentially benefits both parties: investors provide immediate funds to entrepreneurs in return for something of value, most often a promise (IOU) that at some point in the future the money will be repaid, and then some. Depending on the precise form the IOU takes, it might be called a loan, a bond, or a stock (an equity share).

Given the risk that the promise will not be honored, trading IOUs is intrinsically more difficult than trading other goods. Unlike buying gold or carrots or a haircut, the quality of which is readily measured, buying an

IOU is precarious. Because risk and return are positively related (an increase in risk implies an increase in return, and vice versa), those entrepreneurs with the riskiest projects, other things being equal, are the most eager to borrow. Thus, a selection bias known as "adverse selection" exists in the IOU market.

A related problem, called "moral hazard," also impedes the easy trading of IOUs. Entrepreneurs can concoct ways to avoid paying the IOU when it comes due. They might move away, go bankrupt, or falsely claim that they can afford to repay only a fraction of the amount due. More subtly, they can use the funds to engage in riskier ventures than they promised to, forcing added unwanted risk on the lender.

Trading IOUs is not easy, but it is extremely important. Without such trades, potential investors reduce their productivity so as not to accumulate sterile wealth. Moreover, potential entrepreneurs with good ideas but no funds never complete that invention, expand that factory, penetrate that new market, or hire those additional workers. The world, not to mention the entrepreneur and the investor, is left poorer than it would have otherwise been.

Luckily, financial intermediaries and markets can reduce the special problems of trading IOUs. Intermediaries are financial firms that specialize in reducing adverse selection and moral hazard. For at least the past five centuries, two major types of intermediaries, banks and insurance companies, have predominated.

Banks are financial firms that make loans and accept deposits. Depositors are investors who lend to the bank because they are reasonably certain that the bank will honor its IOUs to them, perhaps because the bank's deposits are insured, or because it has been around a long time and owns a valuable building, or because its balance sheets are credible and show it to be in good condition (positive net worth or equity capital, i.e., assets [what the bank owns] > liabilities [what it owes]).[8]

Banks use their deposits or other borrowings to purchase entrepreneurs' IOUs. They are much better at this than the average individual investor because they specialize in screening loan applicants to pick the lowest risks and in monitoring borrowers to reduce the chances that they will default on their IOUs. Banks' gross profits are simply the difference between the return on their assets, the IOUs (e.g., loans) that they purchase, and the cost of their liabilities, the IOUs (e.g., deposits) that they sell. For instance, in 1795 the Bank of North America, an important Philadelphia commercial bank, paid zero interest on its deposits, but received over 12 percent on its assets. After deducting its small overhead for salaries, office supplies, and other business costs, it netted 12 percent on the year. Banks, like the Bank of North America, that issue banknotes—zero-interest bearer IOUs—also earn seigniorage, the profits that accrue to issuers of money. (Today central banks monopolize the power to issue notes, but in early America privately owned banks emitted their own notes.) Banks also supplemented their revenues with fees, the importance of which fluctuated over time and place.

Banks came in a variety of flavors. Commercial banks—the oldest, largest, and most important category of banks—dealt mostly with relatively large businesses. Savings banks, like their modern cousins, mutual funds, specialized in investing the savings of households. Central banks developed and/or implemented national monetary policy, that is, they induced changes in the money supply and interest rates. Investment banks were not banks at all, at least not in the sense of depository institutions. Rather, they served as financial market facilitators.

Banks are "intermediaries" because they are intermediate between investors (depositors or noteholders) and entrepreneurs (borrowers). Investors buy IOUs from the bank, which in turn buys the IOUs of entrepreneurs. Insurance companies are likewise intermediaries because they serve as a link between policyholders (investors) and borrowers. The main difference between banks and insurers is that the IOUs of the latter are usually based on some contingency, for example, someone's death or damage to physical property.

Insurance, like banking, has a long, complex history. Early insurers usually specialized in one of three areas: life, marine, or fire. (Today insurers usually specialize in either life and health or property and casualty [tort liability]. The former encompasses term and whole life insurance, life annuities, disability insurance, and medical cost reimbursement, the latter indemnity from losses on everything from automobiles to homes to medical malpractice.) The contingent nature of insurers' IOUs placed large technical demands on them that slowed the pace of their development relative to banks until a series of empirical, conceptual, and computational hurdles were overcome in the eighteenth, nineteenth, and twentieth centuries, respectively. For instance, reliable mortality tables—statistical predictions of death rates at different ages—were a product of the second half of the nineteenth century.[9]

The second major institution that helps to reduce the problems associated with trading IOUs are financial markets. Although market facilitators like investment banks or brokerages may serve to introduce buyers to sellers of IOUs, financial markets are open forums where investors directly buy entrepreneurs' IOUs.[10]

IOUs come in a variety of specific contract forms: simple loans, where the lender takes the interest at the end of the loan term; discount loans or discount bonds, where the interest is taken up front; amortized installment loans, like modern home mortgages, where borrowers make interest and principal payments concurrently at stated predetermined intervals; balloon loans or coupon bonds, where interest payments are made at stated predetermined intervals and the principal comes due at the end of the contract; equity, where investors receive a share of a business's assets and profits; various hybrid securities that are part equity and part bond or that are convertible from one type of IOU into another. All of those types of IOUs have long histories, but some, like simple and discount loans, were more important early on, while others, like hybrid securities, did not come into their own until the nineteenth century.

IOUs also vary in their maturity, which is to say the length of time the promise encompasses. IOUs that promise repayment within one year are considered short term; they are called "commercial paper" if sold by a business firm and "bills" if sold by a government. The markets for them are called "money markets." Short-term IOUs denominated in the currency of a foreign nation is called foreign exchange; markets for foreign exchange IOUs are crucial for international trade. Intermediate-term IOUs mature, or pay off, in one to ten years. IOUs for periods greater than ten years are considered long term. Markets for intermediate and long-term IOUs are called "capital markets." Securities markets—foreign exchange, money, and capital markets—have been around many centuries. The markets today are larger and faster than their ancestors were, but little else has changed, save the increased use of sophisticated financial derivatives like forward and futures contracts, options, swaps, and combinations thereof.

The economic growth spurts of the northern Italian city-states, Holland, England, the United States, and Japan in the sixteenth, seventeenth, eighteenth, nineteenth, and twentieth centuries, respectively, were each proceeded by financial revolutions, periods of intense innovation in banking, insurance, securities markets, and monetary policy. Now, just because A happens before B does not mean that A *caused* B. But when A almost always precedes B, and B almost never occurs without A, one begins to suspect a causal relationship, particularly if one can tell a compelling story about how A leads inexorably to B. The story related here is compelling: the financial system taps entrepreneurial energy by ensuring that good wealth-creating ideas do not die of neglect. In this view, Americans, or "Yankees," were not any more ingenious than other peoples; they simply found it easier to sell their IOUs to fund the creation of their inventions and improvements.[11]

↙○ No industrial or postindustrial economy can long thrive without access to a modern financial sector such as Wall Street. No country better bears out that claim than Japan. In the 1980s, "Japan Inc." appeared poised to buy up the entire world, including the United States. American pundits and policymakers called for the adoption of Japanese-style trade and industrial policies and financial arrangements. Happily, such reforms were not implemented. By the early 1990s, Japan's economy was moribund and it has yet to recover. Though a variety of factors helps to explain the end of the Japanese economic "miracle," the failure of the Japanese financial system is high on most experts' lists. As it turns out, Japanese banks managed to hide billions of dollars of bad loans for a very long time. When news of the banks' de facto insolvency broke, the Japanese stock market, which had been flying high for a decade, crashed and Japanese real estate prices also rapidly returned to earth. Suddenly, the Japanese were not so rich anymore. They eventually sold back many of the high-profile U.S. purchases they had made, taking big losses in the process.[12]

Wall Street's record is also imperfect. Many blame the 1929 stock market crash for the Great Depression. That is something of an exaggeration, but it is clear that the damage done to the financial system by the crash and the subsequent economic downturn was responsible for the Depression's unprecedented depth and length. Little wonder, then, that financial panics and corporate governance defalcations usually provoke rapid and vigorous policy responses.[13]

The first line of defense against financial panic is the Federal Reserve System, America's central bank. Though like most federal agencies it is headquartered in Washington, D.C., the real heart of the beast is the Federal Reserve Bank of New York (FRBNY) in lower Manhattan, just north of Wall Street. One of the Fed's major goals is to promote financial and economic stability. It does so almost exclusively by increasing the money supply, by ordering the FRBNY to purchase IOUs in the open market. In exchange for the IOUs, sellers receive deposits or Federal Reserve notes that they can use to make payments to other parties. Apparently, nothing calms nerves more than truckloads of new cash.[14]

Except during crises, though, the Fed is reticent to increase the money supply too quickly. Creating money does not increase wealth but instead simply causes prices to rise. So, many times the FRBNY finds itself decreasing the money supply by selling IOUs in the open market. In such cases, the buyers give up cash in exchange for the securities. Once safely at the Fed, the cash is no longer part of the effective money supply (unless it is later returned to active circulation in the economy). By engaging in such "open-market operations," the FRBNY makes daily adjustments to the money supply that the Fed hopes will keep the economy on an even keel. That means keeping inflation in check, interest rates stable, unemployment low, and per capita output growing. For the last twenty years or so, the Fed has done an outstanding job.[15]

The Fed is also charged with regulating many of America's most important banks. Regulation of the financial aspects of other types of companies, though, falls mostly on the shoulders of the Securities and Exchange Commission (SEC). The SEC, working in conjunction with the stock exchanges and the Financial Accounting Standards Board (FASB), tries to ensure that publicly traded companies disclose important financial information to potential investors and the general public. Frauds and scandals still occur, but they are usually quickly squelched before they do serious damage to the financial system or the economy.[16]

Despite high-profile examples, like the Martha Stewart insider trading scandal, the simple fact is that the financial sector has generally provided U.S. businesses and consumers with reliable high-quality products. Almost every American has, at one time or another, had a checking or savings account, obtained a loan, made a payment with a money order, or worked for a company that used the financial system to get started, stay afloat, or meet payroll.

For most (though by no means all) Americans, the financial system is a ubiquitous, if too infrequently appreciated, part of their lives. From birth to death, the financial system cradles them in a web of "private security" even more important to their well-being than the government's "social security." At their birth, if not before, their parents take out life insurance policies on themselves—just in case. Many babies and children save via bank accounts, savings bonds, and, increasingly, 529 education saving plans. Their parents save for retirement with 401k or 403b plans, Roth IRAs, life annuities, and a potpourri of other financial vehicles. Long gone are the days when parents "saved" for retirement by having more children! Most Americans also insure their worldly possessions, including their homes, businesses, automobiles, and personal effects, from loss. They even insure themselves against liability suits and identity theft. Moreover, they use services, like medical and home repair services, safe in the knowledge that the providers are bonded and insured as well as licensed.

Americans are also prodigious borrowers. They borrow long term to fund the purchase of automobiles, education, and homes. They borrow short term, via convenient plastic cards, to smooth their consumption and to fund Christmas and vacation expenses. Though denigrated by some, credit card debt increases Americans' freedom by temporarily unleashing them from income constraints. Though some of the debts, even the long-term ones, inevitably go bad, the financial system anticipates and accounts for the losses.

Businesses also benefit from Wall Street's expertise, of course. The U.S. economy is the most productive in the world. Much of the thanks for that goes to the financial sector. Although some businesses can grow by plowing profits back into the company, most cannot. If they are to grow to reach their efficient scale (size) or scope (breadth), companies must borrow by obtaining loans, selling their bonds, or selling shares in themselves. And al-most no nonfinancial company can easily match their receipts, which tend to come in irregular clumps, with their expenditures, which tend to be reg-ular, like monthly payroll, rents, and utility bills. Accordingly, most compa-nies use the financial sector to obtain short-term financing to tide them over until they collect the next big boost of revenue. They do so by obtain-ing bank loans or lines of credit; larger ones sell their commercial paper, short-term bonds, directly to investors.

Finally, the financial system is the most efficient way to make or collect payments from numerous distant suppliers and customers. Cash couriers would simply be too inefficient in most instances. Without such seemingly innocuous services as checks, insurance, and loans, the pace of business in America would slow and perhaps even grind to a halt.[17]

The financial sector is an important one in the economy in its own right. In 1997 America's financial sector was composed of over 200,000 different firms employing some 5.835 million people. The sector generated over $2 trillion in revenues and was directly or indirectly responsible for almost all payments made in licit transactions. Competition within most parts of the industry is intense, so financial firms continually seek ways to cut costs and boost output. Many have already shifted back office operations to cheaper areas outside of population centers and in some cases out of the country entirely.

Most major U.S. financial firms remain headquartered in Manhattan, but that could quickly change. Like most modern service providers, financial firms' value lies in their employees and databases, not in their physical cap-ital. Should conditions warrant, firms could relatively cheaply and quickly shift functions to new locations or even relocate entirely.[18] In a world of virtual states, hollow companies, and decentralized networks, the continued predominance of Wall Street, the physical place, is by no means clear. The only certainty is that the financial sector, regardless of its physical locations, will remain an important part of the continued growth of the American economy, as it has been since 1790. Wall Street and the U.S. financial system, after all, have not always been synonymous. In the nation's first decades, Philadelphia's Chestnut Street led the American financial sector and hence was the brain center of the new nation's burgeoning economy.[19]

✓○ I do *not* mean to suggest that Philadelphia was *entirely* responsible for America's transition from colony to world power. After all, financial developments similar to those described in this book took place throughout much of the North and in a few pockets in the South. Philadelphia *led* the charge to modernity, but New York, Boston, Baltimore, Charleston, and, a little later, New Orleans also played important roles. But Chestnut Street predominated, at least until 1836, for four basic reasons.[20]

First, Philadelphia was the nation's political capital most years between the revolutionary tumults of the mid-1770s and the official founding of Washington, D.C., in 1801. Moreover, early Washington was no threat to becoming a financial center. It was not a "real" city but rather just a meeting place for Congress a few months of the year. A British diplomat noted that "one May take a ride of several hours within the precincts without meeting a single individual to disturb one's meditations." The capital's vacant, muddy streets and anemic commercial activity certainly could not challenge Philadelphia's financial supremacy.[21]

Second, Philadelphia became the new nation's commercial capital, replacing London as the focal point of mercantile information. It was home to the country's first and most important business periodicals—simple but valuable sheets of paper containing current prices, the names of ships entering and leaving port, and political news important to trade or the general health of the economy. Merchants throughout the nation and, indeed, the Atlantic world subscribed to Philadelphia's periodicals; local newspapers throughout the land often reproduced some or all of the most important prices. In short, everyone in trade wanted to know "What is happening in Philadelphia?"

Third, Philadelphia's early financiers were the nation's greatest innovators, responsible for America's first forays into negotiable ground rents; marine, fire, and life insurance; commercial, savings, and investment banking; building and loan societies; and securities markets. Only after those early financiers—men like Clement Biddle, Stephen Girard, Michael Hillegas,

Robert Morris, and Thomas Willing—had passed away did Wall Street have a chance to overtake Philadelphia. Financial innovators also graced other cities. But in the early years, Philly firms were always the first to the American market.

Last but hardly least, the headquarters of both early U.S. central banks, the first and the second Bank of the United States, graced the Chestnut Street district. Today attention centers on the Federal Reserve because, like those early central banks, it exerts much influence over the size of the money supply and hence interest and inflation rates. It was no different in the eighteenth and early nineteenth centuries, except that "Fed watchers" were then called "national bank observers." So only after the second Bank of the United States followed Philadelphia's early financiers to the grave could Wall Street emerge as the nation's preeminent financial center.[22]

As simple and important as this story is, scholars and teachers have, until very recently, largely ignored it. Financial history is almost completely absent from high school and college curricula. Far too few Americans, therefore, recognize the financial sector's crucial contribution to the American way of life. In fact, many Americans evince fear and misunderstanding of financial institutions, markets, and their participants. Far too many think of finance as a form of gambling or, worse yet, stealing. They suffer the creation and perpetuation of regulations, many of which are unnecessary and some of which are outright pernicious.

Maybe this book, with its patient descriptions of the essential contributions that financial institutions and markets made to early U.S. economic growth, will help to change the public's perception of finance. If you take away the banks, the insurance companies, and the securities markets, you also take away the farms, factories, and infrastructure that separated America from most of the rest of the world. This book is the textbook that Americans should have read in high school or college. Readers should come away from it with a deep and abiding respect for the "capitalists," "financiers," "moneyed men," and "speculators" who drove the financial services sector both then and now. They will also gain a basic understanding of today's financial scene. For although the subjects discussed are over a century and a half old, the basics have not changed. A bond is still a bond; moral hazard is still moral hazard. Readers will not be able to get a job on the foreign exchange desk at a major investment bank just for having read it, but CNBC reports and the *Wall Street Journal* should start to make a heck of a lot more sense.

Chapter 2 shows that already in the colonial period, Philadelphia was a leading financial innovator. Nascent banks, insurers, and securities markets thrived in the Delaware Valley even before Independence. Those institutions were but pale imitations of what the Revolution would bring forth, the commercial banks and securities markets that form the subject of chapter 3. The next four chapters, 4 through 7, describe Philadelphia's role in early American monetary systems, its central, savings, and investment banks, and its insurers.

The next three chapters, 8 through 10, describe the reasons for Wall Street's ascendance. Chapter 8 demonstrates that although Philadelphia invested heavily in Pennsylvania's transportation system, it lost most of its trade to New York, Baltimore, and New Orleans. Less trade meant fewer deposits, Chestnut Street's lifeblood. Chapter 9 shows that the lifeblood of Chestnut Street's financiers also ebbed away. It does so by exploring in detail the life and death of one of Philadelphia's finest financiers, Michael Hillegas. The death of men like Hillegas decreased Chestnut Street's initial advantage in human capital. Chestnut Street lost its final advantage, the second Bank of the United States, in a "Bank War" that pitted Philadelphia banker Nicholas Biddle against the indefatigable Andrew Jackson and a crafty politician named Martin Van Buren. Chapter 11 concludes with a discussion of the role that the dethroned Chestnut Street played in the economic development of the Delaware Valley in the decades leading to the Civil War.

Throughout all, the focus remains squarely on people and how the financial system helped them to lead better, healthier, wealthier lives. I wish that that story were more complete than it is. The sad fact, however, is that many crucial sources have been lost to the ravages of time and archivists uninterested in financial matters. A particularly sad case was that of Howard Terry, who in 1927 found "the remains of an old book . . . in an old house in Holmesburg," a neighborhood in Philadelphia's Frankford section. Although the book contained the names of many prominent early Philadelphia individuals and organizations, neither the Historical Society of Pennsylvania, the Frankford Historical Society, nor the Bucks County Historical Society saw fit to take it off his hands. His urgent letters remain, but not the source itself, save for one tantalizing folio that strongly suggests that the book was one of the missing ledgers of the Bank of the United States, America's first central bank. Oh, the tales that I could have spun had those records not perished! Luckily, enough of the early financial record survived to make this book possible.

~ 2

COLONIAL PRECEDENTS

By the late colonial period—say, 1765—Philadelphia was the crown jewel of British North America. Its people and institutions, rather than its physical characteristics, allowed the Quaker metropolis to surpass Boston as the colonies' leading city. The capital of Pennsylvania, one of the most recently settled colonies, Philadelphia lay nestled along the Delaware River, just north of that mighty river's confluence with its most important tributary, the Schuylkill. (One joke asserts that only a native Philadelphian can pronounce the name of the latter river correctly. The rest of us can get by with "scoo-kull.")[1]

The location was not a propitious one for an ocean port. For starters, the Delaware is not a deep river. Unlike the Hudson, which is essentially a deep trench that filled with water, the Delaware cut its own ever-shifting channels. Oceangoing vessels had to navigate through those channels or run aground, never a good thing. So rather than sailing into port, captains had to stop at the Capes, well south of Philadelphia, and wait until an experienced pilot came aboard to guide the ship safely to its wharf. Outbound, captains had to help pilots, who successfully navigated them through the channels, to return to shore. Captains who decided to sail away with the pilot still aboard faced stiff penalties. Regardless, the pilots had to be paid and the legislature obligingly fixed their fees quite high. In short, the port of Philadelphia was a costly one in terms of both time and money.[2]

Another costly problem was that almost every winter the Delaware froze solid through. That fact might shock readers familiar with recent Philadelphia winters, but the explanation is quite simple: the climate was colder then and the factories that

14

continually warm the river's waters today did not yet exist. Due to the thick ice, business in Philadelphia usually shut down two months each year. Deep saltwater ports like New York rarely faced such difficulties.[3]

Intermittent yellow fever epidemics, though not solely a Philadelphia problem, also disrupted the city's business, usually for months at a stretch. Yellow fever was a particularly nasty disease, dispatching as it did about half of those unfortunate enough to contract it. Worse, those who died did so in an excruciatingly painful weeklong process. Appearance of the dread disease, the cause of which was then unknown, literally caused panic. After a few confirmed cases, those who could afford to flee the city usually did so, posthaste. Only the fall frosts stopped the spread of the fever, so Philadelphia, one of the southernmost of the continent's major ports, faced particularly long viral epidemic seasons.[4]

Given those physical disadvantages, why did Philadelphia thrive instead of stagnate? Luck and freedom. Or perhaps freedom and luck. The lucky thing was that early eighteenth-century Maryland specialized in tobacco production. Due to the nature of the tobacco economy, with its heavy reliance on slaves and British capital investment, Baltimore did not develop until after the Revolution. It proved in the nineteenth century that, as a seaport, it was far superior to the Quaker City.[5]

Philadelphia's freedom was less tangible, but not less important. Pennsylvania's founder, Quaker outcast William Penn, established an enlightened, liberal polity. Religious differences were tolerated; any free person with male genitalia could vote. (In most colonies, voters had to own a penis *and* a substantial amount of property.) Philadelphia means "the City of Brotherly Love," after all. Slavery was present but only in small doses, and the "peculiar institution" was not allowed to stain the colony's development. Indeed, slaves played little role in Pennsylvania's economic development. When Pennsylvania passed legislation in 1783 to gradually emancipate slaves, a few bondsmen were present in the state. Some were house slaves in Philadelphia and other urban areas, but most were the property of farmers in the agricultural counties, like Bucks, that surrounded Philadelphia. Pennsylvania gave up its slaves easily because, to be perfectly frank, they were unprofitable to urban professionals and farmers alike. Climate was certainly a factor. Philadelphia merchant William Pollard, for instance, noted that his "black Boy Jem" was "not worth a Groat [roughly, two dead flies] . . . during our Winter which is very cold." The young man stayed in the "Chimney Corner" and became very sullen. Easy work and good food, Pollard intimated, made Philadelphia's slaves "fatt Indolent & Impudent." The crux of the problem went even deeper: there was little work for slaves during Pennsylvania's long, cold winters, and it simply did not pay to feed them. It was cheaper to hire seasonal labor. Moreover, the Quaker majority was always quite uneasy with slavery.[6]

The Quakers were tolerant of others because they had suffered terribly at the hands of Anglicans in Britain. They couldn't hold high public office there, and in the worst periods, they were harassed, robbed, and even murdered by the king's minions. Steadfast pacifists, Quakers could not retaliate, nor could they take out their frustrations on others, not even Catholics. The painful experience taught Quakers one thing—don't persecute people for their religious beliefs. That didn't stop them from persecuting each other in their monthly, quarterly, and yearly meetings, but that is a different story. The point here is that the Quaker republic on the Delaware was a liberal gem, a bastion of freedom in a world of religious chains. And that made all the difference.[7]

The city's relative freedom attracted and retained the continent's best and brightest minds, including Enlightenment philosopher-scientists like Benjamin Franklin and David Rittenhouse. It also attracted shipload after shipload of industrious Europeans, eager to breathe deeply the colony's free air and to work its almost free land, perhaps after serving a brief indenture period. Those hardworking Germans, Swedes, Scots-Irish, and Englanders, in turn, summoned forth high-quality merchants eager to exchange the farmers' produce for British fineries and the wines, teas, sugars, and coffees of fairer climes. The merchants, in turn, attracted a variety of craftsmen (aka artisans) eager to supply merchants with everything from horseshoes to hats. Early Philadelphia was an eager place, indeed.[8]

Pennsylvania's people and institutions, in short, outweighed the Delaware's ice and sand. Financial flexibility was part and parcel of that "Philadelphia freedom," a term that admittedly today has a somewhat gayer connotation. "Liberty to manage their affairs their own way," Adam Smith argued, was just as responsible for colonial wealth as "plenty of good land" was. In fact, Philadelphia's financiers found freedom as fertile as farmers found the rich red soils of Lancaster County to be. Early financiers in Philadelphia were quite happy because they had some room to maneuver, and maneuver they did. By the time the Revolution erupted in 1775, Philadelphia was North America's most financially advanced city.[9]

∽ We do not know much about Jacob Roth other than the fact that he was a Philadelphian and that he earned a living as a potter. Likely, he was one of thousands of artisans who quit Europe to ply their trade, and try their luck, in the New World. Why he chose Philadelphia over Boston or

New York we know not. The winds may simply have carried the ship upon which he shared a miserable bunk and a few greasy blankets to the Capes of Delaware instead of Cape Cod or Sandy Hook, New Jersey. More plausible, Roth and other skilled artisans were attracted to Philadelphia because of its "ground rents." One thing is for certain: Roth did make use of that innovative financial institution. In 1764 he purchased of merchant-judge Thomas Willing an 18-by-86-foot lot on Third Street. In exchange for the land, Roth promised to pay Willing, or the current owner of the ground rent, 6 pistoles (a type of Spanish gold coin worth £1 7s. Pennsylvania currency) per year forever. He also promised that within seven years he would construct on the lot a building or buildings worth at least £100 Pennsylvania currency. (For the meaning of the term "Pennsylvania currency," see chapter 4.)[10]

Why would Roth and Willing make such a deal? Both men must have valued it more than the other possibilities that they faced. Roth first. Though we know little about this poor potter, he was human, so we can safely surmise that he had human dreams and aspirations. Likely, he strongly preferred to be his own master, to run his own shop in his own way on his own terms, over serving as an employee. The only serious barrier to his dream in Philadelphia's free market was money to buy tools, start-up materials, and, most importantly, a stall or workshop. Money, though, was not easily procured. By the time that Roth could save up enough, his productive years, and quite possibly his life, would be over. His dream would die with him. Worse, from society's view, some portion of his talents and energy would be wasted because as an employee he would not have as strong an incentive to work hard or to innovate.[11]

But all was not lost. Instead of buying his shop outright, Ross could have leased it. That was the relatively inexpensive path that most artisans in most colonial cities took. Leasing was not without its problems, however. For starters, lease terms were often short, as little as a year. After the lease expired, the landlord could easily eject the artisan or, perhaps worse, force a rent increase. The cost of the uncertainty and risk inherent in the lease weighed heavily on artisans' shoulders. Frequent moves cost the artisan time, money, and perhaps even his hard-won customer base. Rent increases moved the artisan ever closer to mere subsistence and ever further from the independence that only ownership could bring.

Even if the landlord was not a capricious tyrant, other dangers lurked. What if the artisan needed to expand the shop or to change it to meet the exigencies of his trade? Would the landlord pay him for making such "improvements"? Or would the landlord sue for "damages"? Or might he even use the improvements as an excuse to increase the rent? Though perhaps better than eking out an existence as an employee, leasing was fraught with risks.

Artisans like Roth could also try to borrow the funds that they needed to set themselves up in business. Much business was carried on by credit, so presumably Roth could have acquired tools and raw materials and paid for them later. The problem here was that merchants that sold on credit often charged exorbitant rates of implicit interest. A tool priced at 10 shillings for cash today might go for 15 shillings for credit at six months and a full pound (20 shillings) for a year's credit. And if he failed to pay the supplier, there would be hell to pay. Imprisonment for debt frequently meant illness, even death, and always spelled ignominy.[12]

Roth could also have borrowed to purchase a plot and a shop. But in an age before federal guarantees or mortgage insurance, who would lend? Colonial capital markets were largely undeveloped. According to eminent Pennsylvania businessman and politician William Allen, "We have among us ten Borrowers to One Lender." And people living in the other colonies could offer no respite. According to Allen, capital flows between colonies were unusual because lenders could not "readily at a Distance command a punctual payment of their Interest."[13]

In fact, for many years the colony itself was the largest lender in the economy. The General Loan Office (GLO) was a government entity that made loans of paper money to Pennsylvanians. Two issues, however, made the GLO an unlikely option for Roth or other poor artisans. Foremost, the GLO lent only on the security of valuable assets like real estate or silver plate. To borrow money from it, in other words, you already had to have "money" (technically, wealth)! Moreover, the interest rate the GLO charged was too low. That is right, too low. It was usually well below the market rate of interest. So everybody and their grandmother wanted a GLO loan. The institution could not lend to everyone, so it had to ration the loans by other means. In some colonies with similar institutions, like Massachusetts, "the longest swords"—that is, those with the most physical and political clout—received the loan office's largesse. Pennsylvania was slightly more advanced than that. Like modern wannabe concertgoers or Soviet homemakers, early Pennsylvanians queued up for GLO loans. The result, predictably, was only a little different from that in Massachusetts. Those who could afford to stand in line, the rich and powerful, got the loans. Of course, they then had more funds to lend to men like Roth, only at higher interest rates.[14]

Lending at high interest rates, always a precarious operation, was extremely risky in colonial Philadelphia for two reasons: First, the borrower might default; second, he might turn the lender over to the sheriff for breaking the law. Yes, Philadelphia was relatively free, but it was not completely so. In fact, to this day usury laws cap how much interest lenders can charge. The rate now, however, is much higher than the 6 or 7 percent that prevailed in colonial Pennsylvania.[15]

Despite those hazards, Philadelphians did sometimes trade IOUs known as bonds and mortgages. The problem with both was that often the principal value fell due after only a year. "Very few that lend out money," a writer for the *Pennsylvania Chronicle* noted in 1767, "will lend it for longer time than a year." Moreover, "when the time of payment comes," lenders would "not receive it in part, but insist upon the whole." Such behavior, the chronicler pointed out, "frequently embarrasses, if not ruins the borrower." With just a year to save up, the borrower usually did not have enough money to repay the principal amount, so he had to sell his land or borrow again, often on less advantageous terms, or default. In the last instance, the lender had to initiate a series of costly and lengthy legal proceedings that enriched no-body—except judges and lawyers.[16]

Philadelphia artisans like Roth, however, enjoyed another option, the ground-rent contract. Despite its name, a ground rent was really more of a perpetual mortgage than a lease. The buyer got full title to the land. So long as he paid the annual "rent," which was actually the interest on a perpetual loan, he could do with the land as he pleased. He could even sell it, subject to the ground rent. Best of all, the rent could never increase and the contract never expired. For just a few coins each year, he could secure his economic independence. Before ground rents were effectively outlawed late in the nineteenth century, hundreds of thousands if not millions of people took advantage of their unique attributes.

But what was in it for sellers like Willing? Why not insist on getting their money up front? For starters, Willing knew that Roth was not likely to be able to muster the 100 pistoles he wanted for the lot. Some form of financing was necessary. But what was the best form for that financing to take? Willing could have written up a bond or mortgage, but, as noted above, collecting the principal sum on such instruments was difficult and beguiling legal niceties abounded. If the borrower had the temerity to pay the principal when due, Willing and other colonial investors faced the serious problem of profitably reinvesting it. Because financial markets were still in their infant—nay, prenatal—state, finding a profitable outlet for large sums of cash was a difficult, time-consuming task. The next borrower might not pay any interest, much less repay the principal on time!

So Willing and other investors actually liked the idea of collecting interest forever. They got the idea, no doubt, from British ground rents. They may also have had British Consols, perpetual bonds issued by the mother country, in mind. The bonds dutifully paid (indeed, still pay) interest, but never principal. They were great long-term investments: buy them, then kick back and receive the interest year after year, decade after decade, century after century. They were especially convenient to fund annuities for widows and minor children. Pennsylvanians could buy Consols and a few rich Philadelphians did, especially during wars or periods of economic dislocation. As Pennsylvania bigwig William Allen explained, though Consols offered relatively low returns, they were much "safer" than mortgages and bonds. But given the distance to London, the transaction costs of buying or selling them were not inconsiderable. In addition, Consols were denominated in sterling, but Pennsylvanians reckoned prices in their own currency, a currency that purchased amounts of sterling that varied over time, even day to day. So there was exchange-rate risk involved too. Philadelphia investors therefore developed ground rents to serve as their own private form of low-risk perpetual debt.[17]

Willing often assigned the ground rents to his sisters and daughters. The payments provided them with a steady annual income. Moreover, those income streams were pretty safe. When a default occurred, the sheriff simply entered any shop or house on the lot and took away enough personal property to satisfy the debt. If the sheriff could not find enough personal property to seize to pay the ground rent due, the property reverted to Willing, who could then sell the land to a new buyer outright or for a new ground rent. Such foreclosures were extremely rare because the sums involved were almost always quite low in relation to the property's value, so buyers were loath to default. Moreover, property financed by ground rents could be protected with fire insurance, of which more anon.

Importantly, sellers like Willing understood that they could obtain the principal by simply selling the ground-rent contract to another investor. In exchange for a lump sum, Willing would assign the right to receive the annual interest payments to the new investor. So both Roth and Willing could extricate themselves from the contract at will; newspaper advertisements replete with references to ground rents are proof positive that both buyers and sellers took full advantage of the flexibility inherent in those safe and liquid capital market IOUs. Only Pennsylvania, Delaware, and Maryland had them, and they were unimportant in the latter two places until after the Revolution. (Readers may recall that Delaware was essentially a part of Pennsylvania until the Revolution.)

Like all successful IOUs, ground rents were "win-win-win" contracts. Willing received a safe, flexible investment immune from exchange-rate or reinvestment risk. Roth got to live his dream of owning and operating his own shop. Society won, too, because Willing had a way to ensure that his loved ones would never become wards of the state and Roth undoubtedly worked harder and smarter for himself than he would have for an employer.

⟋◯ Philadelphia dry-goods importer Stephen Collins felt that he knew what his fellow citizens wanted to purchase from Britain. A Quaker of modest means, Collins feared risking his slim capital to bring those wares to Pennsylvania. What if a war broke out and some French privateer seized his stuff on the high seas? What if a gale sank the ship? Or a drunken captain tried to make his way up the Delaware River without a trained pilot at the helm? What if any number of other plausible disaster scenarios occurred, leaving Collins destitute? It was a chance that he could not take. Without insurance, that is.[18]

Any colonial merchant like Collins could purchase marine insurance—by writing to London. In an age when it took ships up to twelve weeks to make the eastward passage across the Atlantic, that was rather inconvenient, indeed. Worse, though well versed in general trade conditions in the western Atlantic, London-based insurers knew little about specific ships, captains, or merchants. Their premium rates, therefore, were rather generic. That meant that risky shippers paid too little and safe ones too much. Moreover, during wars, which were all too frequent in the eighteenth century, premium rates skyrocketed. The policies were decent, covering a wide variety of perils, many colorful:

> The Seas, Men of War, Fire, Enemies, Pirates, Rovers, Thievers, Jettezones, Letters of Mart and Counter Mart, Surprisals, Takings at Sea, Restraints and Detainments of all Kings, Princes, and People, of what Nation, Condition or Quality soever, Arrests, Barratty of the Master, and Mariners, and of all other Perils, Losses, and Misfortunes that have, or shall come to the Hurt, Damage or Detriment of the said Goods and Merchandize or any part thereof.

But the insurance was not in effect if the ship went off course or, in particularly dire periods, if it did not travel under armed escort or in a convoy. Given such restrictions, premiums were too high and too unfair, and obtaining coverage was too cumbersome. America needed its own marine insurers. Philadelphia led the way.

As early as May 1721, Philadelphia merchant John Copson advertised his services as a local insurance broker. Copson proposed to introduce shippers to local underwriters for a small commission. That proposal, and several others proffered later in the 1720s, apparently came to naught. The trade of the city was still quite small, consisting in 1735 of only 192 arrivals and 207 clearances (about one-quarter to European ports, one-quarter to other mainland colonies, and one-half to various isles in the West Indies), so having a homegrown insurance industry was not of paramount importance. But as the years ticked by, Philadelphia's trade grew and the need for local underwriters waxed strong.

By the late 1740s, Joseph Saunders had established a successful marine insurance brokerage in Philadelphia. For shippers, obtaining coverage with Saunders was much easier and faster than writing to London. Saunders took applications and circulated them among a pool of local underwriters who decided how much, if any, of the risk that they wished to assume. His business thrived, attracting at least two competitors by the outbreak of the Seven Years' War.

Still, most of the marine insurance on ships owned by Philadelphians was underwritten in London because of the superior reputation of the mother country's underwriters. (Nobody wants insurance underwritten by a person who cannot, or will not, pay in the event of a claim.) In 1757 Philadelphia merchants Thomas Willing, Attwood Shute, Charles Stedman, Alexander Stedman, John Kidd, and William Coxe sought to obviate London's advantage by forming Thomas Willing and Company, a partnership with Willing serving as cashier and accountant.

Willing, the ground lord we met above, was clearly the moving force here. Born of a prosperous Philadelphia merchant in 1731, Willing obtained a proper British education, including training in the law at the Inner Temple, London. Willing was only twenty-three when his father died and he had to assume control of the lucrative family business. Lucky it was that Willing inherited a thriving concern because he found himself charged with the welfare of his mother and eight siblings, the youngest an infant. Willing went on to become one of the nation's leading financial practitioners. In addition to his leading role in the development of Philadelphia's ground-rent market, he presided over two of America's most important banks, the Bank of North America and the Bank of the United States, and later helped to launch the U.S. life insurance industry. Conservative by nature, contemporaries dubbed him "Old Square Toes." His conservative business practices, however, helped to ensure the success of the banks he led. They also allowed him to accumulate wealth slowly but steadily. When he died in 1821, Willing was one of the nation's richest men, and not the slightest hint of scandal or fraud hung over his fortune.[19]

The same could not be said of Willing's mercantile partner, precocious orphan, and erstwhile apprentice Robert Morris, who took Shute's place in the insurance company in 1758. Early in his career, Morris found it easy to make money. He knew what and when to buy and what and when to sell. During the Revolution he took bold risks, most of which panned out, and hence he reaped large returns. He became so rich that by the end of the war he was able to circulate his personal IOUs *as money,* a feat that few individuals have ever achieved and that the Continental Congress itself could no longer pull off by 1781. But with riches came scandal. Though never convicted of fraud, many, perhaps jealous of Morris's success, thought him guilty of stealing from the public trough. After the war Morris continued to take big risks. Increasingly, though, his gambles went sour. Massive land speculations—he once owned almost all of western New York—ended up breaking him and his fortune. He died in poverty in 1806 after a prolonged stint in debtors' prison.

Of course, that all lay in the future. In the late 1750s, Willing's insurance company attracted much business but could not satiate all of the demand for marine insurance. So in 1762 a second underwriting company, this one headed by John Kidd and John Nixon, formed. That same year Kidd and William Bradford began to run a brokerage out of the London Coffee House, a popular hangout for Philadelphia merchants. By 1766 competition had so lowered premiums that underwriting became only marginally profitable. The underwriters responded by forming an agreement, essentially a cartel, designed to sustain premiums at or above agreed-upon rates. The cartel quickly disbanded, as most do, due to repeated defections. Philadelphia shippers and consumers didn't complain.[20]

Once again, we find that an IOU created a win-win-win situation. Thanks to the insurance, Collins decided to begin importing dry goods from England. He eventually became an important merchant both commercially and politically. (His daughter Elizabeth married Richard Bland Lee, a northern Virginia Federalist who served in the first three Congresses.) The insurer also earned a profit, on average.

Most Philadelphians were not merchants. What did *they* gain from the existence of insurance? A higher price for their purchases because merchants passed the cost of insurance on to them? Probably not. The risk of loss *did* inhere in the price of goods, but that risk existed whether the merchant chose to "hedge" or reduce it with insurance or not. The fact that merchants could reduce risk through reasonably priced insurance undoubtedly made more people willing to engage in commerce. That meant more price competition and a larger volume of trade. So the existence of insurance likely *reduced* prices for consumers.[21]

✐ Colonial Philadelphia financiers also innovated in the two other major branches of insurance, fire and life. Both helped people to reduce some of the risks they faced, but neither grew very large or important until after the Revolution. The important point here is that once again we find colonial Philadelphia leading the way in the importation and adaptation of British know-how in important financial fields.[22]

Philadelphians remained self-insured against fire until 1752. Until then the cost of conflagrations, like the one that caused some £5,000 of damage to shops near Fishbourne's Wharf in April 1730, fell entirely upon the shoulders of those whose property went up in smoke. Denizens of the city were not entirely without protection as firefighting equipment, including buckets, hooks, and fire "engines"—primitive hand-cranked water pumps— were available. Indeed, in the 1730s several private fire companies organized. By 1752 seven such companies were in existence. But if your house or warehouse suffered fire damage, you were SOL.

In March 1752 Benjamin Franklin and eleven other prominent Philadelphians formed the Philadelphia Contributionship for the Insurance of Houses from Loss by Fire. Joseph Saunders, the marine insurance broker, became clerk of the new institution, and John Smith, a devout Quaker merchant, became its treasurer. Modeled after London's Hand-in-Hand Fire Office, the Philadelphia Contributionship was organized as a mutual. In other words, the policyholders themselves owned the company. As in the Hand-in-Hand, members made a "deposit" to the company based on the value insured and the insured building's major construction material (usually stone, brick, or wood). The contributionship invested the premiums in IOUs and used the interest income to pay claims. Because it was a mutual, any earned interest not used to pay claims was returned to the policyholders / owners as a "dividend."

The contributionship grew but slowly. On its tenth birthday, it insured only £25,415 worth of property on premiums, mostly invested in ground rents and mortgages, totaling £368. Soon thereafter it stopped paying dividends because the sums involved were simply too small and difficult to calculate. In 1768 the association received a royal charter, one of only a handful of American businesses to receive the Crown's formal sanction. For the balance of the colonial period, the company plodded on; its frame was solid but still extremely small. The directors understood from the first that the key to success was not to insure the full value of a building, because to do so invited carelessness and even outright fraud. The contributionship also used its weight in the legislature to enact and enforce laws that imposed heavy fines on Philadelphians who did not regularly have their chimneys properly swept. Unswept chimneys were the number-one cause of house fires in the period.[23]

Fire insurance was another win-win-win IOU. If you owned a policy and your house burned down, you received a cash payment to help you to re-build or move on. If your house never burned, the dividend mechanism and mutual structure ensured that your premiums were not unfairly large. The uninsured benefited as well. Because the contributionship kept its payouts below the insured property's market value, few people deliberately set blazes. So predictions that the existence of insurance would lead to more fires proved unfounded. Moreover, fearful that fires would spread from uninsured homes, the contributionship persuaded the legislature to pass basic fire safety laws that protected everyone.

Life insurance, in contrast, couldn't do much about people dying, but it could help breadwinners to protect their families if the Grim Reaper appeared. Benjamin Franklin long espoused the virtues of life insurance. "A policy of Life Assurance is the cheapest and safest mode of making a certain provision for one's family," he argued in 1769, over forty-five years after first publicly calling for increased use of life insurance. Few heeded Franklin's call. In colonial Pennsylvania marine insurers wrote term-life contracts, but the practice appears to have been rare and costly. After 1759 Presbyterian ministers could procure life insurance through a real mouthful, the Corporation for the Relief of Poor and Distressed Presbyterian Ministers, and of the Poor and Distressed Widows and Children of Presbyterian Ministers. After 1769 Anglican ministers could do likewise through their own corporation with an equally unwieldy name. Most others had to "self-insure," that is, shoulder the risk of the premature death of a bread-winner themselves. Both minister life insurance companies were tiny by any standards. Like the Philadelphia Contributionship, they suffered greatly during the Revolution due to the depreciation of the Continental dollar. One of the life companies also suffered at the hands of a treasurer more loyal to the Crown than to his customers. After the Revolution, as we will learn in chapter 6, marine, fire, and life insurance thrived.[24]

The point here is that even before the Revolution, Philadelphians experimented with financial institutions virtually unknown elsewhere in the colonies, or anywhere in the world outside of London or Amsterdam, for that matter. In only one area, public securities—that is, IOUs issued by gov-ernment—did Philadelphia lag slightly. Its second-place finish, however, was due to its financial strength, not any weakness. The full story is too long and sordid to get into here. Suffice it to say, issuing paper money was (and unfortunately remains) a convenient way for governments to borrow—all they needed was a printing press, some paper, ink, and a law mandating that people accept the stuff. Some colonial governments, especially those in New England, resorted to this expedient too frequently. As more and more of the money entered circulation, the value of all of it eroded. Readers who lived through the "great inflation" of the 1970s will recognize the feeling.[25]

Things got so bad that Massachusetts undertook monetary reforms. Britain also interceded, forbidding the other New England colonies from is-suing more fiat zero-interest paper junk. Thereafter, Massachusetts had to borrow honestly, by selling interest-bearing government bonds known as treasury notes. The notes did not circulate as money, serving instead as a relatively safe and lucrative investment. Boston, ergo, enjoyed a relatively active public securities market by the mid-1760s.

Colonial Pennsylvania's paper money, on the other hand, upheld its value quite nicely. When Pennsylvania's government needed to borrow, it could do so quite cheaply by issuing its zero-interest paper bills of credit. Only on a few occasions did it find it necessary to pay interest for current funds. So Philadelphia's public securities market was not as large or ad-vanced as that of Boston, but only because Pennsylvania was more credit-worthy. In fact, Pennsylvania's experience with government securities did not begin until the French and Indian War. During that conflict, which many historians count as the first truly global war, Philadelphia merchant-politician Isaac Norris, already an experienced investor in British Consols, pushed a so-called Indian Trade Bill that empowered the colony's Indian trade commissioners to borrow up to £4,000 on bond at 6 percent interest for five years. The Pennsylvania Assembly raised the commissioners' debt ceiling to £10,000 the next year. Due to the state's high credit rating, in-vestors gobbled up the bonds. Isaac Norris himself bought some, as did merchant Thomas Clifford, but by far the most numerous investors were Philadelphia's leading ladies, including Mary Coates, Hannah Allen, and Susannah Head. This was the first of a small number of laws allowing vari-ous Pennsylvania government agents to deficit finance their operations by issuing fully negotiable interest-paying bonds. The bonds did change hands, but the total volume of outstanding bonds was not high enough to warrant the formation of an active secondary market.[26]

In contrast, Philadelphia and New York ran neck and neck in the private securities market. Colonial New York boasted at least one person who explicitly called himself a broker, Hendrick Oudenaarde. Apparently, Oudenaarde matched buyers to sellers of private promissory notes. But his newspaper advertisements were too vague to draw any other conclusions from, and no other information about that aspect of his business has been found. Brokering promissory notes was but a small part of his business, so although Oudenaarde identified himself as a broker (actually as a "brooker," a Dutch bastardization of the word), his techniques were probably no more advanced than those of colonial Philadelphia's rudimentary brokers, men like William Ibison, Enoch Story, William Smith, and James Hume.[27]

✍ Financiers in colonial Philadelphia tried to implement additional innovations as well, but British authorities rebuffed them at every turn. Perhaps the most ambitious of those failed forays was Robert Morris and Thomas Willing's attempt to form a commercial bank in the mid-1760s, when several new imperial regulations conspired to significantly reduce Pennsylvania's money supply. Things got so bad that residents of Bucks County, just north of Philadelphia, resorted to squirrel-scalp bounty money. That was not quite as gross as it sounds. Rural Pennsylvanians did not make payments with dead squirrels, at least with any regularity. Rather, they turned the squirrel scalps over to local magistrates, who, lacking coins, wrote out IOUs in payment of the statewide bounty on the fecund little crop eaters. (Americans then were not quite as interested in environmental protection as they are today.)[28]

Despite the obvious need for a bank, Morris and Willing met stiff resistance. British authorities, in line with mercantilist theory, more or less said "colonists can't engage in profitable activities like commercial banking." Such high-handed tactics may have worked elsewhere in the empire, but in late colonial America they would not play. The reason was simple: Columbia was growing strong enough to kick John Bull's butt, and Americans knew it.

Indeed, by the late colonial period, the older, more densely populated areas of Pennsylvania began to resemble England demographically and economically. The emergence of textile manufacturing was a sure sign that the colonies were rapidly maturing. As Philadelphia merchant William Pollard explained to a correspondent in April 1773, "The Manufactory of Coarse Linnen increases fast in the Country." The reason? When farmers died, they split up their "good Plantations" among multiple children. After several generations, the lots became too small to further subdivide. "Rather than go farther back into the Country where Lands are cheap, or undertake the arduous Task of Clearing new Lands," Pollard explained, many thousands of young people turned to manufacturing, "as in many parts of England."[29]

Those and other similarities to the old country helped Americans to realize that they were not inferior colonial lowlifes. They were as good as Britons and hence entitled to the same rights to life, liberty, and property. Once enough of them realized that the king was taking more from the colonists than he repaid them in services, a break became inevitable. That break, we learn in the next chapter, had an important but until recently little understood financial component. Somewhat ironically, the war also sped the development of Philadelphia's financial sector. So it could be said without contradiction that financial development caused the Revolution and that the Revolution caused financial development.

3

REVOLUTIONARY DEVELOPMENTS

Over the course of the eighteenth century, the mainland colonies of British North America underwent profound economic, social, and political changes. Many volumes have described, assessed, analyzed, celebrated, deprecated, or searched out the causes of those changes. Almost all of them, however, ignore the important role that finances played in the coming—and ending—of the American Revolution.[1]

The colonies were, at their root, business enterprises designed to enrich the British government and individual Britons. The hope was that colonists, like dutiful sons, would create economic value out of the wilderness, keep a small portion to reproduce themselves, and remit the balance to the mother country to pay for taxes, insurance, interest, and British manufactured goods. Almost every act or decree, almost every aspect of British commercial regulation of the colonies, had a single purpose: the extraction of wealth from North America. Basically, Britons lent wealth to colonists in exchange for which the colonists returned the wealth, with interest, and pledged, in most instances, to deal only with British merchants. Those arrangements—known as the mercantile system—functioned tolerably well for over a century.

Early Pennsylvania was well endowed with the marketable fruits of nature. Johan Christopher Sauer noted in 1724 that compared to the Old World, Pennsylvania was rich with wildlife and metallic ores. "Many a man," he boasted, "has bought a property for 100 Florins and found 1000 Florin" in natural resources, including iron ore, on it. Sauer didn't note what happened to people who had not saved up 100 florins, but Pennsylvania was a relatively prosperous place for all. In fact, contemporaries often called it the "best poor man's country." Most people were too busy trying to get rich to worry about the systemic exploitation inherent in the mercantile system. Moreover, early colonists had been born in Europe. They were few in number and faced grave threats, including the threat of an early grave, so they saw Britain's control and protection as necessary and even good.[2]

As the number and proportion of native-born colonists swelled, and the burden of the payments exacted by the British grew, the grumbling of discontent became increasingly audible. It reached a crescendo in the 1760s and 1770s, when the onerous side of Britain's colonial monetary and trade policies became blazingly obvious. In the eighteenth century, most British policymakers and political economists were so-called mercantilists, not free traders. They thought it necessary to control trading routes in order to ensure a steady flow of gold, silver, critical war materials, and other raw materials to the British Isles. British policies—including the infamous Navigation, Sugar, and Currency Acts—were therefore designed to prevent Americans from controlling their own trading routes or money supplies. Such policies certainly helped Britain, but they injured the colonists by allowing colonial business cycles and interest rates to vacillate wildly, exposing colonists to net-worth deterioration, liability runs, bankruptcy, and ruin.

It is a well-established fact that the market prices of bonds, stocks, real estate, and slaves vary inversely with interest rates. If you could, with the same amount of work and risk, net 10 percent investing in a farm or 5 percent lending money, which would you choose? If you are like most people, you'd choose the farm. If many people indeed choose the farm, what happens to the price of farms? They increase. If you could net 10 percent in a farm or 15 percent lending, which would you choose? Again, other factors being equal, most people would choose the higher return, in this case the lending. What will happen to the price of farms in that instance? They will, of course, decrease. So as interest rates increase, the price of land decreases. Early Americans also clearly understood that as interest rates decreased, the prices of long-term investments like farms and bonds went up. We know that because they noted it time and time again.[3]

Armed with this simple fact, imagine, if you will, a colonial firm—say, a family farm—that owned real estate purchased for £50 and various tools, crops, household items, and the like initially valued at an additional £50. Imagine, too, that the farmer possessed £25 of equity (net worth) and owed £75 worth of debt, in the form of bonds, notes, and book accounts. Imagine further that all of those assets were purchased and all of those IOUs were sold when interest rates were 6 percent per annum. If some shock, like a war or a new imperial policy, increased interest rates to 12 percent per year, the farmer would still owe £75, but his real estate would plummet in value, to approximately £25.

At that point, the farm would still be solvent, but its net worth would have vanished. If interest rates continued upward, to 24 percent, by no means an outlandish figure, the market value of the farm's fixed assets would sink to a mere £12.5. The farmer's other assets would have probably also lost value, but even if they did not, his total assets would now be worth only about £62.5. But he would still owe £75. Although the farmer did nothing "wrong," he would now be technically insolvent. If he died or his debts were called in, his family would be beggared as wealthy foreigners snapped up property for just pence in the pound (cents on the dollar).

This is not idle speculation. Many colonial firms went bankrupt largely due to policy decisions made by London bureaucrats. In 1772 and 1773, the colonies suffered through the last of several great waves of policy-induced bankruptcies. Faced with extremely high interest rates, many Philadelphians, like merchant John Mitchell, found that they could no longer pay their debts. The sheriff seized all of Mitchell's physical assets and tried to sell them, but a general scarcity of circulating cash—brought about by meddling British regulators—meant that there were few buyers. Mitchell's stuff eventually sold, but at bargain prices. He lost everything, as did untold others. Many of those unfortunates found early graves due to the stresses of debtors' prison and the shame of "failure." So much for government protecting life, liberty, and property.

Some people may have shrugged off losses like those described above. Many American colonists, however, could not stomach such losses because they believed, as followers of seventeenth-century political theorist John Locke, that it was the job of good government to *protect property rights,* not to steal from the people indirectly through manipulation of the money supply and interest rates. The familiar outcries against "taxation without representation," which many scholars have correctly termed outlandish or hyperbolic given the tiny size of the explicit taxes to which the colonists were subjected, make more sense when viewed as marginal shocks. The infamous taxes on stamps and tea, in other words, were merely the straws that broke the camel's back. The tremendous weight of imperial monetary and trade regulations was the load that stretched the colonial camel's spine to the breaking point in the first place.[4]

The American Revolution, I argue, was as much a monetary phenomenon as a fiscal (tax) one. In addition to shaking off those pesky little taxes, the colonists rebelled to gain control over the domestic money supply and interest rates and hence, as we've seen, the market value of their property. Ironically, the financial stress of the Revolutionary War created monetary chaos, rampant inflation, extremely high interest rates, and large property value fluctuations. Out of those difficulties, however, emerged a modern financial sector that laid the basis for America's ultimate political unification and economic development.

⟋◯ The Patriots barely won the American Revolution. On numerous occasions, they could have lost the contest had circumstances turned out even slightly differently. Perhaps the rebels got lucky. A more sympathetic view is that the colonies rebelled at the precise moment when they were just strong enough to achieve victory. Either way, de facto independence did not come easily. And it certainly did not come quickly. One problem was that the colonists were deeply divided. About one out of every three adults thought rebellion treasonous. Many such Loyalists helped the redcoats by serving in their ranks or by providing them with succor and information. Another third of the colonists didn't take sides unless forced to. They wanted to live their lives, not die protecting a king they never knew or promoting abstract ideals they never believed possible. So only a third of the adult population were ardent Patriots. They had their work cut out for them, and then some.[5]

The rebel governments that formed in 1775 and 1776 faced an immediate pressing need—money. Money for guns, money for ammo, money for ships, money for sailors and soldiers, money for officials' salaries. Raising significant sums through taxation was out of the question when two out of three taxpayers did not recognize the rebel governments' right to collect it. And everyone complained that they were being asked to pay too much. Pennsylvanians from every part of the state claimed tax exemptions—the westerners because they had to fight the Indians, and the easterners because they had to take on the Loyalists in their midst. Quakers and some Germans argued that they could not in good conscience pay taxes during wartime. Members of other denominations wondered why they should pay to liberate a bunch of foreigners and peaceniks from the yoke of imperial oppression. And the merchants who evaded the British blockade were not about to turn their booty over to the taxman—if they could help it. Worst of all, many Pennsylvania tax collectors fell prey to brigands like the infamous Doane Gang. The four Doane brothers ransacked Bucks County, just north of Philadelphia, until a posse was able to shoot one, hang two others, and force the fourth bandito to seek asylum in Canada.[6]

The new governments also tried to borrow what they needed. But except in Boston and Philadelphia, Americans were unaccustomed to lending money to government. Besides, what were the chances that the new governments would survive long enough to repay the loans?

Unable to tax or borrow what it needed, the rebel governments had only one other option available: print up their own money. And so they did. Here there was significant precedent because all colonial governments had at some point printed their own money, so-called bills of credit, or paper money. The concept was simple: take some paper, have a printer engrave different denominations on it, induce some government officials to sign it, get it into circulation by using it to buy goods and services or by lending it to citizens, and keep it in circulation by passing a law forcing people to accept it and by promising to redeem it in the future for taxes or loan repayments.

As in the colonial period, the ploy worked well but only for a while. The bills had a familiar look and feel, and if one did not want to hold them, they were easily exchanged for coins or goods. As the imperial crisis turned into full-blown war and the volume of bills in circulation grew, and grew, and grew, something had to give. And that something was the market value of the paper money. As early as late 1776, sellers began to demand that those who wished to pay in paper money had to submit to higher prices. In the parlance of the day, bills of credit "depreciated." In more modern terms, inflation had set in. And it was not going away anytime soon. In fact, by 1778 it was accelerating. The British did not help the situation by counterfeiting rebel paper money in large quantities. The redcoats put downward pressure on the money's value too. The British army wreaked havoc in lower New York, large swaths of the South, and, in September 1777, southeastern Pennsylvania. The redcoats stole or ruined £187,000 in Philadelphia alone. That sum included books and portraits lifted from Benjamin Franklin's personal library.[7]

Although the rebels responded in kind against Loyalist property when they could, their depredations could not destroy faith in British money, which was composed largely of gold and silver. British destruction of Patriot property, in contrast, injured the value of the Continentals, which were ultimately backed by taxes and hence expectations about the future productivity of American merchants, artisans, and farmers. For example, the productivity of George Brinton's farm, located in Birmingham, Pennsylvania, must have diminished substantially after redcoats raided it for supplies. As figure 3.1 details, the redcoats took or destroyed everything from hay to sugar.

Too many real bills circulating promiscuously with reams of valueless

Figure 3.1: Example of Destruction of Patriot Property in the Delaware Valley, 1777

Damages Suffered by George Brinton at the Hands of British Troops,
September 11–16, 1777

4.5 tons of hay	3 pails
200 bushels wheat	2 pounds sugar
35 bushels corn	1 pound coffee
30 bushels rye	1 pair flatirons
15 bushels buckwheat	1 new great coat
5 acres of grass "fit for the scythe"	7 coats
10 bushels barley	10 waistcoats
1 likely young mare	8 pairs breeches
3 horses	3 hats
2 bullocks	1 fur cap
7 cows	1 pair boots
3 yearling heifers	1 hundred weight cheese
2 spring calves	1 pair spatterdashers
25 sheep	2 feather beds with pillows
6 large swine	9 coverlets
9 smaller swine	6 pairs blankets and sheets
1 young mare	4 pairs pillow cases
2 falling axes	3 chaff beds
1 broad axe	2 pairs bedsteads
1 pair compasses	5 bed cords
2 chisels	2 cloth cloaks
1 shovel	1 calico quilt
1 handsaw	1 camlet petticoat
1 pair steelyards	1 double gown
1 gun	6 linsey petticoats
1 sword	6 gowns
1 pistol	22 shirts
2 pairs sheep shears	8 aprons
1 bolt blue linen yarn	6 yard striped linen
7 handkerchiefs	8 pairs striped trousers
3 canisters	1 diaper table cloth
1 brass warming pan	5 common table cloths
1 soap box	6 pairs stockings
1 double case of razors	2 pairs gloves
"a number" of bottles	sundry children's clothes
6 bushels of dried apples	1 calico bag
6 blind halters	2 pairs stays
1 set of bells	6 pairs of shoes
5 pairs of harness	1 beaver hat
5 collars	1 pewter pot

continued

Figure 3.1: (*Continued*)

5 pairs of chains with backbands and belly bands	9 pewter plates
	2 pewter dishes
1 cart saddle	3 tin pans
1 iron square and post axe	1 coffee pot and funnel
desk, bookcase, and case of drawers damaged; 3 chairs destroyed	1 looking glass
	1 set china cups and saucers
1 bible	9 milk pans
"a number" of books	2 copper teakettles
2,821 rails	1 copper saucepan
762 stakes	2 large iron pots
12 bags	2 candlesticks
1 frying pan	1 dozen knives, forks, and spoons
1 churn	2 cider tubs
1 pewter bottle	

Source: Historical Society of Pennsylvania.

counterfeits combined with military setbacks and depredation of property like that detailed in figure 3.1 all spelled a loss of confidence in Congress's ability to redeem its bills. That, in turn, meant inflation. The rebel governments tried to tax and to borrow, but they never quite got the hang of either, so they kept on printing money. Not everyone complained. Inflation elated Americans who owed large debts. As prices spiraled ever upward, debtors found it increasingly easy to repay their obligations. In 1774, when, say, a new hat cost about $1, a debt of $100 would have weighed heavily on most colonists. By 1778, when new hats went for $60 each, even a day laborer would have little problem paying off a $100 debt. Obviously, lenders were not happy to lend the equivalent of a hundred hats in 1774 only to receive two hats in return four years later![8]

Wartime inflation hurt many Americans—indeed, anyone on a "fixed income," that is, anyone who received a salary or interest payments. The reason is simple: prices went up, but income did not. Pennsylvania Supreme Court chief justice Thomas McKean calculated that debtors who repaid their obligations in depreciated bills cost him £4,723 (specie value) and that he suffered a loss of £2,759 (specie) because his salary did not keep pace with inflation. Perhaps McKean could afford to suffer such losses, but many others could not. When rebel paper money was effectively repudiated in 1782, Catharine Ray Greene "had with the Rest . . . lost by Paper money." Benjamin Franklin helped her out, but he could not aid all of the nation's widows and orphans, most of whom suffered in silence.[9]

Like all great innovators, foiled colonial bankers Robert Morris and Thomas Willing perceived opportunity where others saw despair. Instead of accepting the status quo, they decided to act. Freed from the imperial shackles that had stymied their colonial banking scheme, the duo created a bank, designed along the lines of European banks like the Bank of England, that they hoped would help to thwart the nation's currency crisis. Their creation, the Bank of North America, issued money made of paper. But unlike the government's bills, the Bank's notes could be redeemed—upon demand—for gold or silver coins at fixed known rates. The notes could also be turned into deposits, a type of money that had no corporeal existence at all. Transfers of deposits from one person's ownership to another were carried out by means of checks, much as today. Deposits were also convertible into coins or notes at the holder's option. So the Bank offered three types of money (notes, coins, deposits) to the government's one. Moreover, most governments accepted the Bank's money in payment of taxes. So banknotes could do everything that bills of credit could do, and then some. Little wonder, then, that most people soon came to strongly prefer bank money to the government's stuff.[10]

The Bank of North America began operations in January 1782. Although it was not an immediate success, by late spring it was fairly well established. On April 20, 1782, in fact, Spain's unofficial representative in Philadelphia, Señor Rendon, told his superiors that the Bank's notes were freely accepted at par because Philadelphians knew that the Bank made only short loans on good security. Its credit with the public may have been further enhanced by the Bank's ostentatious displays of gold and silver coins. According to legend, Willing, the Bank's first president, enjoined the tellers to magnify the Bank's riches by carting the same coins in the front door, out the back, then back in the front, over and over, all day long. Such stories sound implausible, but banks as recently as the 1980s, during the Savings and Loan Crisis, were known to employ similarly deceptive tactics. Whatever the Bank did, it worked, because soon its notes, deposits, and equities (shares) were highly coveted assets.[11]

In 1784 commercial banks also sprang up in New York and Boston. Both eagerly sought, and received, important technical advice from the Bank of North America. The banks were especially interested in learning how the Philadelphia institution limited counterfeiting. They realized that any counterfeits that slipped past the tellers would be a deadweight loss to the institution and its stockholders. Even those counterfeits that the tellers caught, however, would still hurt the bank by injuring its reputation. And unlike the government, the banks could not execute counterfeiters, at least not legally. As a result, the Bank of North America and other early banks worked assiduously to make their notes as counterfeit-proof as possible by using fancy papers, watermarks, secret marks, and other devices. Though not perfect, such strategies generally worked. Before the great proliferation of banks in the 1830s, counterfeit coins were far more common than counterfeit banknotes.[12]

✑ One major outcome of the wartime currency fiasco was the almost complete renunciation of government paper money for the better part of a century. By the war's end, many Pennsylvanians had already learned that bank money was better than government money because it was more difficult to counterfeit and because it was immediately convertible in specie, notes, or deposits, at the holder's option. Nevertheless, after the Revolution, several states, including Pennsylvania in 1785, again resorted to issuing bills of credit. In all instances, the bills failed miserably. Pennsylvania's bills of credit, for instance, slowly depreciated about 7.5 percent until June 1786, when they suddenly dipped another 15 to 20 percent. By September of that year, they had rebounded to 10 percent below par (face value) but on July 14, 1787, the bills stopped circulating entirely. Only the threat of civil disorder forced the bills again into circulation, albeit at a slightly steeper discount. The ugly affair produced, in the words of future U.S. president James Madison, "a wound which will not easily be healed." The Virginian was correct.[13]

By late summer 1787, the bills had depreciated by as much as 30 percent. In November the Pennsylvania Assembly noted that "the bills of credit emitted [by this state] . . . have suffered a considerable depreciation." To stop the depreciation, the legislature began pulling the bills out of circulation faster than planned. But even that tactic failed to restore their value. In February 1788 the legislature noted that its bills were roughly 33 percent below par. By the end of March, one needed £140 to £150 in bills of credit to extinguish a £100 specie debt. (New Jersey's bills of credit were similarly depreciated.) The value of the bills never recovered. On September 17, 1788, the *Pennsylvania Gazette* reported that "for some time past" bills of credit of the 1785 emission "ceased to pass as a currency." "Instead of being a medium of commerce," the *Gazette* continued, the bills "are now bought and sold at much less value than is expressed on the face of the bills." On February 17, 1789, the assembly journal also noted that the 1785 emission "has ceased to be a circulating medium." So it was no accident that newspapers quoted the going prices of the bills next to the prices of loan office certificates and other Revolutionary War debt. All were essentially speculative securities, "junk" debt in modern parlance. Government paper money was so discredited that one of the least controversial parts of the U.S. Constitution prohibited states from issuing more bills of credit. By renouncing paper money, which could be highly inflationary, the United States joined Holland, Great Britain, and a handful of other leading nations that had also made a credible commitment to anchoring their money to the precious metals.[14]

The United States emerged from the trials and tribulations of the 1780s on a specie standard, with a money supply composed almost entirely of bank liabilities (notes and deposits) and foreign coins. In addition to supplying the economy with currency, commercial banks served as intermediaries that linked savers to entrepreneurs. Those with extra cash found the Bank of North America a good place to store it for safekeeping. When they needed it, they could withdraw it in coins and / or banknotes. Or, if convenient, they could order the Bank to pay it to a third party via check. As a rule, they did not receive interest on their deposits, but their monies were callable at will and perfectly safe.

Those who needed to borrow funds for short periods also found the Bank of North America a useful institution. Say a miller sold a thousand barrels of flour to a merchant for shipment to the West Indies in return for the merchant's promissory note. Instead of waiting for the IOU to fall due, the miller, who likely had employees and farmers pressing him for payment, could present it to the Bank on "discount day." If the Bank's directors saw fit, they would immediately give the miller the discounted present value of the promissory note (the value of the note minus the interest due). Once again, an IOU made everyone happy. The merchant got to delay payment, but the miller received most of the funds arising from the sale immediately. The miller's workers and suppliers were happy to get paid immediately too. And the Bank, or more precisely its stockholders, was also happy, as long as the borrower paid his promissory note when due.

Most of the time—indeed, almost all of the time—bank borrowers did pay on time because they knew to do otherwise jeopardized their credit standing in the entire community, not just with the bank. And the bank did not lend to just anyone. It very carefully screened loan applicants, selecting only the best of the best. Because the bank's interest rate was constrained by law at 6 percent, a rate generally well below that charged on Chestnut Street's back alleys, it had the pick of the litter. Anyone with a shot at getting a loan tried the bank first. Of course, the bank had to turn many applicants away. That did not help it politically, but it did ensure its basic economic soundness.

The way to reduce the number of disgruntled loan applicants was to make the Bank of North America larger or to create more banks. Both in fact occurred. In 1784 the Bank of North America merged with the so-called Bank of Pennsylvania after the new bank's successful initial public offering of stock but before it commenced banking operations. Later another Bank of Pennsylvania formed. That one, which at $3 million had a larger capitalization than the Bank of North America, began operations in 1793. By 1814 Philadelphia County was home to nine commercial banks, America to an additional 193. All were based largely on the template provided by the Bank of North America.[15]

✐ As noted above, the rebel governments found it difficult to borrow money. They simply did not have bright enough prospects or a good enough credit record. So they raised very little money domestically from *willing* lenders. But the rebels did have soldiers, and it is amazing how persuasive a few dozen muskets, bayonets affixed, can be. Unlike many armies, the rebel forces as a general rule did not confiscate provisions and supplies. But when the going got rough, and it was often quite rough, they took what they needed and left behind an IOU. Receiving a piece of paper of dubious value as compensation for good horses, wagons, and foodstuffs was a bitter pill for farmers to swallow, but many other armies in history under similar circumstances would have killed the farmer and taken his stuff, including perhaps his wife and daughters. So although the Patriots' tactics seem a tad intrusive today, they were actually quite enlightened.[16]

And, truth be told, the army essentially used the same heavy-handed tactics on itself. Oftentimes the government could not make payroll. So instead of giving soldiers money, it gave them IOUs. The soldiers were no happier than the farmers, who at least did not have to risk their lives day in and day out to receive the seemingly worthless scraps of paper! Of course, there was a chance, however remote, that the rebels would win the war and find the political wherewithal to pay their debts. The fact that some foreigners were willing to lend to the Patriots was a good sign, but not one that could be taken too far. After all, many of the foreign loans came from France and its minion Spain, both of which made them in the hopes of weakening Great Britain, their perennial enemy.

Ironically, despite the fact that the rebel government found it difficult to borrow, it found it quite easy to run up a big load of debts. Almost immediately, those debts began to change hands. Soldiers and farmers in need of immediate cash sold them for pennies to a few dimes on the dollar. The buyers were speculators, men who gambled that the debts would eventually be paid off or, more likely, that they would be able to unload the IOUs in a few days to a yet more optimistic speculator. America's public securities market was born, but as yet it was a tiny fickle beast. Its brokers, specialists who matched buyers to sellers of government IOUs, charged much higher commissions than they would a decade later. Prices were generally quite volatile and price differences between markets were often large and persistent.

Moreover, the sheer number of different IOUs—many of them signed by Philadelphians, like U.S. treasurer Michael Hillegas, serving in the Continental government—even securities speculators and brokers found overwhelming. To reduce the confusion and spur demand for securities, Philadelphia broker Matthew McConnell in 1787 published a tract that summarized the situation. "Ever since public securities have been in circulation," McConnell explained, "their variety were found so great, that a knowledge of them was considered by those who did not attend to their raise and progress, as a profession." Though one of those professionals, McConnell himself found the country's debt structure "extensive" and a subject that required "much attention." Indeed, the detail that followed was almost mind-numbing. The large number of debt issuers—from the Continental Congress to Continental quartermasters to state governments to militia officers—made things difficult. The fact that the debts were denominated in the several state currencies or in dollars added yet another layer of complexity. Primitive communication and record-keeping systems didn't help matters. Despite his best efforts, McConnell found that he could not obtain "all the laws of the different states relative to their public securities." Throw in the fact that some of the debt instruments had been fully serviced, some partly serviced, and others utterly neglected, and the mess was nearly complete.[17]

Other difficulties lurked. As noted, some of the IOUs had been partially serviced. In other words, some interest payments had already been made. Yet all interest remained due on other IOUs, even of the same type. Further compounding matters, many of the interest "payments" were made not with cash but with the issuance of *additional* IOUs. The final straw was that counterfeiters had altered many of the notes. "It is supposed," McConnell explained, "that the ink is extracted with some kind of liquid, and then in place of eight or ten dollars there is inserted many hundred." Banknotes the handwritten government IOUs were not.

Under such conditions, trading volumes were necessarily low, prices widely dispersed, and brokerage fees relatively high. Much of the trading that occurred was localized. Pennsylvania's IOUs, for instance, traded a little in Philadelphia—at speculative prices well below 50 percent of face value. The size and quality of the market paled in comparison to what was to come.[18]

It was little wonder that European investors generally eschewed American securities in the 1780s. As McConnell noted, Europeans did not consider American governments "to be so well organized as to afford security, and believe that much danger is to be apprehended from the Indian natives." More damning still, Europeans found the revenue base of American governments much too slender and precarious. Moreover, the country's greatest asset, many millions of acres of unimproved but fertile land, could not be paid for and settled for a considerable length of time.

McConnell predicted, accurately, that once the government began to pay interest on the debt, the IOUs would become "a kind of active national stock" that would "serve as a medium in trade." But, McConnell lamented, just a few months before the Constitutional Convention was to convene in his home city, government had taken "no decisive measures" to service, let alone pay off, the war debt. "This is owing," he argued, setting the stage for the convention, "not to a want of ability, but to a difference in opinion about the mode of doing it, and a want of energy in the federal government." That all changed after adoption of the Constitution.[19]

✒ Many people know that the distressed state of the national debt helped to bring about the political atmosphere that made the Constitution possible. Few, however, realize that financial theory played an important role in that crucial document's final shape, in the constitution of the Constitution, if you will. The Revolution blessed Americans with a profound understanding of how agency problems affected both public and corporate governance. An agent is any one who conducts business on behalf of an owner of property. Employees, for example, are agents. And real estate and insurance agents are aptly named. If not properly compensated and watched, agents tend to act in their own self-interests rather than in the interests of the owners. Hence, employees "slack off" when they can and in particularly severe cases will even steal from owners.[20]

In good Lockean tradition, Americans saw government officials as mere agents, as individuals deputized to serve the interests of the owners of the nation, the citizens. When Robert Morris vacated the office of superintendent of finance on November 1, 1784, for instance, he published a full statement of his accounts, noting that "the Master [i.e., the public] should know what the servant [i.e., Morris, as superintendent] has done." Government was to serve the people, not the other way around. This might seem trite or obvious today, but in the eighteenth century it was still a radical notion. So it was not at all clear that the idea was a practicable one.[21]

When it became obvious to the colonists that their agents, the king and Parliament, served themselves instead of their constituents, they perceived "tyranny," formally severed the agency relationship on July 4, 1776, and set out to find new agents from among their own kind. As they did so, they paid strict attention to the incentive structures of the political offices that they created. They tried to ensure that every officer was "checked" or monitored by another and that every part of the government was "balanced" by another that, in turn, was backed by a different set of special interests.

Anti-Federalists, those who opposed the passage of the proposed U.S. Constitution, feared that the rapaciousness of government knew no bounds. Moreover, they tended to come from occupations or areas—like farming or the backwoods—where they had relatively little experience mitigating the principal-agent problem just described. They therefore looked upon the creation of a powerful national government with trepidation.

Federalists, on the other hand, believed that constitutional checks and balances, along with the proper alignment of economic incentives, could prevent governmental tyranny. They tended to come from occupations and areas—like wholesaling in cities—where they gained significant experience reducing agency problems. They were therefore confident that they could mitigate the problem in government. For example, Matthew McConnell, the Philadelphia securities broker, thought it "ridiculous to suppose that sufficient power cannot be given to that body [the national government] without endangering the liberty of the subject, when that liberty is so well secured by the frequent election and constant rotation of the members." "In a republic, where legislators are alternately both governors and governed," he argued, "there is an effectual check against usurpation."[22]

With some notable exceptions, Federalists like McConnell were right. The U.S. Constitution and many of the early state governments were models of proper governance, so much so that the plethora of new business corporations that formed in the late eighteenth and early nineteenth centuries copied them closely. Indeed, largely the same set of men who wrote the early state constitutions also wrote the first corporate charters and by-laws. So once again we find Philadelphia, the home of the Constitutional Convention, at the leading edge of U.S. financial thought and innovation.

✐ The American Revolution did more than give the thirteen mainland colonies their political independence. It also led to the creation of a new sort of government, one, as Abraham Lincoln would later say, "of the people, by the people, for the people." That new government, flying the financially astute U.S. Constitution as its banner, laid the foundation for the financial revolution that funded the transportation, market, and industrial revolutions of the nineteenth century.

The precise nature of that financial revolution forms the subject of the next five chapters. In short, the financial revolution ushered forth a stable monetary system (chapter 4), a system effectively regulated by a central bank (chapter 5), and a means of trading three of life's most disruptive risks (chapter 6). It also helped Philadelphia to become the original "City of Homes" (chapter 7) and helped it to join the transportation revolution (chapter 8), the explosive growth of roads, canals, and railroads that took place in the first half of the nineteenth century. But first we start with the basics: money, money, and money.

4

MONEY, MONEY, MONEY

Money is the most widely held financial asset. We all use it, most of us every single day of our adult lives. It is a wonderful thing. It seems simple enough, but in fact few of us have a deep understanding of what turns out to be a rather involved subject. In this chapter, I hope to change that. I also hope to show that when it came to money, Philadelphia was an innovator. In the colonial period, it set the standard for quality government paper money. During and after the Revolution, it led the charge to bank money. By the 1790s, it was also home of the U.S. Mint. Though for all intents and purposes a failure until the California gold rush, the Philadelphia Mint coined most of the slim stock of U.S. coins. This chapter, in other words, is truly about money (bills of credit), money (bank liabilities), money (coins). But precisely what is this elusive subject, this money? A few pages should make its essence crystal clear.[1]

Money is literally *any* "thing" readily accepted in payment for goods, services, or debts. The money supply is simply the sum of all money in an economy at a given time. The set of institutions and markets that creates and redeems money is called the monetary system. Money and monetary systems have taken a wide variety of specific forms, most of which can be reduced into one of three types: barter, commodity, and fiat. Of course, those three systems can coexist, but at any given time, one system typically predominates.

Barter is by far the simplest monetary system, likely dating to roving bands of *Homo erectus* beginning some 2 million years ago. It is simply the exchange of one good or service for another—a hunk of antelope meat for an Acheulean hand ax, a basket of apples for a spear, a necklace of pretty stones for sex. Barter took place during chance encounters, often at the interstices of territories or ranges. Barter within groups was probably quite limited because early bands of hunters and gatherers were likely organized like modern firms. Firm or band members, most of whom were closely related, exchanged goods and services within the group on a nonprice basis. Anthropologists call this behavior "sharing" or "forging ties of mutual reciprocity." It seems extremely unlikely that "sharing" occurred between unrelated bands, so some type of quid pro quo arrangement, or "trading," must have taken place.

Simple trade theory shows that bands that engaged in trading activities would have been better off than those that did not engage in trade, and much better off than those that gave away resources gratis. Trade increases wealth by allowing for specialization of production and hence increased per capita productivity. On a more basic level, it allows people to rid themselves of unneeded items in exchange for more desirable things.

Those "gains from trade," however, were limited because barter is an extremely inefficient method of exchange. The first problem is that each party must desire to acquire the exact good that the other has to offer, including the exact quantity and quality, and at the exact time the other has it to offer. This so-called double coincidence of wants is difficult to overcome within the barter system. Moreover, barter creates an enormous number of "prices," the costs of goods and services in terms of each other. An economy with just ten traded goods and services, for instance, requires forty-five different prices, while an economy with a thousand traded goods and services requires just shy of a half million different prices![2]

Because of the problems with barter, commodity monies typically arise as population densities increase and as economies produce a greater variety of goods. Despite a superficial similarity to barter, commodity monetary systems are a major advance, arguably much more important to prehistoric economic growth than the invention of the wheel or the harnessing of fire. In a commodity monetary system, one good becomes a unit of account, the means by which all other traded goods and services are priced or valued. The commodity becomes a measure of value, answering the question "What is the price of that?" in the same way that inches or centimeters answer the question "How long is that?" or pounds or kilograms answer the question "How much does that weigh?" The unit of account is an abstraction of reality analogous to human abstractions of distance, mass, time, and so on.

Conceptual confusion arises because sometimes the commodity that underlies the unit of account is also used as a physical medium of exchange. In other words, the commodity upon which the abstract unit of account was formed was literally turned over to the seller to make a purchase. It is important to keep in mind, however, that the unit of account and the medium of exchange are *distinct* concepts. For example, imagine a monetary system with the commodity money "clams." (Or, to be more precise, clamshells. I could not resist the pun because the word "clams" is slang for dollars.) All the goods and services in that economy would be priced in clams, not in terms of each other. A bow, for instance, might cost 20 clams, each arrow for that bow 2 clams, a bead necklace 10 clams, a handful of rare medicinal herbs 50 clams. A purchaser of those herbs might actually have paid the shaman 50 clams. Or he might have paid 2 bows and a bead necklace ($[2 \times 20] + 10$), or 1 bow and 15 arrows ($[1 \times 20] + [2 \times 15]$). Whatever the particulars of the case, two concepts should be clear: First, commodity money systems are much more efficient than barter because the number of prices will equal the number of traded goods and services. Second, the unit of account and the medium of exchange need not be the same physical thing. The breakthrough was the creation of an abstract measure of value, not the physical form of the exchange.

Commodity monetary systems have existed in some human communities for at least the last several thousand years and perhaps much longer than that. As self-equilibrating systems, they need no government aid to form or to continue. In fact, they function better when governments leave them alone. Here is how they work: Suppose that clams are the unit of account or measure of the value of things. Further suppose that the economy produces 10 goods and services, A through J. Suppose, too, that at the initial condition, each unit of each good can be produced on average in 1 hour (total) and hence all cost the same in terms of clams, say, 1 clam. To wit, A = 1 clam, B = 1 clam, C = 1 clam, and so on. Now let us suppose that an individual can on average harvest 5 clams in an hour. Obviously, it will be more lucrative to harvest 5 clams in an hour rather than to spend that hour producing 1 unit of A or B, et cetera. Individuals will quite rationally harvest clams and exchange them for A . . . J. By introducing more clams into the economy, however, the clam price of A . . . J will increase. In other words, soon it will take 2 clams to acquire a unit of A . . . J, then 3, then 4, then 5. At that point, individuals in the economy will be indifferent about whether they produce 1 unit of A . . . J in their hour, or if they harvest 5 clams and then exchange the clams for 1 unit of A . . . J.

Of course, the numbers used above are just for the sake of example. If 100 clams could be harvested in an hour, then the nominal clam price would be higher but equilibrium would still be reached. Conversely, if it became easier to produce A . . . J, so that 5 units could be produced in an hour, then the clam price of A . . . J would drop until people would again be indifferent about producing A . . . J or harvesting clams. In other words, commodity monetary systems are self-equilibrating systems where the supply of money grows or shrinks as market forces indicate.

Interestingly, clamshells were a fairly effective commodity money, as were animal teeth, beads, bronze, cattle and other large domesticated quadrupeds, coconuts, feathers, furs, leather, needles, rice, rum, salt, sundry types of shells, stones, tobacco, wheat, wool, and a huge host of other non-rare commodities. As late as the 1960s, monetary theorists in the United States seriously considered a monetary system based on common bricks. The problem with such monies is not their lack of rarity, which, as we will see is actually a great virtue, but rather their lack of uniformity. One variety of tobacco is better than another, insect-infested wheat can be mixed with good grain, and so forth. Heterogeneity creates incentives for buyers (or debtors) to adulterate their payments. Consider the problem from another angle—diamonds, rubies, and other precious stones are extremely rare but almost never become money because it is not easy to distinguish valuable gems from common or flawed ones.[3]

Gold and silver are the classic commodity monies not because of their rarity but because of their homogeneity. They are, after all, elements. Though susceptible to debasement by mixture with lesser metals, there are fairly easy ways, like water displacement and standardized weights, to distinguish between adulterated blocks of precious metals and blocks of specified purity.

The relative rarity of the precious metals actually decreased their effectiveness as units of value. When the gold standard ruled, there were periods of inflation (higher prices) and deflation (lower prices) due to fluctuating supplies of new gold. When new gold supplies slowed, the monetary supply could not keep up with increased demand, and the market price of gold moved higher. The prices of goods and services, therefore, trended lower because each ounce of gold purchased more goods and services. That, of course, induced more people to seek out gold in expectations of above-market returns. After gold strikes, the money supply expanded rapidly and inflation ensued, as with the clam example above. And as with the clam example, there was a natural limit to the price increases because as the aggregate price level rose—that is, as each ounce of gold purchased fewer goods and services—it became less lucrative to mine gold. Eventually the equilibrium point was reached where the return from producing gold equaled the going risk-adjusted market rate of return. The monetary system was again in balance or equilibrium.

The rarity of precious metals turned out to be the main cause of their downfall. The supply of the precious metals was not, in the words of economists, sufficiently "elastic." Unlike common commodities like clams or bricks, which can be harvested or manufactured virtually at will, the precious metals, particularly gold, were often elusive. There were periods when the entire known stock of gold was in circulation or other use. When commodity prices began to fall, signaling a need for more gold money, new natural deposits had to be discovered before equilibrium could be restored. The process could take years, even decades. In the second half of the nineteenth century, many Americans urged moving from a gold standard to a silver standard on the supposition that the supply of silver was more elastic than that of gold. Silverites, like the Populists, ultimately failed. Gold strikes in the Klondike relieved the pressure on gold supplies until the government decided to do away with commodity money entirely.[4]

Only after the coercive powers of the state are well developed does a fiat monetary system have a chance to succeed. In such a system, the government establishes a unit of account literally by fiat or decree. To help make the decree stick, the government often creates a medium of exchange, composed of paper bills and / or metal tokens, that it proclaims to be "legal tender for all debts, public and private." The great strength of such a scheme is that the supply of fiat monies, like today's Federal Reserve notes, is in theory perfectly elastic. In other words, the supply of money can be increased or decreased as needed. That flexibility, however, turns out to be a great weakness. Fiat systems are not self-equilibrating. They are similar to the command economies of communist nations. Unless the commander, like Federal Reserve chairman Alan Greenspan, is an able or lucky one, the results can be disastrous. Often the central monetary authority, the government agency responsible for determining the supply of money, creates too much. That, in turn, causes inflation, as during the 1770s—and 1970s. Sometimes, as in the case of the United States in the early stages of the Great Depression, the central monetary authority creates too little money, leading to deflation and greatly reduced per capita economic output. Over long stretches, fiat monetary systems almost invariably create inflation. The aggregate price level of the United States, for instance, has increased tenfold since it abandoned gold in favor of Federal Reserve money.[5]

⟋◯ After the first few years of initial settlement, colonial Pennsylvanians, like colonists in the rest of British North America, resorted to barter only infrequently. Barter was extremely inefficient, and the colonists knew it. "Bartering one species of property for another," they realized, "would be endless labour." "For some years after the settling of this colony," a Pennsylvanian wrote in 1768, "we had but little specie, and trade was carried on chiefly by truck or barter." "Under such inconveniences," the aged man correctly noted, "it was found impossible for a colony to flourish, or the inhabitants make any considerable progress in their improvements."[6] The legal monetization of country produce, like wheat and beef, helped but was not as efficient as the use of coins, which finally began to circulate after about 1700.

When in the late 1710s and early 1720s "the balance of trade carried out the gold and silver as fast as it was brought in" to the province, domestic trade again temporarily had to be "carried on by the extremely inconvenient method of barter." In response to that crisis, Pennsylvania issued a fiat medium of exchange called "bills of credit." The bills, made of paper, were essentially non-interest-bearing government promissory notes (IOUs). The government redeemed the bills when citizens presented them to government officials to pay taxes or to repay sums borrowed from the government's General Loan Office, or GLO. (When an IOU is returned to its maker or issuer, it is effectively repaid because it is nonsensical to owe something to oneself.) Sometimes the Pennsylvania government issued the bills to government suppliers and called them in via taxes. At other times the government, through the GLO, lent the bills to citizens on the security of land or other assets. In that case, the bills were redeemed when presented by the borrowers to make loan repayments. Between their issuance and redemption, bills of credit passed hand to hand as cash, canceling debts and making purchases. Between 1723 and 1775, Pennsylvania emitted a grand total of just over £1 million bills of credit. Never, however, did the total volume of bills outstanding exceed £500,000.[7]

It is essential to understand that those bills never became Pennsylvania's unit of account. They served only as one of many media of exchange. In other words, the bills *represented* value but did not *define* it. Many modern Americans will have difficulty understanding this point because they are so accustomed to having the unit of account and the medium of exchange coincide. A moment's reflection will reveal that even today, the unit of account and the medium of exchange are conceptually distinct aspects of money. Suppose, for example, that you decide to sell your used car for $10,000. When you draw up the contract, you do not specifically state that the buyer may take possession of the vehicle when he delivers a hundred $100 bills or anything of the sort. In fact, you would probably find it odd if the buyer tendered cash at all. You might want a money order or cashier's check instead of the buyer's personal check, or to maintain possession of the vehicle until the check cleared, but, except perhaps to avoid taxation, you would not expect a cash payment. In other words, when you think "$10,000," you have an abstraction in your mind, a measure of what you can buy with that $10,000, not a particular *thing* in mind. Indeed, if the buyer of your automobile happened to have $10,000 worth of goods and services that you wanted, say a thousand shares of a particular $10 stock that you wanted to own or a thoroughbred racehorse worth $10,000 that you wanted to race, you would be just as happy to take either of them as the money. Importantly, you would not be engaging in "barter" because you would have valued each item according to its current *dollar* price.

If you lived in Russia, or many other areas of the world, the distinction between the medium of exchange and the unit of account would be very clear to you. In Russia and elsewhere, people and firms often express prices and contract terms in U.S. dollars because the dollar holds its value better than the ruble (and many other national currencies). The purchaser / payer / borrower still usually tenders rubles (or other national currency), but the number of rubles s / he forks over will depend on the going exchange rate between the ruble and the dollar. The use of the dollar as a unit of account in Russia is so ubiquitous that "bucks" has become part of the Russian language. A common joke is that when Russian tourists reach the United States, they are amazed to learn that Americans use *Russian bucks.*"[8]

So when a colonial Pennsylvanian made a contract for £100 "Pennsylvania currency," he or she did not have a hundred £1 bills of credit in mind. All that s / he expected was that goods and services totaling PA£100 would be paid to satisfy the contract. The payment might be made in whole or in part in Pennsylvania's bills of credit. But it might also be made in the bills of credit of other colonies, in coins, in bonds, in labor, in livestock, in "country produce," or in any other good or service that the creditor desired and upon which a money price could be ascertained.

Both the Pennsylvania government, then located in Philadelphia, and Pennsylvania's leading businessmen, Philadelphia merchants, had a hand in creating "Pennsylvania currency," the colony's unit of account. Early on the legislature passed laws that regulated the value of coins in the province. In 1723, for instance, the assembly inserted into a bill a clause that stipulated that Spanish pistoles and other gold coins should continue to pass current at £5 10s. per ounce. The British eventually made it clear that they disapproved of such statutes, so the coin-rating business became a private matter. Leading merchants periodically convened, as they did in September 1742 and February 1775, to assess and modify the ratings. Increasing the value of a coin in terms of local currency, of course, tended to attract and retain that coin in local circulation. As water always flows downhill, so, too, does money always flow to where it will "fetch" the most.[9]

By the late 1730s, Pennsylvanians had determined that the Spanish milled dollar, a silver coin, was worth 7 shillings and 6 pence (7s. 6d.) Pennsylvania currency, the rating that held for the rest of the century. Other silver coins also had ratings, based on their silver content. Similarly, Pennsylvanians settled on the values of various gold coins. Almanacs often printed the ratings of the major coins, so we know that the coin ratings did occasionally change but not drastically so.[10]

In their domestic dealings, Pennsylvanians understood that 7s. 6d. and $1 were as interchangeable as 1 inch and 2.54 centimeters or 1 pound and .45 kilograms. Only when they dealt with outsiders did they find it necessary to explicitly equate the two units of value. For example, when in 1757 Philadelphian "Sylvanus Americanus" proposed the publication of a monthly "American magazine" for circulation throughout British North America, he carefully described the subscription price as being "One Shilling Pennsylvania money for each magazine, or its value in the current coin of the several places above mentioned, allowing Seven shillings and Six pence for each Spanish Dollar."[11]

Clearly, Pennsylvania's early money supply was far from homogenous. In 1755 a robber managed to lay his hands on "about Seventy Pounds," fifty of it in bills of credit and the balance in foreign coins. In 1764 a mugger made off with "in Paper Money two Five Pounds Bills, and three Twenty Shilling Bills, and other small Money, which amounted to £17 5 s. 6 d., 4 Dollars, some English shillings, and £45 in Gold, chiefly English Guineas, some Moidores and Doubloons." Similarly, in 1772 a thief stole "about 190 Half Joes, about 30 Pistoles, 8 Moidores, 4 Guineas, 60 Pieces of Eight, and 48 Pounds in Jersey Six Pound bills," not to mention "a number of bonds, to the amount of £1,500."[12]

But were that all! Much early money existed only as notations in account books. Say a neighbor needed a pig for breakfast. Most likely, she would not have any coins or bills with which to pay for it. So the seller and the buyer would mark the transaction down in their respective account books. Maybe the next week the pig seller would want "a plug of tobacky." Again, both parties would dutifully mark down the exchange, noting the money price of the tobacco. Once a year or so, the two parties would settle their accounts. Then, and only then, might cash be tendered to pay a balance down or eliminate it completely. Though this system appears a bit awkward, it was quite efficient and widely used. In fact, the vast majority of purchases, especially in rural areas with stable populations, were made on book account.[13]

Even storekeepers extended credits. "Credit is a thing so very common here," a colonist in Westmoreland County, Virginia, wrote in 1774, "that there is not one person in a hundred who pays the ready money, for the goods he takes up, to a store." (When in high school in the mid-1980s, I worked in a small country store that still extended book credit to steady customers.) In the colonial period, the use of cash was more common in urban centers with more fluid populations, like Philadelphia, but even there the use of book credit was ubiquitous.[14]

The use of book credit declined during the Revolution because the supply of bills of credit increased so rapidly. As inflation began to kick in, people realized that holding the bills for extended periods was a losing proposition because with each passing day a given amount of bills would purchase fewer goods. So the game was to spend your money ASAP, if not sooner. But that was no way to live, so after the Revolution Philadelphians generally supported monetary reforms, including replacing government paper money with private bank money. The U.S. Constitution, which prohibited states from issuing bills of credit, marked the apex of that monetary reform movement. But one final reform was still needed.

✍⃝ Soon after passage of the Constitution, state currencies disappeared, replaced by a national unit of account known as the U.S. dollar, a slightly modified version of the Spanish milled dollar unit, rated at 7s. 6d. The entire nation adopted Philadelphia's rating of the dollar. Indeed, in the 1780s and the early part of the 1790s, the U.S. dollar was often divided into "ninetieths": 7s. times 12d. per shilling plus 6d. So after about 1795, it no longer makes economic sense to speak of Pennsylvania's money supply—U.S. dollars were U.S. dollars, regardless of their state of origin or circulation. But Philadelphia still had an important role to play in American monetary history.

After the final redemption of state bills of credit in the late 1780s and early 1790s, the major media of exchange were foreign coins and bank liabilities, specifically banknotes and deposits. A bank liability is simply an IOU owed by a bank to the owner or holder of the liability. Most readers will be familiar with the bank liability known as "checkable deposits" or "transaction deposits." The principles of such accounts today are the same as they were in the late eighteenth and early nineteenth centuries. Namely, the bank holds a sum of value for the depositor until the depositor requests the funds to be paid to him- or herself (a withdrawal) or his or her assigns (a check). Bank checks were used to make long-distance remittances as early as 1782, when Philadelphia's Bank of North America, the nation's first commercial bank, began full operation. Over the decades, the use of checks exploded as the number of banks grew and the complexity of bank payment networks increased. Provided the maker of the check had sufficient funds in his or her account, checks were payable in specie upon demand. If certified by the cashier as "accepted," checks were literally as good as gold, as long as the bank remained solvent, of course.

Banknotes were also bank liabilities or IOUs. Redeemable in gold or silver on demand, like deposits they did not pay interest to the holder. Unlike checks, notes were bearer instruments designed to pass from hand to hand as cash. Although also composed of paper and physically similar to bills of credit, specie convertibility made banknotes a very different animal, indeed. Unlike fiat bills, the volume of which was essentially at the whim of legislatures, the market largely determined the volume of banknotes in circulation. Specie convertibility served to check bank emissions by forcing bankers to keep larger reserves, that is, higher ratios of specie to liabilities, on hand to meet redemption requests.

It is important to note that banknotes were *not* a legal tender. They circulated as cash to the extent that the bank gained the market's confidence by promptly redeeming any notes presented for payment. The market realized that bankers held only a fractional reserve of specie against their liabilities. Liability holders became anxious only if it appeared that the fractional reserve was too small. Most of the time, most banks held adequate reserves, so their notes circulated locally at full par, that is, dollar for dollar. When *local* notes slipped in value, it was because the market perceived that the bank's reserves were inadequate or, in other words, that the bank was in trouble and might default or because counterfeits were rampant.

Banknotes that strayed very far from the bank of issue traded below par, for example, at 99 cents on the dollar. In most instances, such discounts were not risk premia and hence should not be taken as indications of the supposed instability of the banking system. Rather, such discounts were simply reflections of the cost and time it would take to redeem the notes at particular distances from the bank of issue. Banknotes, of course, were redeemable only at the bank that issued them (or sometimes their branches, but until very recently branch banking was a rare bird in America).[15]

Quotations of the prices of Pennsylvania banknotes appeared in newspapers published in Massachusetts, New York, Maryland, Virginia, South Carolina, Louisiana, and elsewhere. Likewise, Philadelphia papers quoted the prices of notes issued by banks in those and other states. The money supply in the early national and antebellum periods was truly national in scope.

Our story cannot end here because Philadelphia was home to the U.S. Mint, the part of the federal government responsible for manufacturing the nation's coinage. The Mint was of little economic importance in the early decades of the nation's existence because it minted relatively few coins. A political football, the early Mint didn't function terribly well. It did possess sufficient internal and external checks and balances to prevent major frauds. The situation persisted because most banks were content to hold foreign coins and bullion as reserves and most domestic payments were made with banknotes or checks. By the 1850s the nation's monetary situation began to change drastically and the Mint's importance grew many times over. By then, however, Chestnut Street's financial dominance was little more than a memory.[16]

✐ On April 2, 1792, George Washington signed into law a bill establishing a mint, a factory for the production of coins, for the federal government, under article 1, section 8, of the U.S. Constitution. (That same clause also empowered Congress to "regulate the Value . . . of foreign Coin," a power that it also exercised.) The bill drew upon the earlier work on coins and mintage proffered during the Confederation period by Thomas Jefferson, Gouverneur Morris, Robert Morris, and others and the more recent recommendations of Alexander Hamilton, whose "Report on the Establishment of a Mint" Congress had received on January 28, 1791.[17]

The law stipulated that the Mint should "be situate and carried on at the seat of the government of the United States, for the time being," which was simply legalese for Philadelphia. In some ways, Philadelphia was the logical location for the institution. The city, after all, was home to the headquarters of the Bank of the United States, the nation's central bank. Moreover, it was a thriving commercial center. On the other hand, Philadelphia was not a likely candidate for the nation's permanent capital. And, as a more practical matter, the city proper offered little in the way of waterpower and much in the way of disease. Indeed, the Mint suspended operations during parts of 1797, 1798, 1799, 1802, and 1803 due to the yellow fever epidemics that ravaged the city each autumn of those years. The institution also found itself reliant on inefficient horse- and manpower until the introduction of steam presses in the 1810s.

In 1800 the Senate considered the expediency of moving the Mint to Washington, D.C., the nation's new prefab capital. But the Mint was already well ensconced in the Quaker City. The Washington administration had seen to that, instructing the institution to purchase real estate outright rather than to lease. The most suitable available area was composed of three lots located on Seventh Street between Market and Arch, just two blocks north of Chestnut. In the middle of June 1792, Mint director David Rittenhouse, a world-renowned Philadelphia scientist, personally negotiated a price of £1,600 cash on the barrelhead and assumption of a £21 per annum ground rent payable to the Almshouse. After Thomas Jefferson and Washington approved the deal, construction moved quickly. On July 31 the cornerstone of the plain but relatively substantial brick edifice was laid.[18]

Though the lots proved too small for the Mint within just a few years, the institution remained in its original location (and a lot that it rented in the Northern Liberties, then a suburb just north of the city line) until 1833. That year it relocated to a new building—under construction since July 4, 1829—on the corner of Chestnut and Juniper streets near Penn Square. The new building was more spacious and visually appealing than the old, thanks to two Ionic porticos and a complete marble covering. Contemporaries believed that only Girard College—a school for orphaned boys bequeathed by Philadelphia merchant-banker Stephen Girard—rivaled its beauty. The new building was more functional too, as it was fireproof and contained ample room for steam-driven presses and other technical improvements. It was something of a miracle, however, that the Mint survived long enough to acquire such modern posh digs.[19]

The 1792 law charged the Mint with the manufacturing of copper cents ($.01) and half-cents ($.005), silver half-dimes ($.05), dimes ($.10), quarters ($.25), half-dollars ($.50), and full dollars ($1.00), as well as gold eagles ($10), double eagles ($20), half ($5) and quarter ($2.50) eagles, and $3 gold pieces. Half-cents fell out of favor by about 1830 and the $3 gold pieces were not a big hit, but most of the other denominations were popular. (Indeed, most of those denominations are still in use, though gold has long since given way to paper and silver to baser metals coated with a silver-looking finish.) The Mint could purchase copper or accept deposits of specie by private parties (individuals, partnerships, and corporations), but it could not purchase the silver and gold that it needed to coin dollars and eagles, respectively. That proved its undoing.[20]

Active Mint operations began in October 1792. By November 6 of that year, the Mint had successfully produced a special batch of silver half-dimes. Its auspicious beginnings, however, soon gave way to torpor. High copper prices plagued the minting of pennies and half-pennies from the start. Worse still, not until July 1794—almost two years after commencing operations—did the Mint receive a private deposit of silver, some $80,000 of French coins owned by the Bank of Maryland. The first private gold flow into the Mint occurred in February 1795, when New England merchant Moses Brown deposited $2,276 worth of gold bullion.[21]

The Mint paid its officers well, especially considering how little work they did. The director received the same salary as a city bank president, while the other officers earned as much as a bank cashier (the chief operating officer, not a mere teller). The directorship, at least at first, was a very high-profile federal position, so it managed to attract considerable talent. The Mint's first director, for instance, was Philadelphian David Rittenhouse, perhaps the only American with both the mechanical and financial experience requisite for the job. A clockmaker, astronomer, and paper maker, Rittenhouse had long served as Pennsylvania's state treasurer. Even Rittenhouse could not draw blood from a stone; the Mint languished for half a century simply because it obtained precious few deposits of the precious metals.[22]

The 1792 law, after all, made no provision for the Mint to purchase gold and silver bullion on behalf of the public. An act for regulating foreign coins passed in February 1793 authorizing the president to proclaim that foreign coins, save Spanish milled dollars, were no longer legal tender and authorizing the secretary of the treasury to turn over to the Mint for re-coinage all such foreign coin paid to the U.S. federal government. No president made such proclamation, so the Mint relied solely on a trickle of voluntary private deposits.[23]

Between its inception and 1830, the Mint coined, in aggregate, only about $37 million—$18 million of that during the 1820s. By way of comparison, on any given *day* after 1800, the banking system had more than $40 million of banknotes in circulation! Moreover, most of the coins that the Mint did produce immediately flowed out of the country or were melted down. The only remedy—"debasing the coin" so that it was worth more as a coin than as bullion—was a measure that early U.S. politicians were loath to consider.[24]

Working at the Mint, either as an officer or as a laborer, does not appear to have been particularly onerous given the standards of the day. Some of the officers stayed at their jobs for decades, for instance, while others brought, or attempted to bring, friends and relatives into the organization while simultaneously fending off the entreaties of numerous supplicants. Neither practice jived with classical republican political theory, which argued for term limitations and if not for meritocracy, then at least against nepotism. Moreover, the officers often deputized clerks to sign receipts, vouchers, and the like for them. At least one clerk quit when he calculated that "the sacrifices" of time he made "have been nearly equivalent to the compensation allowed me for my services at the Mint." He quit because he was only *slightly* overpaid! The skilled technicians received so little practice at their trades that they botched what little work they did have. One assayer, for example, effectively ruined $974.75 worth of silver by inadvertently mixing it with ashes and broken crucibles.[25]

Laborers and technicians were expected at their posts eleven hours a day. In the 1790s their hours changed with the seasons. By the 1820s they worked a fixed schedule from 5:00 a.m. to 4:00 p.m., except Saturdays, when they could knock off at 2:00 after the weekly cleaning routine; Sundays, of course; and the Mint's two official holidays, Christmas and Independence Day. They received a small extra stipend, called "drink money," during the summer months. The money was for cooling drinks, not alcohol-laden ones, because workers also received stern warnings not to be "found drunk" or to "bring spirituous liquors into the Mint." When in production, the Mint was a dangerous work environment, even for the sober. Indeed, smoking was also forbidden, and long before its prohibition in the workplace became trendy. Because the Mint attracted visitors, workers were also enjoined not to use profane or indecent language. Perhaps as a compensation for such onerous regulations, Mint laborers received paid sick days, a rarity in the era.[26]

With the Mint operating at low volume, the nation's small denomination currency, its pocket change, came from three major sources: foreign coins, fractional banknotes, and various fractional paper currencies—the infamous "shinplasters" emitted by some retail stores, nonbank corporations, and municipalities. The small foreign coins were often severely debased or even counterfeit. They were essentially tokens upon which foreigners earned the seigniorage. Similarly, the seigniorage from the circulation of fractional banknotes went to bank stockholders, not the government. The notes were adequate as small change, as long as they were genuine and the issuing bank remained solvent. Private shinplasters issued by nonbanks were more frequently counterfeited and less likely to be redeemed. Public shinplasters were essentially bills of credit and hence technically unconstitutional. But they circulated within the community of their issuance anyway.

None of those sources of small change was as good as an ample supply of domestically produced small coins would have been. Many politicians, egged on by private firms that wanted to win contracts to produce small coins for the government, found the small-change situation disagreeable and laid blame squarely on the Mint. Joshua Coit—a Connecticut Federalist who died in 1798 at the age of only forty—fired the first round, introducing a motion to investigate the Mint. Elias Boudinot, a staunch Hamiltonian Federalist from New Jersey, then rose and attacked the Mint as inefficient. William Smith—a representative from South Carolina who had been born in Bucks County, Pennsylvania, in 1751—opined that the Mint was "of little or no use whatever." So in early 1795, an anxious House of Representatives investigated the Mint in order "to render the institution more beneficial." The committee, chaired by Boudinot, thoroughly examined the institution for several months, before submitting a significant report to the House on February 9, 1795.[27]

First, the committee reviewed the Mint's organizational form and the duties of its officers. At the top of the hierarchy was the director, whose duty was to oversee "the whole business in all its various departments," including all of its "contracts and purchases" and "all improvements, buildings, machines, and whatever." The director was also the final inspector of "all receipts and issues of the mint." Reporting to the director were the assayer, the chief coiner, the engraver, and the treasurer. Gold and silver are rarely found in pure form; they are usually mixed with each other and also with baser metals like copper. It was the duty of the assayer, therefore, to examine specie deposits to determine their quality and value. (At first, the assayer also had to melt and refine the deposits, but that function soon devolved on a new officer, the melter and refiner.) The chief coiner was in charge of the actual coining of the precious metals from the ingots supplied by the assayer (later the melter and refiner). This was the key productive function of the Mint. The engraver engraved and otherwise prepared the dies, hubs, and punches that stamped impressions upon the metals to form the coins. As his job had to be completed before the chief coiner could set to work, he sometimes employed an assistant. The treasurer was in charge of all specie deposits. He paid them out to the assayer (and later the melter and refiner) for coinage and received back the completed coins. He kept track of all movements of metals within the Mint and their assayed values. He also made all payments on account of the Mint and rendered the Mint's accounts, each quarter, to the U.S. Treasury Department.

The committee discovered that the Mint's officers employed three clerks, one for the director and assayer, one for the chief coiner, and one for the treasurer. The director's clerk maintained the Mint's daybook, letter book, and contract book. He also physically secured the Mint's dies and hubs. The chief coiner's clerk also served as clerk to the melter after the latter's office was established. He kept track of all metals received by the chief coiner and all coins turned over to the treasurer. The Mint also employed a number of workmen who physically moved the specie from location to location within the Mint and who operated the forges, furnaces, lathes, rollers, presses, and milling machines that transformed the raw metal into coins.

Next, the committee made "strict enquiry into the causes why the product has not been greater, in so long a time as two years and an half from its institution." It concluded, basically, that making coins was a difficult, technical work of a type virtually unknown in America. In short, the Mint's employees "were not masters of their business." The committee's claims were not entirely true. Small mints had been established in the colonies at various times. Massachusetts ran a mint for over thirty years in the seventeenth century; Virginians tried to mint copper coins in 1642, 1726, 1769, and 1772, but without much success. Some expertise had developed at the private mints, like Connecticut's Company for the Coining of Coppers, that sprang up after the signing of the Declaration of Independence.[28]

It was true, however, as the committee made clear, that the Mint had to construct its own buildings, make its own tools, then build its own machinery, all from scratch. Moreover, the Mint rightly refused to settle for anything less than excellence. Its patience paid off. The coins "lately executed," the committee claimed, "are superior to any made in Europe." Such claims were common throughout the period. (But the claim did not amount to much because the government-owned mints in Europe produced rather shoddy coins in the eighteenth and early nineteenth centuries.)[29]

The committee then argued that the great expense of the Mint compared to its meager output was simply a function of the novelty of its product and the high start-up costs associated with any new business. Indeed, most of the institution's expenses were unavoidable ones for land, buildings, machines, copper, and payroll. The committee insinuated that Congress itself was to blame for some of the Mint's difficulties because the original law failed to establish the important post of melter and refiner and because it did nothing to discourage the depositing of gold and silver of inferior quality. The Mint, therefore, attracted gold that contained too much silver and silver that contained too much copper. Already the Mint had spent £500 to refine substandard specie. The committee spotted a variety of smaller problems too, all of which it hoped to remedy with its suggestions.

The House committee made seven major suggestions, most of which were quickly adopted:

1. That the position of refiner and melter be lawfully established and a suitable person appointed to pre-process precious metals into "bars or ingots fit for

the rolling mills" for the use of the coiner. This was to speed up production and also to maintain "the propriety of positive checks, throughout the whole of the business of the mint." The committee understood that the assayer could easily defraud depositors if he was also in charge of the refining process.

2. That a charge to depositors of between 2 and 6 cents per ounce for substandard metals deposited at the Mint be allowed. That charge would dissuade people from foisting off debased specie on the Mint.

3. That the Mint give preference to deposits of bullion at the standard or higher. This was to encourage deposits of high-quality specie and dissuade deposits of specie inferior to the standard.

4. That deposits be made of at least 200 ounces of silver and 20 ounces of gold. This was to keep the Mint from having to gear up production for a small job. The Mint and the committee, in other words, recognized the economies of scale inherent in coin production.

5. That the silver standard be increased to nine parts silver and one part copper. That measure was to prevent the coins from turning black as they wore out.

6. That the president be authorized to reduce the weight of the copper coin, up to two pennyweights per cent, at his discretion. That was to prevent pennies from costing more to produce than their nominal (face) value.

7. That the U.S. treasurer be authorized to distribute coppers at the public expense by sending them to a bank or collector in each state. That was to ensure the proper dispersion of small change throughout the country.

The committee also reported that it had thoroughly examined the accounts of the Mint and thought the accounting procedure protected "the public against every avenue of deception." Furthermore, the Mint seemed well prepared for civil unrest or robbery. A loaded musket, with bayonet affixed, two loaded pistols, and a sword were always kept at the ready. A watchdog and a watchman under "secret instructions" kept the Mint secure after hours. The bullion was safely lodged in a vault and secured with two locks, one kept by the treasurer, the other by the assayer. The Mint was also insured.[30]

Apparently not everyone was satisfied that the Mint was secure from depredation, especially of the insidious insider variety. By November 1795 Elias Boudinot, the Mint's third director in less than a year, found it necessary to publish a long pamphlet that detailed the accounting procedures at the Mint. Boudinot took the opportunity to point out that the Mint carefully screened and monitored its workmen, imposed heavy fines for security breaches, and immediately dismissed workers who did not follow the

Mint's strict procedural rules. It was forbidden, for example, for a worker to leave the Mint "without permission first obtained." A Mint worker was even forbidden to "carry about him any of the same denomination of coin, at that time striking at the Mint." Each officer also kept track of the name, age, country, size, and profession of each of his employees, just in case. Of course, those precautions made the Mint more expensive to operate.[31]

Pennsylvania law promised to fine and imprison at hard labor anyone, including employees, convicted of stealing or embezzling the Mint's coins. The federal government's punishment for embezzlement was death. In addition, the assayer ($1,000), chief coiner ($5,000), and treasurer ($10,000) had to obtain bonds conditioned on their good behavior and faced stiff fines for lesser breaches of protocol.

Perhaps those harsh penalties explain why no instances of major peculation at the Mint survive in the historical record. Reports of rapaciousness, however, repeatedly rocked its reputation. David Rittenhouse's successor, Henry William De Saussure of South Carolina, faced the first barrage. He resigned after "certain persons in the government" made some "invidious and illiberal . . . insinuations" about the Mint and "the manner in which it was conducted." A congressional investigation discovered no wrongdoing, and President Washington noted that De Saussure's conduct as Mint director "gave entire satisfaction." De Saussure told correspondents that he quit because Rittenhouse, who had been ill for some time before resigning, had left the institution in a state of lethargy. The Mint therefore required so much of De Saussure's attention that he could not serve the Mint and simultaneously engage in his profession as the government had promised he could. (He also seems to have missed Charleston and the bosom of his friends.)[32]

De Saussure's successor, Elias Boudinot, also found himself facing charges of incompetence and wrongdoing. According to Boudinot, the Mint was in sad shape when he assumed control in late 1795. Boudinot struggled to improve the efficiency of the institution, but he at first made little headway in the face of repeated yellow fever epidemics, internal squabbling, the removal of the capital to the Potomac, difficulties importing copper, and repeated political investigations.[33]

In 1800 a Senate committee complained that the Mint had spent over $165,000 to produce just shy of $2 million worth of coins. The circulation of the coins, the committee claimed, was "very limited, and mostly confined to places in the vicinity of the Mint." The committee recommended doing away with the Mint entirely and leaving it up to banks, especially the Bank of the United States, to regulate the value of foreign silver and gold coins in circulation in the United States. It further argued that because the Mint had proven with its "efforts of almost seven years" that it was not even competent enough to produce copper coins efficiently, that function should be outsourced to private contractors. The issue festered.[34]

In 1802 the Mint again came under attack, prompting Senator Uriah Tracy, a Federalist from Connecticut, to beseech Boudinot to put together a correct statement of the Mint's operations. "This mint institution," Tracy confided, "has been viewed with an evil eye by some men, who ought to have known better." "I am & always have been in favor of preserving this institution," he informed Boudinot. Tracy was of no effect in the House, which voted to abolish the Mint, but he managed to stop the measure in the Senate.[35]

Boudinot got the message loud and clear. In 1803 he managed to cut expenses some 38 percent while simultaneously increasing output. Moreover, Boudinot, engraver Robert Scot, and others signaled that the Mint was about to become profitable by offering to undertake the coinage by private contract. Furthermore, most of the Mint's assets, aside from the land on which it sat, had no market value except to a firm in the business of making coins. The government, therefore, would have suffered a large loss from its liquidation. Thanks to such considerations, the Mint was saved from the political forces that swirled against it.

Internal dissension, however, threatened to destroy the Mint from within. Mint treasurer Dr. Benjamin Rush, a Philadelphia Republican infamous for his mercury purge therapies, and Boudinot, the maternal uncle of Dr. Rush's wife, accused each other of wrongdoing in a bitter family feud that lasted several years. Rush accused Boudinot of using a Mint smith to fix his carriage, of personally profiting from the disposal of the dung of the Mint's five horses, and of taking kickbacks from the agent that he employed to make copper purchases on the Mint's account. Boudinot retorted that he would have used the Mint's smiths to help any distressed carriage owner, that before his tenure the Mint used to pay for the disposal of dung and now it had it carted away gratis (the carter sold it as fertilizer), and that the copper agent that he surreptitiously employed managed to negotiate lower prices than Mint officials and clerks could obtain when sellers knew that they were dealing with the government. Boudinot also counterattacked, claiming that Rush did not fulfill his duties as treasurer. Rush intimated that Boudinot was becoming senile.[36]

The feud appeared poised to move to the courtroom, but Alexander J. Dallas, the U.S. attorney for the Philadelphia district, dropped the entire matter as too trivial to pursue. Boudinot would not allow the matter to end and retaliated by annoying Rush at every opportunity. He accused Rush of using the Mint's funds for his own personal use for over a year. When that accusation proved groundless, he intimated, again apparently in error, that one of Rush's clerks had absconded with important Mint records. Rush responded to Boudinot's treatment by spending as little time at the Mint as possible. That hardly helped the Mint's productivity.[37]

Until the Boudinot-Rush squabble, Mint officers had gotten along just swell. The tussle, therefore, negatively impacted the institution's morale. The other officers wrote that they deplored "the dissentions that unhappily subsist between the Director and Treasurer of the Mint." Laborers responded by repeatedly breaking the rules against admitting unauthorized visitors and smoking. In 1805 Boudinot stepped down in favor of new blood, University of Pennsylvania mathematics professor Robert Patterson. Rush clung to his office until his death in 1813.

In 1853 the Mint again faced public humiliation when Richard McCulloh, the melter and refiner of the Mint, accused Franklin Peale—the son of famous portrait artist Charles Willson Peale and namesake of Pennsylvania's most revered Founding Father—of rampant corruption and mismanagement. McCulloh claimed that Peale, the chief coiner, had illegally used the Mint's resources to strike commemorative medals. Congress and the public clearly condoned the use of the Mint for the striking of *public* medals. As early as 1795, government documents mentioned the practice. The Mint struck numerous medals in praise of public figures over the years. As one newspaper reported in 1842, "The custom of rewarding great public services and commemorating important public events by striking, conferring, and distributing medals is as ancient as civilization." But Peale had taken the business a step further, using the Mint's machines to make medals for *private* parties, including corporations and at least one couple celebrating fifty years of marriage! As late as 1821, the legal status of striking private medals at the Mint was unclear. Surviving records do not make it clear if the private medal production turned a profit or, if it did, who took the proceeds. The uncertainty of the situation made it almost inevitable that someone would make a stink on Chestnut Street.[38]

McCulloh further alleged that Peale instructed idle Mint workers to make furniture for Peale's personal use. More damning, McCulloh claimed that the Mint systematically added more copper to gold coins than that allowed by law and that it reserved the seigniorage from the new 3-cent silver coins, which contained only 2.5 cents worth of silver each, for itself, both of which accusations were substantially true. Mint officials explained, however, that assaying and coining were imperfect arts and that no nation's

coins were quite as pure as professed. Even so-called "fine" gold was only
.995 gold. France, not the United States, varied the most from its own legal
standard, its louis d'ors containing only a little over .900 gold on actual empirical measure, though the professed standard was .91667! Some gold coins
minted in New Orleans were slightly below the minimum legal standard,
but U.S. coins were not systematically deficient of precious metal. As for token 3-cent coins, the Mint showed that lawmakers had intended for the
profits that they generated to help to defray the Mint's overhead costs.

McCulloh published his gripes, but little came of his accusations. As
noted above, his two most damning accusations, while technically true,
were easily explained. Moreover, the public may have discounted his claims
because he was involved in patent disputes with Peale. In fairness to Mc-
Culloh the governance structure of the Mint did get soft by the late 1840s.
The director signed off on too many items without keeping adequate tabs
on what his managers, like chief coiner Peale, were up to.

In 1856 another scandal erupted, this time pitting Mint director James
Ross Snowden against an outside contractor named James Barclay. Barclay,
bearing an U.S. Senate resolution, attempted to induce Snowden to allow
him to conduct a series of coinage experiments using the Mint's metal and
machines. Snowden demurred, nimbly destroying each of Barclay's suggested improvements. When Barclay suggested, for example, that coins
would wear less quickly if they had a smaller diameter, Snowden shot back
that the increased thickness of the coin would make them liable to "split-
ting," a counterfeiting process whereby the valuable center of a coin is
scooped out and replaced with a base metal. And when Barclay implored
that U.S. coins possessed no "special test of fraudulent reduction," Snowden retorted, correctly, that "the familiar tests of the genuineness of coin
are the senses of sight, smell, hearing and feeling" and that "the balance"
was the best method and could be used with any coin. Barclay lost on the
technical merits of his arguments and due to the fact that Snowden's boss
was the secretary of the treasury, not the U.S. Senate.[39]

As noted above, the federal government authorized the production of
token silver coinage in 1853. Like the coins in use today, the metal content of
the silver coins of the 1850s was worth less than its market price. Holders,
therefore, passed them from hand to hand instead of melting them down or
using them to make payments overseas. The coins were, in effect, federal
(and hence constitutional) bills of credit made of a little silver and baser
metals instead of paper. The tactic worked; by 1857 the government could
finally remove the legal tender status of foreign coins.

The California gold rush also helped to strengthen the indigenous coinage system. Supplies of new coins, most minted in Philadelphia, helped to improve the quality of the money stock. Banknotes and deposits remained the main components of the money supply, but individuals found it easier and cheaper to obtain coins when needed, and banks found it relatively easier and cheaper to maintain strong specie reserve ratios. That is not to say that the Mint seamlessly accommodated the sudden influx of California gold. Improved machines and procedures had to be put into place so that the Mint could increase output from about $100,000 to several million dollars per month. The Mint had always managed to employ skilled scientists and technicians, like David Rittenhouse and Christian Gobrecht, inventor of an innovative new method of "medal ruling"—a technique for copying coins and medals with great precision. However, the Mint had not always been able to implement new technologies or to purchase new machinery.[40]

In 1838 the government had established branches of the Mint at New Orleans, Louisiana; Charlotte, North Carolina; and Dahlonega, Georgia. New Orleans was chosen because it was the main commercial center of the burgeoning West. The other two branches were near the relatively minor gold and silver strikes made in the southeastern states in the latter part of the 1820s. As late as 1852, the Philadelphia factory still produced over 91 percent of the nation's coins, by value. So Philadelphia bore the brunt of the change. Not only did demand for its services increase; the very nature of its business changed because California gold contained an enormous amount of silver that had to be separated before the gold could be coined. In the words of Mint director George Eckert, the influx of California gold "required new constructions, extensive enlargements, a new arrangement of the space within the mint, and new machinery." By 1853, the first year that it turned a substantial surplus, the Mint was playing an enlarged role in the economy.[41]

In one sense, that was more than a little ironic given that Wall Street had long since dethroned Chestnut Street. In another sense, it wasn't ironic at all because domestic coinage was such an inconsequential part of the financial system. Even if Philadelphia's artisans had never struck a single dollar or eagle, Chestnut Street would still have been the early nation's financial center. Adam Smith had it right: gold and silver do not matter much. What does matter was precisely what Philadelphia had: financial markets and institutions. A good many of those markets and institutions were forged, if you will, in the crucible of the Revolution and minted during the tenure of Treasury Secretary Alexander Hamilton. To Hamilton's vision we now turn.

5

HAMILTON'S VISION

Alexander Hamilton was born a literal bastard in the West Indies sometime in the 1750s. Orphaned as a teen, he came to America on the eve of the Revolution on the eighteenth-century equivalent of a college scholarship. Within a few years, he was already a published author and a military officer distinguished for his physical courage in battle and the clarity of his thought and expression. Through the trials and travails of the miserable living conditions at encampments in Valley Forge and Morristown, and numerous battles in New York, New Jersey, Pennsylvania, and, finally, Yorktown, Virginia, he forged an almost father-son bond with General George Washington. In the meantime, Hamilton managed to marry well and to establish himself as one of the nation's leading financial theorists. After helping make the Constitutional Convention a reality, Hamilton joined the Washington administration as treasury secretary. A leading member of the Federalist Party, Hamilton died in 1804 as the result of a wound inflicted by Vice President Aaron Burr. Although some politicos rejoiced at the death of a potent foe, most Americans mourned the loss of a truly great American patriot.[1]

Hamilton also committed adultery. That is indisputable; he admitted as much. Apparently most U.S. politicians, then and since, have strayed, at least on occasion. Thomas Jefferson and William Jefferson Clinton come immediately to mind. Few of Hamilton's fellow adulterers, however, could match his contribution to this country's success. A profoundly creative genius, Hamilton was arguably *the* architect of modern America. Though a low-bred foreigner, Hamilton, and Hamilton alone among the pantheon of Founding Fathers, understood the crucial role that financial development and economic growth would play in the continued existence of the tender young Republic. Moreover, though but a mere lad compared to elder statesmen like Benjamin Franklin and George Washington, Hamilton, and only Hamilton, had a clear vision of the actual policies that would bind the new nation in a virtuous web of self-interest and prosperity. Others, most notably Robert Morris and Gouverneur Morris, "the rake who wrote the Constitution," managed to snatch glimpses of the overall vision. But only Hamilton saw the whole clearly enough to make the vision a reality. And he did most of his best work just a few blocks from Chestnut Street.[2]

Within just a few years of the adoption of the Constitution, Hamilton, with the support of Washington and a Federalist majority in Congress, managed to implement all of the major planks of his financial modernization plan. First, the dollar became the national unit of account. Second, the Bank of the United States, working in conjunction with the treasury secretary, became the nation's central bank. Third, the federal government established a tax base sufficient to service the Revolutionary War debts of both the national and state governments. Fourth, a thriving market for those debt securities arose and flourished. Finally, a private financial services sector composed of banks, insurance companies, and brokerages developed. Resting on the solid base provided by the first four innovations, those new financial markets and institutions drove early U.S. economic growth.

True, some early Americans deprecated Hamilton's financial revolution. But most, like William L. Smith, favorably contrasted the flourishing 1790s with "the deplorable and wretched State of this Country before the adoption of the new Constitution:—the languid state of commerce, navigation and manufactures, the general want of confidence and credit at home and abroad." The nation backed Hamilton's financial system with the hope, now realized, that it would lead to the "restoration of public and private credit, a revival of the public faith, encouragement to navigation, commerce, agriculture and manufactures."[3]

✒️ We saw in chapter 4 that the specie *definition* of the dollar was far more important than the actual coinage of dollar-denominated coins. What mattered was that people understood what a dollar meant in terms of purchasing power and that that value did not fluctuate very much. The stable unit of account meant that Americans would no longer be cheated out of their property as they had been at times in the colonial and revolutionary periods. Recall that those fluctuations had given impetus to the political movements that ultimately led to the Declaration of Independence and the Constitution.

To keep the new nation together, therefore, it was essential to keep the dollar stable and interest rates in check. To help ensure the stability of the dollar, Hamilton established the Bank of the United States, the nation's second "central bank"—a bank charged with implementing the government's monetary policy. Today central banks are state-owned or state-controlled, exert considerable control over the money supply—usually through the issuance of fiat notes and bank reserves—and act as a lender of last resort during financial crises. They are charged with maintaining the stability of macroeconomic variables like employment, interest, and inflation rates. The Bank of England, the Bank of Japan, the European Central Bank, and the Federal Reserve System of the United States are just such textbook examples of central banks. Scholars note, however, that at least six major types of central banks are possible:

1. Private institutions under considerable political direction
2. Private institutions under little political direction
3. Government departments under considerable political direction
4. Government departments under little political direction
5. Direct political control by the executive
6. Direct political control by the legislature[4]

The early United States enjoyed three of the second type of central banks, and all three were headquartered in Philadelphia:

1. The Bank of North America, which served as the nation's central bank during the tumultuous 1780s and continued in existence as a commercial bank during the remainder of the period under study
2. The Bank of the United States (or BUS, 1791–1811)
3. The second Bank of the United States (or SBUS, 1816–36)

Each of those banks, working in conjunction with the finance minister or the U.S. Treasury Department, attempted, usually quite successfully, to keep inflation low, interest rates within a reasonable range, and business cycles from oscillating too violently. They also on occasion acted as a lender of last resort. And they usually acted as the federal government's financial agent, the depository of its cash, the source of its short-term credit, and the payer of its bills.

That is not to say, of course, that the early central banks always succeeded in keeping the economy on an even keel. After radicals revoked its charter in 1785, for example, the Bank of North America was forced to stop lending. A recession naturally ensued. "Our wharves look on a week day as they used to look on Sundays," a contemporary noted in the midst of the downturn. "Only a few houses are building . . . and not a ship on the stocks." Continuation of such conditions, he predicted, would soon ruin both "the farmer and mechanic," not to mention "day labourers of all kinds, who were supported by these tradesmen."[5]

The Bank of North America eventually got its charter back, but its heyday as the nation's central bank had passed. In 1791 Hamilton's brainchild, the first Bank of the United States, began operations with a capital of $10 million, an enormous sum for the day. Within a year the BUS proved that it could stymie financial panic, and within five years it showed that it could fight inflation. The BUS eventually established eight branches, one each in Boston, New York, Baltimore, Norfolk, Charleston, Savannah, Washington, D.C., and New Orleans. Its reputation for strong, conservative leadership held it in good stead.[6]

Some foreign analysts argued that the BUS was simply too large to be profitable. They found it difficult to believe that the former colonies were rapidly approaching the mother country in terms of population, manufacturing output, and trade. Well-informed Americans, like New York merchant William Constable, knew better and tried to persuade skeptical Europeans that the BUS was not too big for the nation. In fact, it was not even too big for Philadelphia. Even though the BUS employed much of its capital in Philadelphia, most observers in the 1790s believed that Philadelphia possessed an insufficient amount of bank capital. As Constable noted in 1794, "It is well known that 3 times" the present bank capital "might be occupied there."

Constable also argued that the "natural Increase" of the U.S. population was very high and that "Emigration from Europe" had been "considerable." He further noted that though American manufactures and commerce did not yet match that of England, both already far surpassed that of Scotland, which boasted two royal and many private banks capitalized at about $9 million. European investors soon came to agree with Constable. In 1809 foreigners owned some eighteen thousand of the BUS's twenty-five thousand shares.[7]

They were not disappointed, at least not by the Bank itself. The BUS was profitable but not unusually so. Like other large urban banks in the era, it consistently paid dividends ranging from about 8 to 10 percent per year. Interestingly, however, its stock price was generally lower than that of other large urban commercial banks, probably because market participants understood that its profitability in the future might suffer if it had to act, in its capacity as central bank, for the greater good. Moreover, despite the institution's economic success, its continued existence was tied up in national politics and hence was by no means assured. Its charter set to expire on March 4, 1811, the BUS on April 20, 1808, petitioned the U.S. Senate for recharter. Its argument was concise and direct:

> That contemplating the extensive operations of the bank; the intimate connexion of the institutions with the public credit and finances; and the dispersed and distant residence of many of the stockholders; your memorialists deem it a duty to the government, and to the commercial world, as well as to themselves, to submit at this period, to the legislative consideration, the expediency of protracting the duration of their charter. Without an early assurance upon this subject, every motive of prudence and justice will enforce the adoption of adequate measures, to prevent the dangers and mischiefs of a sudden dissolution of the corporation.

The petition then ticked off the contributions the Bank had made to the government and the entire economy, that is, the government's profits from its ownership of BUS stock, the millions of dollars the BUS lent to the government, and the BUS's banking services that enabled the government "to collect its revenue, and to perform its pecuniary engagements, with ease, economy and security." It noted, too, that it established branches "not always for the general emolument of the institution, but sometimes (on the suggestion of the secretary of the treasury) for the peculiar accommodation of the public."[8]

The Senate immediately referred the Bank's petition to Albert Gallatin, the treasury secretary, who responded in writing in March 1809. Born in Geneva, Switzerland, in 1761, Gallatin emigrated to America in 1780, a year after graduating from the academy, because he wanted to experience the American Revolution firsthand. After bumming around a bit in Boston, Philadelphia, and Richmond, he settled on Pennsylvania's frontier, then located in the vicinity of Pittsburgh. He impressed nearly everyone he met, including his rough-hewn neighbors, who continually elected him to office, even ones that as a recent immigrant he was not legally allowed to hold! Some credit him with almost single-handedly preventing the Whiskey Rebellion, western Pennsylvania's protest against federal excise taxes on the production of whiskey, from turning violent. By the late 1790s, he was a Republican Party stalwart and, with his European education, the only Republican clearly qualified to join the Jefferson administration as treasury secretary. (Philadelphia merchant Tench Coxe could have handled the job as well, but nobody was quite sure if he was a Republican or not. He switched sides several times in his career.)[9]

Gallatin dissected the Bank's balance sheet, then concluded that the BUS's affairs "have been wisely and skilfully managed." He further noted that the Bank's efforts allowed the United States "to collect with so great facility, and with so few losses, the large revenue derived from the impost [tariff or tax on imports]." Gallatin not only urged Congress to recharter the BUS on terms similar to its first charter, he suggested that the Bank's capital be increased from $10 million to $30 million, with $15 million of the new stock reserved for "such states as may desire it." If adopted, that plan would have tied the interests of the several states more closely to the national institution. As Gallatin put it, "The bank itself would form an additional bond of common interest and union amongst the several states." Such an alignment of economic interests probably would have profoundly changed the monetary history of the United States.[10]

But ultimately Congress rejected both Gallatin's plan and the BUS recharter altogether. Hamilton's argument about the constitutionality of the Bank to the contrary notwithstanding, some congressmen believed that the BUS was an illegal usurpation of federal power. Others disliked the idea that the discretionary portion of U.S. monetary policy was largely in the hands of a private citizen, not a government official. Still others hoped to replace the BUS with a new bank or banks that they could personally control. Perhaps most importantly, the political party that had created the BUS, the Federalist Party, was no longer a potent political force. Nevertheless, the votes in both the House and Senate were close ones, coming down to a single vote in each instance.[11]

The BUS passed peacefully out of existence when Philadelphia merchant Stephen Girard purchased most of its assets, including its stunning building near Chestnut Street. Girard was a reclusive French émigré who proved, in the end, to have a heart of gold. An orphan from Bordeaux who settled in Philadelphia in 1776, Girard could never discard his thick French accent. Naturally reclusive, he preferred working diligently at his desk to frittering away time in the mercantile coffee shops, as many of his fellow merchants did. His reputation suffered further because his wife, his entrée to Philadelphia's social scene, went insane. Some probably truly disliked the fact that Girard put his wife into an asylum and then took a series of mistresses. Most, however, were probably envious of Girard's growing fortune. The Frenchman had an uncanny ability to "time" markets, that is, to buy very low and to sell very high a short time later. He concentrated first on commodities like coffee but later turned his clairvoyance to the financial markets. Girard, it turned out, was not a miser, not the "Stephen Graspall" that some claimed. In the early 1790s, he *personally* attended to many of the victims of the dreaded yellow fever, proclaiming, in effect, that Frenchmen were more difficult to kill than Americans. In fact, Girard had developed an immunity to the disease during his business trips to the West Indies. Nevertheless, working in a yellow fever hospital took considerable physical courage, a strong stomach, and an intense public spirit. That public spirit really showed through after Girard's death in 1831. Instead of bequeathing his considerable fortune to his many siblings and their children, the childless Girard established a school for orphans in Philadelphia that functions to this very day.[12]

Although Girard hired the BUS's most important employees, his bank was not a new central bank—it didn't even have a charter. For the first time in thirty years, the United States was without a central bank. And for the first time in thirty years, the United States was again in a shooting war with Great Britain. Unsurprisingly, the results were again disastrous. As during the Revolution, the national government found it difficult to borrow, difficult to make payments, difficult to fight on all cylinders. The war dragged on through 1812, 1813, and 1814. By time word that the war was over finally reached the United States in early 1815, most Americans had rediscovered the need for a Hamiltonian central bank. By 1816 they had one that they could live with, at least for the time being.[13]

Capitalized at $35 million, the second Bank of the United States was three and a half times as large as the BUS. Unfortunately, it was not three and a half times as good, at least not at first. Under the drunken stewardship of its first president, a political appointee named William Jones, the SBUS proceeded to run the economy into the ground by first extending far too much credit, then quickly restricting it. A financial panic ensued, followed by a steep recession that saw interest rates spike, farm produce prices plummet, and unemployment soar. People were understandably pissed (in the American sense) of the pissed (in the British sense) president and his institution. The preceding three decades of solid growth, however, had created more than enough goodwill to stymie any thoughts of revolution. And within a few years, the SBUS, under Langdon Cheves and Nicholas Biddle, had turned itself, and the economy, around. By 1823 the U.S. economy was again growing and the central bank was again doing what it should, preventing recessions, not making them. But the seeds of resentment had been laid, and in a dozen years the trees that those seeds brought forth would bear bitter fruit, indeed—the details I leave for chapter 10, "Wall Street Ascendant."

✑ Hamilton's third accomplishment, after defining the specie dollar and establishing a central bank to regulate it, was to lower the nation's tax burden. That accomplishment, one rarely achieved by politicians, was closely related to his fourth plank, funding the national debt, so the two will be treated together.[14]

Taxes and debts were the two great bugaboos of early American politics. As we have seen, both combined to foment the Revolution and then the movement for the Constitution. Due to the volatile interest rates and deteriorating balance sheets that had confronted them in the colonial and Revolutionary periods, late eighteenth-century Americans feared and disdained debt of any sort. They knew firsthand that when interest rates jumped, the value of their assets—land as well as bonds—plummeted, ripping their net worth to pieces and exposing them to runs by liability holders. Under such circumstances, it was best not to have any liabilities, any debts, outstanding. Early Americans also hated taxes, as much as we do today if not more so. Taxes that had to be paid in cash—specie or bills of credit—were particularly onerous because cash was often in short supply.

When Hamilton took office, the nation was caught between a rock and a hard place. The Revolution left it with a seemingly huge debt, a debt that many believed had to be dealt with quickly lest it corrupt the young Republic the way that it allegedly had Britain. But to quickly expunge the debt would require massive taxation. Especially after Shays's Rebellion, a nasty tax rebellion in western Massachusetts, the rapid approach appeared politically inexpedient to say the least.[15]

The other major alternative was to repudiate the debt, to thank the thousands of public creditors for their contribution to the cause of freedom and tell them to take a hike. The debt holders were not thrilled with that option, which amounted to nothing more than a tax that would fall only on their shoulders and all at once. Shays's Rebellion would have been but a Sunday picnic compared to the tumult that would have occurred in the aftermath of such a bald-faced repudiation.

Through history, many nations have found themselves in similar pickles. Most have made the wrong choice and suffered the consequences for years, decades, and, arguably in some cases, centuries. Not so America. Hamilton found the perfect mix. He subtly repudiated a part of the debt, lowered taxes, and turned the national debt into a national blessing. The details are mind-numbingly complex. The overall picture that emerges, however, is a thing of beauty.

The key to the repudiation part of the plan was to induce government debt holders, a motley mix of speculators, widows, farmers, businessmen, and former military men, to *voluntarily* accept a reduction in interest. Most did, essentially because they valued the liquid (easily salable) nature of the new bonds that Hamilton offered them in exchange for their original bonds, which were highly variegated and difficult to sell.[16]

The new bonds bore 3 or 6 percent interest, payable semi-annually, some beginning immediately, some, the "Deferred Sixes," beginning in 1801. Though individually registered with the U.S. Treasury, the new bonds were easily transferable. Moreover, because all the many types of old bonds had been reduced to just three types of new ones, there were a lot of each type. Almost every business day, some of them traded. Their prices made it into the newspapers in the big seaport cities, including Philadelphia. Religious scruples somewhat dampened the speculative spirit in Philadelphia. In 1791 the Philadelphia Yearly Meeting, a large gathering of pacifist Quaker policy-makers, decided that "dealing in publick Certificates issues as a compensation for expences accrued, and services performed in the late War . . . is inconsistant with our peaceable Testimony and principles." But newspapers bear ample evidence of active trading of the three major types of U.S. government debt in Philadelphia. The availability of good price information made the bonds even easier to sell because both the buyer and the seller could easily determine the going price.[17]

The first public securities broker in Philadelphia may have been Francis White. As early as October 13, 1784, he advertised that "all public securities [were] bought and sold" at his office "in Chestnut Street." White's business was impressive. He brokered and dealt in a wide variety of public securities, including Nicholson's, Stelle's, Story's, and Pierce's Certificates, Pennsylvania militia certificates, the bills of credit of Maryland and Pennsylvania, Virginia land warrants, and "every other sort of Continental or State Securities." Thanks to Hamilton's refunding plan, the job of White and all the nation's brokers got much easier in the early 1790s because all those securities became just three.[18]

The result of the voluntary refunding of the debt was that instead of paying an average of 6 percent interest per year, the federal government reduced its interest burden to approximately 4 percent. That interest reduction relieved some of the tax burden. Efficient collection of taxes reduced the burden yet further because the new federal government, unlike the state and local governments, did not waste large sums merely collecting the tax. Hamilton managed that feat through the implementation of revenue tariffs, that is, taxes on imported goods. Such taxes were easy to collect because import points were limited. Also, the rates were so low that there was no incentive to smuggle and little need to curtail consumption. Moreover, the persons who initially paid the taxes were rich merchants with access to bank credit.

All that was needed, therefore, were a few collectors monitoring inbound ship cargoes. The import merchants paid the appropriate tariff to the collectors, who then paid it into the treasury, usually via the BUS. The importers then passed the taxes onto their customers in the form of higher prices. So the tax was fair in the sense that everyone who consumed foreign goods paid it in proportion to the rate of their consumption. The low tariffs did not decrease trade very much, and most of the money collected went directly into the government's coffers, which is to say the vaults of the BUS.

The government ran into a bit more trouble when it implemented a more intrusive tax on the production of whiskey. Such excise taxes were common in the colonies, including colonial Pennsylvania. It was somewhat ironic, then, that western Pennsylvania put up a stink about the federal levies. In an overwhelming show of force, the national government stamped out a minor rebellion, the infamous Whiskey Rebellion, in the autumn of 1794. Though not quite as efficiently collected as the tariff, the whiskey excise stayed in effect, making its contribution to the national budget.

The real value of Hamilton's plan can be seen, ironically enough, in the state budgets in the 1790s. With federal assumption of their debts, their defense, and sundry other of their functions, state and local governments could cut taxes. And they did. Those cuts won the public over to the new arrangements and undoubtedly helped to fuel the economic boom of the 1790s.

∽ The burgeoning private financial system deserves a good deal of credit for that boom too—indeed, for America's general prosperity from the passage of the U.S. Constitution until the Panic of 1819. Hamilton's first four accomplishments made completion of this fifth and final plank possible. Control over the money supply and interest rates was incomplete and the business cycle persisted, but relative to the colonial period, U.S. firms could better predict future business conditions. With important macroeconomic variables under some degree of domestic control, Philadelphia businesses could seriously consider implementing productivity-enhancing projects. Because the initial outlays for most such projects were beyond the means of most businesses, entrepreneurs had to turn to external sources to finance expansions and other improvements.[19]

Philadelphia businesses that desired to acquire external financing faced two major options: direct and indirect finance. They could borrow directly from investors for long terms in the so-called capital market, or they could borrow short term in the money market. Or they could borrow short or long term from investors indirectly through financial institutions known as intermediaries. If they tapped the direct route, the firms had to decide whether to sell equity (stock), debt (bonds, mortgages, ground rents), or hybrid (e.g., preferred stock) instruments. If they decided to obtain funds from intermediaries, they had to decide whether to approach commercial banks, savings banks, insurance companies, trusts, or other types of intermediaries.

In the late 1990s, initial public offerings of stock were all the rage. The 1790s were not radically different. Most early bank initial bank offerings (IPOs) were hot affairs. Like Internet IPOs, the stock subscriptions filled quickly, leading to big jumps in share prices in the "after market." Other companies found it more difficult to sell shares in themselves. It took the Schuylkill Permanent Bridge Company, for instance, two years to fill its subscription books.[20]

Most early U.S. IPOs were of unseasoned companies, that is, new firms without proven track records. Potential subscribers therefore wanted to know who had already signed on the dotted line. Subscriptions by prominent men or savvy investors signaled the worth of the company to others. Charles Babbage, a celebrated calculator, argued that most investors paid too much heed to the names of "men of wealth and character." "The respectability of an undertaking," he lamented, "is too often inferred from the names under whose sanction it is introduced." "The facts stated in the prospectus are believed to have been examined into," he continued, though they seldom were. Still, well-known gentlemen were unlikely to risk their valuable reputational capital. Investors knew that, as did company promoters. For example, Josiah White was unable to interest anyone in Lehigh Navigation Company stock until Jacob Shoemaker—a founding director of two financial intermediaries and actuary of the Pennsylvania Company for Insuring Lives—famous political economist Condy Raguet, and capitalists John Stoddart and James Spencer each pitched in $10,000. That opened the floodgates, and the rest of the subscription filled within a day.[21]

Shares took the physical form of stock certificates, embossed with the company seal and emblazoned with the signatures of at least two top company officers. The certificates were usually numbered and listed the number of shares as well as the shareholder's name (and other identifying information, if necessary). Many early companies, like the Pawlings Ford Permanent Bridge Company, tried to make their shares transferable only in the presence of a corporate officer. Other companies allowed their shares to be assigned by mere endorsement. The Delaware and Schuylkill Canal Navigation Company tacitly allowed transfer by assignment because it realized that ease of transfer increased demand for its shares. But all companies required eventual registration of the new owner's name. After all, each company had to know who owned it, so that it could send out dividends and meeting announcements to the correct persons.

Early Americans maintained a love-hate relationship with their commercial banks. An anonymous author writing in 1834 pretty much summed up their ambivalence: "Banks are engines calculated to do much good if well managed, much evil if badly administered." Early U.S. banks were quite modern in form and effect. Like banks today, they carefully screened and monitored borrowers. Also like modern banks, they held government bonds as liquid secondary reserves and maintained contingency funds to meet defaults. "Several of our most solid banks," policy pundit Thomas Law noted in 1826, "keep stock in preference to specie, to a certain amount, relying upon its convertibility into cash, and retaining it because it yields an interest and diminishes their dead capital in the precious metals."[22]

But the very efficiency of early banks brought scorn. Government regulations, particularly usury laws (interest-rate ceilings), forced banks to engage in nonprice rationing (essentially "discriminatory" lending practices) that had profoundly negative political implications for the institutions. Because early banks were very choosy lenders, they suffered few defaults. William Constable claimed that the Bank of New York made only "one bad Debt of about twenty pounds" through the first seven years of its existence. The Bank of North America was such a prudent lender, legend has it, that its name was always spoken with veneration. But when a debt did go bad, though, banks did not hesitate to sue, a point that their enemies never failed to make.[23]

Moreover, many people honestly wondered how banks that purported never to lend at more than 6 percent interest could pay dividends of 8, 10, or 12 percent. Bank dividends could exceed the usury rate because, as Albert Gallatin explained in 1809, "every bank lends, not only the whole of its capital, but also a portion of the monies deposited for safe keeping in its vaults." "Experience," Gallatin explained, "has taught the directors what portion of the money thus deposited they may lend, or in other words how far they may with safety extend their discounts [loans] beyond the capital of the bank and what amount of specie it is necessary they should keep in the vaults." Not everyone knew or grasped this, however.[24]

Furthermore, because commercial banks issued cash-bearer liabilities (banknotes) in addition to deposits, they aroused the suspicions of politicians and theoreticians and found themselves blamed for the economy's intermittent woes. Seemingly shady accounting practices also hurt. Commer-

cial banks in Pennsylvania, for example, sometimes issued "stock notes,"
long-term loans to stockholders secured by the hypothecation of their own
stock. Many contemporaries deprecated stock note usage, but ultimately
the practice mattered little. Banks could have functioned without any capital at all. Moreover, were the borrowers to default on their notes, the banks
would have immediately taken possession of the shares, which they could
have sold to raise cash or cancelled to reduce their liabilities. The practice,
in other words, was perfectly sound.[25]

Contrary to repeated assertions based more on innuendo than empirical
evidence, early banks lent to a much wider group of people than just merchants. The main criterion was creditworthiness, not occupation. Philadelphia banks, of course, did not lend to the "absolute Poor," nor usually to the
more numerous class of "Citizens in straightened circumstances who from
the want of small Sums are exposed to great difficulties." The risk was simply too high for the net return, which was paltry given the high fixed costs
of lending and collecting numerous small sums and the low usury ceilings.
Realizing this, some Philadelphians concocted a plan to lend small sums to
"respectable Citizens to whom" small loans would be "highly beneficial,"
like tradesmen with apprentice and inventory costs. The plan called for the
creation of a city-owned and -operated not-for-profit pawnshop that would
charge double digit interest rates, for example, $3.25 for the use of $50 for
thirteen weeks. The city never got into the small-loan business, but after
about 1810 many private pawnbrokers did.

A wide segment of the population, however, was able to borrow from
banks to fund business projects. Each spring the Bank of Harrisburg lent
considerable sums "to the hardy and adventurous class of citizens, whose
countless rafts, launched at every point along this stream and its numerous
tributaries, float down upon the swelled bosom of the Susquehanna." Similarly, after 1820 roughly half of all loans made by Stephen Girard's bank
were for less than $500; most of those smaller loans went to small retailers
and artisans.[26]

Artisans clearly needed credit to make a go of it. They were, after all,
small businesspersons. As early as 1786, a Philadelphia mechanic complained of the dearth of credit with which to "carry on his business." It was
customary for artisans to extend credit to their customers. In addition, businesses that sold perishables, such as brewers of "small beer" (light beer),
had to move product or suffer spoilage. Such businesses often extended
generous credits to keep the beer taps flowing. God bless them.[27]

Artisans in more staid businesses also found it necessary to extend credit.
On July 30, 1808, for instance, Philadelphia tailors Wilkins and Atkinson

made a "suit of cloathes" for Morgan Delaurs for £3 7s. 6d. Delaurs took the clothes and repaid the tailors later. Nathan Field, James E. Smith, and Nathan Atherton did likewise. All told, that day Wilkins and Atkinson extended about $20 worth of credit. To stay afloat until their customers repaid them, the tailors had to obtain loans.[28]

In many businesses, significant inventories tied up capital for long periods. Brewers of porter had to age their products for up to a year. Thanks to the financial system, Philadelphia breweries, though smaller than those of London, dwarfed those of the Continent. In 1819 German immigrant Ludwig Gall marveled at the city's "enormous breweries." Size brought with it scale economies, the ability to produce more with less.[29]

Businesswomen also needed, and received, liquidity loans. Elizabeth Helm, one of many examples, enjoyed extensive dealings with the Bank of North America as early as 1792, when over $18,000, a princely sum for the day, flowed through her account. She made large cash deposits every fortnight or so, continually drawing down her balance with checks made out to her suppliers. When her account fell a little short, a quick loan bridged the gap until her next deposit.[30]

When they could no longer obtain loans from established banks, artisans sought, and sometimes obtained, charters for their own banks. The legislature chartered the Southwark Bank, for instance, to afford "facilities in business to those whose occupation depends upon ship building and the arts connected with it." "It was for the special benefit of the shipwrights, of the rope makers, of the block makers, of the ship chandlers, &c. of Southwark, that this bank was instituted," a contemporary noted in 1834.[31]

But direct access to bank loans was not necessary for artisans to benefit from the banking system. Banks would not lend at usurious rates, but many individuals would. Often those individuals borrowed from banks, then turned around and lent to artisans and others at illegal rates. Derisively referred to as "note shavers," such men provided a valuable service, loans to people who needed them, at rates that they were willing to pay. Though some such lending merely "grinded the faces of the poor," most of it helped younger, poorer men get the loans that they needed to expand their businesses. And women too. Margaret Moulder ran an extensive flour wholesaling business in the 1790s. Her largest open accounts ran into the many hundreds of pounds Pennsylvania currency per year. Moulder may or may not have borrowed from the bank or money market herself. But her customers, men like Jonathan Bonsall and Thomas Pedrick, clearly did. They paid Moulder in cash, and sometimes their accounts ran ahead. In essence, they advanced cash to her by prepaying some of their flour purchases. They were able to do so because they had access to bank or money market discounts. So whether Moulder directly benefited from the emerging financial system herself is beside the point. It helped her customers (and probably her suppliers too) and hence aided her indirectly, whether she realized it or not.[32]

Banks also indirectly aided an even larger group, everyone involved in the economy, with their notes and deposits. Both were extremely convenient means of making payments and purchasing the goods and services of strangers. Bank money, as the saying went, "greased the wheels of commerce." But even here, banks came under political attack. Some people simply could not, or would not, understand that banknotes by their nature would pass at an increasing discount the further they strayed from their bank of issue. The discount stemmed from two forces: first, the transaction and interest costs of transporting the notes back to the bank for redemption in specie and, second, to the risk of nonpayment (default). Table 5.1 illustrates the difference. Note that in 1816, the notes of all the country banks at a considerable distance from Philadelphia suffered from the same discount, 10 percent. Clearly, high interest rates and the time and cost necessary to remit the notes for redemption were the main culprits. In 1820, by contrast, some notes depreciated only a little, while others lost a large percentage of their value. The small discounts covered the expense of remittance; the large discounts were largely a function of perceived default risk.

Note issuance was, of course, quite profitable. (Anytime you can get people to accept your zero-interest promissory note, you are in an enviable position.) State governments accordingly had to clamp down on the issuance of moneylike notes, usually allowing only banks, often only legally chartered banks, to issue them. When monetary conditions were deranged, however, state governments often looked the other way. In 1820, in the aftermath of the Panic of 1819, at least fifteen corporations issued notes, although they had no legal sanction to do so. As figure 5.1 shows, several, like Girard's Bank, were unincorporated banks, but most of the note-issuing transportation companies were making small change, not loans. Most of those companies retired their notes, derisively called "shinplasters," when small coins returned to circulation. But inevitably a few defaulted, leaving numerous people to suffer the loss of $.25, $.50, even $.75. These "enormous" losses also got blamed on the poor banks for keeping specie in their vaults while the rest of humanity had to suffer to use slips of paper.

Hitherto, historians have been all too eager to accept the early critics' views of America's commercial banks. For the most part, the banks did an excellent job, especially given the legal, political, and economic constraints

Table 5.1: Pennsylvania Banknote Discounts, 1816 and 1820

Bank	May 6, 1816	January 31, 1820
Bank of Gettysburg	10	3
Harrisburg Bank	par	1.5
Carlisle Bank	10	3
Bank of Chambersburg	10	3
Westmoreland Bank	10	12.5
Lancaster Trading Company	10	2
Marietta	10	33
Centre Bank	10	25
Farmers' Bank of Reading	10	8
Alleghany Bank	10	50
Germantown	10	par
York	9	3
Farmers' Bank of Lancaster	10	par
Swatara	10	3
Easton Bank	par	par
Pennsylvania Agricultural and Manufacturers Bank	10	40
Bank of Washington	10	45
Northampton Bank	10	2.5
Juniata Bank	10	40
Delaware Bank	par	par
Chester County Bank	par	par
Bank of Beaver	10	50
Bank of Pittsburgh	10	4
Huntingdon Bank	10	25
Monongahela	10	12.5
North Western Bank	10	35
Union Bank	10	50
Northumberland, Union & Columbia Bank	10	50
Bucks County	10	par
Farmers' and Mechanics' Bank of Pittsburgh	10	40
Farmers' and Mechanics' Bank of Greencastle	10	35
Montgomery Bank	par	par
Silver Lake Bank	10	40

Source: *Journal of the Senate of Pennsylvania, 1819–1820*, 336.

Figure 5.1: Corporations that Illegally Issued Notes in 1820

Stephen Girard's Bank
Connelsville Navigation Company
State Bank at Camden, New Jersey
Youghiogany Bank of Perryopolis
Columbia Bridge Company
Greensburg and Pittsburgh Turnpike
Greensburg and Stoystown Turnpike
Somerset and Mount Pleasant Turnpike
Pittsburgh and New Alexandria Turnpike
New Alexandria and Conemaugh Turnpike
Chambersburg and Bedford Turnpike
Bedford and Stoystown Turnpike
Harrisburg, Carlisle, and Chambersburg Turnpike
New Hope Delaware Bridge Company

Source: *Journal of the Senate of Pennsylvania, 1819–1820*, 337.

that they faced. The same can be said of the rest of the financial system. The best evidence of that comes not from biased historians but from those who had real resources on the line—early investors, particularly foreign investors, who presumably were interested in risks and returns, not patriotism. After adoption of the Constitution and the appointment of Alexander Hamilton to the post of treasury secretary, foreigners bought extensively of U.S. bonds. "Considerable shipments" of specie came into the country from Europe in the early 1790s, William Constable noted in 1794, "to buy into our funds."[33]

By 1796 so many U.S. bonds and shares of the Bank of the United States were trading in London that British investment primers, most notably Thomas Fortune's *Epitome of the Stocks,* began to take note of their existence. In both London and Amsterdam, brokers and dealers arose to facilitate the exchange of U.S. securities for a fee of .25 percent of the value of the transaction. Importantly, European investors looked at the U.S. securities as investments, to be bought and held for the reliable income stream they produced, and not as speculations, to be held only so long as they could be jettisoned for a few more dollars than they cost.[34]

The U.S. bonds were nominally denominated in dollars, but they were essentially convertible into sterling at the fixed rate of 4s. 6d. sterling per dollar. So a London or Amsterdam investor who purchased a U.S. Six Percent bond with a principal value of $100 would receive $6 or £1 7s. sterling (6 × 4.5s. = 27s.) per year, payable quarterly, *in Philadelphia.* To have that sum remitted, the investor could ask the BUS to do so, which it did free of charge, but subject to the prevailing exchange rate, which of course fluctuated. Moreover, agents in London who received the funds charged .5 percent of the sum remitted for their services. The bonds and bank stock passed by endorsement in Europe, but any holder could have his or her ownership officially registered by writing a U.S. government loan office or the BUS, respectively.

Foreign investment in America was nothing new. Indeed, many of the colonies were founded as business ventures. What was new in the 1780s, and especially the 1790s, was the large-scale purchase of American financial assets by foreigners. Foreigners purchased 13 percent of the Bank of North America IPO, and by 1803 they owned over 50 percent of the U.S. national debt, over 60 percent of the Bank of the United States, and 35 percent of America's state-chartered banks. They also held small percentages of U.S. insurers, turnpikes, and other corporations. British citizens made slightly over half of that foreign portfolio investment. Dutch citizens made about a quarter, and sundry other foreigners the remainder. The same general pattern held through at least 1853. Moreover, early U.S. life insurance companies, many of which functioned mainly as trust companies, managed to attract significant deposits from abroad.

Foreigners were free to sell as well as to buy U.S. securities, so their relative importance changed over time. Table 5.2 documents fluctuations of foreign ownership of the U.S. national debt in selected years between 1803 and 1853. Foreign ownership of other types of American financial assets followed a similar pattern. European investors realized that they could earn higher returns in America than in Europe, even after adjusting for risk, and American entrepreneurs realized that if they worked hard and smart, they could earn enough to repay the loan with interest and have some left over for their trouble. The point here is that late eighteenth- and early nineteenth-

Table 5.2: Foreign Ownership of the U.S. National Debt, Selected Years, 1803–53

Year	Total public debt (in millions)	Held by foreigners (%)
1803	86.7	56
1818	99.0	26
1824	83.8	31
1828	58.4	33
1853	58.2	46

Source: Mira Wilkins, *The History of Foreign Investment in the United States to 1914* (Cambridge, MA: Harvard University Press, 1989).

century foreign investors held more "stock" in early America than modern historians do. The foreign investors grasped the importance of Hamilton's vision. Maybe someday American historians will too.

⟋◯ Contemporary Pennsylvanians certainly understood Hamilton's vision and they made it reality. By 1810 Philadelphia and its suburbs were home to 5,635 stables and workshops, 15 cotton or woolen factories, 15 rope-walks, 44 copper, brass, or tin shops, 11 breweries, 18 distilleries, 28 soap and candle makers, 14 glue manufactories, 7 paper mills, 27 tobacco and snuff factories, 16 potteries, 2 glassworks, 3 iron foundries, 17 carriage makers, 3 oil mills, and 28 cutlers. Though nothing compared to what would come, it is clear that the Quaker City was chock-full of entrepreneurs. And its hinterland was full of farmers. By 1810 southeastern Pennsylvania was a thriving land "form'd into neat farms with portions of irrigated meadow, woodland & open fields" and dotted with "country retreats" large and small. Its farms boasted of "substantial barns, fine private dwellings, excellent breed and condition of live stock, and superior cultivation." Even English travelers likened them to "Old England." Further in the interior, manufactories thrived in major towns like Lancaster. By 1818 Pittsburgh considered itself a "Birmingham" because it was already home to scores of factories.[35]

All of that contrasted sharply with areas with similar resource and human capital endowments, like Canada, that did not enjoy a vibrant financial system. Numerous knowledgeable observers pointed to Canada's relatively backward financial system as the main reason it lagged behind the northern United States economically. John Duncan traveled through Canada and the United States in 1818 and 1819. He noted that in America "scarcely has an infant settlement numbered a hundred houses, till a corporation for the manufacture at least of bank notes, if it be nothing more, is immediately set on foot." "The commercial capital of Canada, on the other hand, with a population of about twenty thousand, and a trade employing annually about 150,000 tons of shipping," he explained, had just formed its first bank. Duncan thought the Americans more commercially precocious than the merchants of Montreal but pointed out, too, that high illiteracy rates made banking in Quebec a challenge. "As an expedient to assist those who cannot read," Duncan noted, the new Canadian bank "exhibited a row of dollars upon the margin of each of their notes, corresponding in number to its amount."[36]

In the 1820s James Buchanan, the British consul in New York, also described Canada's relative "torpidity, and indolence." He explicitly attributed the difference to Canada's immature financial system. In 1833 George

Hebert, another British observer, also lamented the sorry state of Canada's economy. He, too, attributed the dearth of intermediation facilities as a major cause of the north country's economic backwardness. "Bank notes circulate very little beyond the towns in Lower Canada [Quebec]," he argued, adding that by forbidding interest payments, "the Catholic clergy" induced the faithful to hoard specie rather than to suffer "the risk of lending it for nothing." Steep discounts of 20 to 25 percent for cash payments indicated high implicit interest charges on book accounts, Hebert explained. Such high interest rates explain why Canadian farms sold for much less than comparable farms in the northern United States. "Money is so scarce in Upper Canada [Ontario]," he further explained, "that most of the farmers are obliged to pay their labourers with grain." It is not likely that Hebert exaggerated. According to another source, the money supply of upper Canada in 1825 was only £135,000 Canadian currency (i.e., $540,000, or $3.58 per capita).

Early 1840s traveler William Thomson also argued that Canada lagged behind the Northeast in "wealth, cultivation, and internal communication." John Robert Godley thought that foreign investment made all the difference: the United States could attract it but Canada could not. "The prosperity of America, her railroads, canals, steam navigation, and banks, are the fruit of English capital," he argued. "England," he claimed, "has sunk nearly £40,000,000 in the States." "On the other hand," Godley lamented, "hardly a shilling of English capital has found its way into this province."

Finance, in short, was fundamental to growth. Canada and New York were physically indistinguishable. Culturally and politically, both were a mix of British and continental influences, albeit New York's was Dutch and Canada's French. Yet until late in the nineteenth century, after it finally began to emulate Yankee finance in earnest, Canada remained an economic backwater. Hamilton's vision, in short, appears to have been a key factor in the launching of America on its historic growth trajectory.

Less abstractly, the financial system also enriched Americans' lives by helping them to save for the future, to purchase a home, and to share risks—big ones. In so doing, it transformed America by helping to unleash the entrepreneurial drive that so many European travelers both admired and deprecated.[37]

✒6

HAZARDOUS VOYAGES

Hannah was like any other girl born in early nineteenth-century America. She was extremely lucky to survive her first year, very lucky to get through her second, and lucky, indeed, to make it to her third birthday. By the time she was five or six, however, she was likely to live a good, long time, provided her parents earned enough to keep her warm, dry, and fed until a suitor or master whisked her off to wedded bliss or an apprenticeship. Like girls born anywhere, anytime, her parents loved her dearly and dreamed that she would live a better life than they had. Everything was fine in Hannah's little world until the night that her father, a blacksmith, did not answer the call for supper. The gruesome scene in his small shop on the first floor of his home told the story: he had tripped and smashed his head on his anvil. He was still alive, but barely. His blood, now cold, seemed to suffuse every nook and cranny in the floor. The doctor who was summoned managed to keep Hannah's father alive for several days. But, as her mom explained to her daughter while the tears streamed down both of their shattered countenances, Daddy's time to meet Jesus had come.

As late as the 1820s, widows often took over their deceased husbands' businesses and ran them successfully. Hannah's mom, though, was no blacksmith. She could cook, clean, and even do a little stitching, but mending horseshoes was not in her repertoire. She had no choice but to sell the family home. Unfortunately, interest rates had risen since the family had purchased the property almost ten years before. And the shop, the most valuable part of the structure, was more than a little worse for wear. Even the best offer was not enough to cover the family's debts, recently enlarged as they were by the physician, preacher, and casket maker. Hannah and her mom scrimped to get by. Gifts from friends and family helped, but eventually poor diet and thin clothes caught up to Hannah. After a brief illness, she joined her father and Jesus, having spent eight years, four months, seven days, and twenty hours on this earth.[1]

Mary, another little Philadelphia girl, probably would have suffered the same fate had not her father, a lowly countinghouse clerk, purchased a very special IOU. The IOU stated that the Pennsylvania Company for Insurance on Lives and Granting Annuities would pay $1,000 to Mary's mother if he died. With that money, Mary's mother paid her deceased husband's "final expenses" and other debts. The remainder, about $500, she invested in U.S. government bonds. With the family free of debt, the $30 yearly interest kept Mary alive and well until she married. (I suspect that Mary encouraged her husband to purchase life insurance soon after informing him of her first pregnancy.)[2]

Despite its obvious need, life insurance emerged relatively late and grew very slowly at first. The Insurance Company of North America, primarily a marine insurer, continued the colonial practice of writing term insurance on the lives of mariners. It did very little of that kind of business, however. By one estimate, fewer than a hundred American lives were insured in 1800. Change would come, but for the Hannahs of the world it would be painfully slow. In 1807 a London life insurer called the Pelican Life Insurance Company (est. 1797) advertised its wares in Philadelphia through the agency of Israel Whelen, a Chester County Quaker who was an active merchant and a director in the BUS and Lancaster Turnpike Company.

If Englishmen could sell life insurance in Philadelphia, then why couldn't Philadelphians sell life insurance in Philadelphia? After all, most of Philadelphia's financial innovations had European, and usually British, roots. Philadelphians kept a keen eye out for new ideas, maintained extensive European contacts who kept them apprised of the latest and greatest, and knew how to mold foreign institutions to Pennsylvania's laws and America's customs. It was only a matter of time, therefore, before they launched their own life insurance company.[3]

The Pennsylvania Company for Insurance on Lives and Granting Annuities first showed signs of life in December 1809 when articles of association were drawn up. The Pennsylvania Company obtained a formal charter on March 10, 1812, but soon after that America went to war with Britain. The company delayed its IPO and did not write any life policies until 1813. The Pennsylvania Company, the nation's first joint-stock life insurance company, had gotten off to a rocky start. Things would not get easier for some decades. Early life insurers had difficulty selling whole life policies because the cost of the policies was prohibitively high and their marketing and sales techniques were too simplistic. The Pennsylvania Company, like most early life insurers, found it easier to sell trust services and life annuities—IOUs that made an annual payment for the duration of the policyholder's life. Where life insurance protected widows and minor children from the shock of the breadwinner's early death, annuities protected individuals from the curse of superannuation, of living "too long" after their economically productive years had ended. So while the Pennsylvania Company did not help many children like Mary at first, it did keep many a "spinster" and "retired merchant" from penury, the public dole, or private charity.[4]

Annuities were relatively cheap. For instance, for a lump sum payment of $100, the Pennsylvania Company promised to pay a fifty-year-old $7.72 annually for life, no matter how long the IOU holder, called an annuitant, lived. The Pennsylvania Company's life insurance policies, however, were quite pricey by later standards and astronomically expensive compared to today's. (Early policies were also much less liberal than later ones, so early policyholders paid more and got less.) Early premiums were expensive due to two primary causes. First, the Pennsylvania Company had very little relevant statistical information about death rates to go on. A few published mortality rates were available, but none measured how many *Philadelphians* of different ages would die in the next year. And none of the macabre tables yet accounted for adverse selection, the nasty fact that people who are more likely to die are more likely to seek insurance. So the Pennsylvania Company's actuaries had to make guesses, educated guesses to be sure, but guesses nonetheless. They always erred on the side of the company, not so much out of greed as out of the realization that the company's survival was of paramount importance to beneficiaries.

The second reason premiums were so high was something of a catch-22. High premiums meant few sales. That, in turn, meant that early life insurers had to invest some of their premium receipts in liquid but low-return assets so that they could quickly sell them to meet death claims. Lower returns on invested assets of course spelled higher premiums, and high premiums meant few sales. It took the industry several decades to break that vicious cycle.

Some scholars point to religion as the main reason why life insurance was slow to catch on in America. It is true that contemporaries generally viewed property and casualty insurance companies, primarily marine and fire insurers, much more favorably than they did life insurers. Most early Americans correctly understood that insurance of ships and buildings against gales, pirates, and fires was the antithesis of gambling. Gamblers, after all, sought to *increase* the volatility of their returns while policyholders sought to *decrease* the volatility of theirs. The insurance was merely a reimbursement in case of loss.

Life insurance, on the other hand, seemed to offer a bonanza to the beneficiaries of the deceased. Much to the chagrin of early life insurers, some early Americans were slow to accept the notion that life insurance was not akin to a lottery on the life of an individual but rather was, like fire and marine insurance, a reimbursement, not of the ultimate "value" of a human being, but rather of the individual's expected future income. That insight, though, does not explain why insurers sold so little life insurance in the early years. As the widespread popularity of wagering pools, lotteries, and tontine schemes shows, early Americans, even Philadelphians as we will see, were avid gamblers. So if anything, the perception of life insurance as a gamble should have increased demand for the product. Moreover, there were good religious reasons for obtaining coverage—or so the insurers argued. The husband, they noted time and again, had as much a sacred duty to provide for his family in death as he had in life.[5]

Clearly then, price was the main factor limiting sales. As soon as prices (premiums) came down, sales increased, and all while Americans' religiosity (and propensity to gamble) stayed more or less constant. With lower premiums, life insurers could turn the vicious cycle into a virtuous one. As they sold more policies, they created a steady stream of premium revenue that always exceeded claims. They quickly learned that they would no longer have to sell assets to meet claims. That allowed them to become quintessential long-term investors, preferring relatively high-yielding but illiquid mortgages over government or corporate bonds. Now the catch-22 worked in favor of yet lower premiums and yet more sales. By the Civil War, life insurance IOUs were important savings vehicles for America's middle and upper classes. By the close of the nineteenth century, a sizable percentage of the poor invested their pennies in life insurance. One reason why America never embraced socialism was that most of its workers were capitalists, indirect owners of capital through their insurance policies.

What brought premiums down? You guessed it, Chestnut Street. Its life insurers were the industry's elder statesmen and its leading conservative voices. The Pennsylvania Company along with the Girard Life Insurance, Annuity and Trust Company—chartered in 1836 and named after famous Philadelphia financier Stephen Girard—were especially noted for their conservatism because they clearly favored safety over new sales. Life insurance meant family protection. Its value lay in the certainty of its payment, not its rate of return. For that reason, the early Philadelphia life insurers, unlike some later upstarts, also enjoyed a reputation for paying valid claims promptly, without litigation. No man, it was said, wanted to bequeath his widow and small children a lawsuit or a claim against a bankrupt corporation.

Despite their conservatism, Philadelphia's early life insurers were not stodgy or unwilling to innovate. Competition ensured that. A quarter of a century after its incorporation, the Pennsylvania Company was still of modest size. The company leveraged its twenty-five years of hard-earned experience, however, by updating its tables "based upon rates of interest conformable to their experience in the improvement of funds, and upon rates of mortality observed among actual insurers and annuitants in Europe and America." That brought lower rates for insurance and higher rates for annuitants. Part of the impetus for the lower insurance rates was the entrance of the Girard Company, the premiums of which were lower than those of the Pennsylvania Company. More importantly, the Girard Company's policies were "participating." In other words, the company promised to repay premiums to policyholders should its mortality, investment, and expense assumptions prove too conservative. Those "dividends" provided the solution to the premium paradox because it allowed the company to offer perfectly safe policies, at the lowest possible cost.[6]

Participating policies eventually revolutionized the life insurance industry. But in 1837 only about three hundred Philadelphians had insured their lives, and for a total of only about $400,000. Moreover, most of those policies were one- or seven-year term policies, not whole life policies. The recession that crippled the U.S. economy in the late 1830s and early 1840s hurt asset values but did not bring in the rash of claims that so injured marine and fire insurers. Moreover, the main business of the early life insurers, the trust business, emerged from the recession largely unscathed. Trusts were basically financial accounts held "in trust" for children, widows, and charitable institutions; most arose out of estate proceedings. Many people thought institutional trustees superior to individual ones, who often died, went bankrupt, or neglected their charges' interests. Many institutional trustees, including the Pennsylvania Company, offered customers a guaranteed rate of return and the almost perfect safety of the capital invested.

For some years after Chestnut Street gave way to Wall Street as the nation's financial capital, Philadelphia continued to lead the industry—but in a bad way. The first mutual life insurer to be chartered, Mutual Life, was stillborn in 1844. But three years later, Penn Mutual Life formed and thrived by selling relatively low-cost participating policies, half for cash, half for credit. The 1840s also witnessed the advent of the commissioned sales agent. Lower costs and higher pressure led to greater sales volume. Greater sales meant greater economies of scale could be achieved, mostly through lower unit expenses.

By 1850 the life insurance industry faced a new problem—it was growing too fast for its own good. Contemporary analysts, including Philadelphia actuary Harvey Tuckett, chastised life insurers for focusing on growth instead of the safety of the investment. Tuckett noted, correctly, that whole life policies and fire or marine insurance were fundamentally different because, on the one hand, death is "a certainty," with only its precise moment in doubt. On the other hand, it was not at all certain that a ship would sink or a house burn during the contract period. Ergo, he argued, property and casualty insurers could "close their accounts at the end of every year, and arrive at a correct conclusion of their profit and loss." Life insurers could make no such determination, because ultimately their profitability rested on their *long-term* mortality, investment, and expense experiences. Any attempt by life insurance companies to distribute profits over the short term, therefore, was to confuse "the shadow for the substance." Tuckett derided mutual life insurers and stock insurers who offered high, frequent dividends on participating policies.[7]

Tuckett was correct—when he wrote in 1850. Many life insurance companies, including those headquartered in Philadelphia, did engage in sundry unsound practices. Some charged premiums that were unrealistically low. Others charged relatively high premiums but rebated most of it through "bonus," "dividend," or other profit-sharing mechanisms. Others charged reasonable premiums and made rational dividends but allowed policyholders to "pay" their premiums with personal promissory notes. Some insurers risked their assets for too little reward. More than one Philadelphia life insurer dabbled in many such abuses simultaneously until it failed. The key problem was that the Pennsylvania legislature allowed life insurers to keep their liabilities secret and allowed them to use sham auditors. Market participants, therefore, often believed they had a better understanding of each company's financial situation than they actually did. If they managed to cut through the fog, they quickly sold their stock or dropped their policies.

Few balance sheets of early Philadelphia life insurers are extant. Those that survive are somewhat frightening. Consider the condition of the Equitable Life Insurance Company of Philadelphia, shown in figure 6.1, on April 15, 1850, when that company had in force 212 policies with a total face value of $319,920.

Figure 6.1: Balance Sheet of the Equitable Life Insurance Company of Philadelphia, April 15, 1850

Assets:	
Bonds of Pennsylvania, Philadelphia, Pittsburgh, and Cincinnati	$16,552.84
Bills receivable	$1,199.91
Mortgage	$400.00
Cash	$869.06
Balance due on 1,350 shares of its own stock	$19,021.81
Total	$38,043.62
Liabilities:	
Capital stock (installments received)	$15,800.00
Premiums received	$16,973.45
Interest received	$1,144.20
Surplus (undistributed profit)	$4,095.97
Total	$38,013.62

Source: J. A. Fowler, *History of Insurance in Philadelphia for Two Centuries (1683–1882)* (Philadelphia: American Publishing and Engraving Co., 1888).

Basically, though the company had a small surplus, it assets were not broadly diversified and, in the case of its stock notes, were not remunerative. Worse yet, the company's expenses were very high. After a few of its shares sold at auction at 40 percent of par, the misinformation fog lifted and policyholders began dumping their policies en masse.

Tight finances like those of Equitable Life led to "sharp" business practices. Policyholders, in effect, got what they paid for. Low-cost Philadelphia insurers tried to weasel out of claims by alleging that applicants had lied about their age or health, forcing widows and orphans to litigate or settle for pennies on the dollar. Tuckett claimed to "have heard of an office the trustees of which boasted of their power to litigate a claim for three years." Tuckett quickly pointed out, however, that "the number of offices which act upon these principles are few." But there were enough to damage the city's reputation. With many of the new techniques exposed as unsound, the locus of innovation and entry shifted to Massachusetts, home of the brilliant actuary-regulator Elizur Wright (no relation, honest), and later to New York.

By the Civil War, life companies had learned to estimate fair and proper dividends with accuracy. The better companies always erred on the side of caution but returned any excess profits to the policyholders. By 1910 mutual companies dominated the life insurance industry and would continue to do so until the final years of the twentieth century. Though scandals plagued the industry in the 1900s and 1990s, the life insurance industry for the most part had a positive impact on the savings rate and the fate of millions of families, but precious little of its success owed anything to Philadelphia. Today little remains of the city's once-glorious life insurance sector. The same can be said of its fire insurance sector.

↪ Premature death of the breadwinner was not the only predator that stalked American families. Fire could bring both death and physical destruction of home and shop. To lose a heavily mortgaged property to fire would make financial insolvency well-nigh inevitable, an exceedingly unhappy prospect in an era when bankruptcy—for any reason, even accidental—led to imprisonment. Many would rather perish than languish in debtors' prison. For starters, imprisonment for debt stained the debtor's reputation more or less forever, an experience as humiliating as wearing Hester Prynne's scarlet letter A. Worse, imprisonment was downright dangerous. Conditions in Philadelphia's Prune Street (now Locust Street) debtors' prison, for instance, were severe. Contemporaries described it as a "human slaughter house," a "dismal cage," and a "loathsome storehouse"—and those are the printable descriptions. Prisoners—the lucky ones, that is—lived off the charity of friends and family. The unlucky ones died slow, agonizing deaths from starvation and disease as the jailers callously looked on. The government provided prisoners with nothing but the prison walls and the guards. One judge vindicated the state's attitude by arguing that the debtors should be allowed to die "in the name of God" for their "presumption and ill behaviour."[8]

House fires were extremely common in early America. The reason is obvious. Aside from the sun, fire was the main source of both heat and light. A spark from a fireplace, a forgotten candle, or a broken oil lamp was all it took to turn a home or shop into smoldering ash. Then there were the neighbors. If they did not have their chimneys swept regularly, the built-up soot would eventually catch fire and shoot out the top of their chimneys like a blowtorch. One ember on a wood-shingled roof and that was all she wrote. If conditions were right, an entire block could go up in smoke.[9]

Big cities like Philadelphia were home to numerous private fire companies. But the firefighters simply did not have the technology or incentive to effectively combat big blazes. Today's fire crews are professionals equipped with flame-retardant suits, oxygen masks, high-pressure water hoses, ladder trucks, and other marvels of modern firefighting technology, but even they often can do little more than prevent the spread of the conflagration. Early firefighters relied on bucket brigades to fuel their hand-powered "engines," pumps that created about as much pressure as a modern garden hose. They were amateur volunteers to boot and likely owned no life insurance. They bravely tried to rescue people but were not about to turn themselves into cinders to save someone else's house.

For all those reasons, fire insurance was pretty darn important. That is why, as we have seen, it emerged in rudimentary form in the colonial period, in Philadelphia. Though Philadelphia was free of the large fires that swept Manhattan during the Revolution, the war nonetheless severely injured the Philadelphia Contributionship. The culprits were not arsonists but the legal tender laws and the depreciation of the Continental dollar. Borrowers used the opportunity to pay off their indebtedness to the Contributionship in nearly worthless paper dollars, and the tender laws forced the company to accept the payments at their full nominal value. So the company lent, say, £100 in 1770 only to receive back £1 in 1780.

Under dire financial stress, the directors of the Contributionship made a bad business decision in 1784 when they declared that henceforth no house would be insured or reinsured if a tree stood in front of it. The directors feared that the tree might catch fire and engulf the house or that it might impede firefighters' efforts to dowse a blaze. The decision almost immediately spurred the entry of a competitor, the Mutual Assurance Company for Insuring Houses from Loss by Fire. Headed by Plunket Fleeson, an interior decorator and state assemblyman, and Quaker merchant George Emlen, the new company came to be known by its emblem, a green tree, because it insured houses with trees as long as the home owner paid an additional premium and trimmed the tree at least once a year to keep it below the house's eaves. The new association received a formal charter from the state legislature in 1786.

Both early Philadelphia fire insurance companies insured only structures, not their contents. Though primarily a marine insurer, the Insurance Company of North America (ICNA) sought to exploit that contractual weakness by insuring contents as well as the buildings themselves. Demand for the policies was weak at first, so the ICNA began to advertise widely. The ads worked. By 1796 it insured $288,250 worth of goods on fire risks ranging from western Pennsylvania to Massachusetts to Georgia. The ICNA found profit margins for fire insurance much stronger than those for marine insurance. Through the end of 1802, it received $81,253.76 in fire insurance premiums but paid out only $30,116.59 in claims. Other marine insurers could not resist such profitability, so many emulated the ICNA and began to offer fire policies as well as marine ones.

The two mutuals, the marine insurers, and some foreign insurers met

Philadelphians' need for fire insurance until 1810, when the state legislature banned the sale of insurance policies by foreign companies. In 1810 about sixteen thousand dwellings housed the ninety-six thousand or so residents of the city proper and its outlying districts. Many of the owners of those dwellings recognized the need for fire insurance but simply found it too expensive. They supported the formation of the American Fire Insurance Company of Philadelphia, hoping that it would supply enough new IOUs to bring premiums down to more affordable levels. But the American, a stock company, simply filled the void left by the exiting foreign insurers. It hired Israel Whelen, an important local agent used by many of the foreign insurers, and with his help assumed many of the foreign insurers' existing policies.

The next year, 1811, the Bucks County Contributionship Insurance Company formed. A mutual originally modeled after the Philadelphia Contributionship, it at first took deposits. Soon it switched to the assessment method, where each member paid a pro rata share of claims as they arose. In 1817 an association of sixteen firefighting companies formed the Mutual Fire Association of Philadelphia. The notion was that any profits arising from the insurance would go to improve the firefighting capabilities of the member companies. The association formally incorporated in 1820. It summoned forth enough competition to induce price concessions by the ICNA and other fire insurers.

The market for fire insurance, however, remained far from saturated as only a small percentage of the population opted to purchase protection. Part of the reason for the low rate of market penetration was that the early fire insurers tended to avoid risks rather than rate them. In other words, they simply refused to write business on riskier structures rather than to attempt to determine an appropriately higher premium. They preferred to underwrite faraway but comfortable risks rather than insure all local risks.

In 1829 the state legislature terminated out-of-state agencies as it had foreign agencies almost two decades earlier by imposing a tax on premiums of 20 percent. The new law attracted an entrant, the Franklin Fire Insurance Company, named after Benjamin Franklin. The Franklin pushed the Philadelphia companies to carefully rate risks rather than simply accept or reject applications. Its other major innovation was the insurance of buildings under construction, crops in the barn or field, and ships and their cargoes while in port. The company was, of course, located on Chestnut Street, "163 1 / 2 Chestnut street, third door below Fifth street" to be exact. By 1832 Philadelphia was home to eight dedicated fire insurers. Entry came hot and heavy in the 1830s, mostly in the form of stock insurers headquar-

tered in Philadelphia's suburban districts, including Kensington, Spring
Garden, and Southwark.

The business need for fire insurance was amply demonstrated in 1836
when Charles Lennig's drug manufactory burst into flames, causing $150,000
in damages and two deaths. Lennig recouped about $100,000 of the loss,
mostly from American Fire and the Franklin. The shock of that loss, the
largest in the city's history to that time, was nothing compared to the shock
of the panic and recession the following year that sent asset values spiraling
downward. The balance sheets of fire insurers strained as high interest rates
sent the market value of their stocks, bonds, mortgages, and real estate
plummeting. Worse, as real estate values sank, the moral hazard increased
and the number of claims, especially large claims, jumped. As in the marine
industry, such pressures led to the proliferation of mutual fire insurers in
the 1840s. But the heyday of Philadelphia fire insurance had clearly passed.

∕◯ A third type of insurance was also important, though most people
need not buy it directly. Whether plying the Seven Seas or inland waterways
like the Delaware and Susquehanna rivers, barges, barks, boats, frigates,
ships, sloops, snows, steamships, and other water-going vessels could catch
fire, run aground, spring a leak, capsize, or fall into the wrong hands. The
vessels themselves were big investments, and when laden with valuable
goods, they were *huge* investments. To ship off without insurance was to
court financial disaster. Little wonder, then, that even in the eighteenth century, marine insurance had a very long history, indeed.[10]

As described above, colonial Philadelphians were no strangers to marine
insurance. In the early eighteenth century, they purchased coverage from
London, perhaps with the help of a broker. By midcentury entrepreneurial
Philadelphians wrote insurance policies for their fellow merchants. Thomas
Willing and half a dozen others even established a special partnership to underwrite marine risks. The Revolution disrupted the sector. Rates were, of
course, very high during wartime. The return of peace, however, brought
more trade, lower rates, and a sectoral resurgence.

One of the more colorful types of insurance written in the early national
period was ransom insurance. The IOUs promised to pay ransoms should a
mariner be taken hostage by pirates. Their day was short-lived: colonists
had had no call for them, protected as they were by His Majesty's navy; the
policies fell into disuse after 1795 when the U.S. government began to pay
tribute to Algerian pirates. Within a few years, the United States decided it
would be cheaper to defeat the pirates than to continue to bribe them. It
was right. The need for ransom insurance ebbed until a new species of land-

based pirate, vultures who kidnap and ransom wealthy Westerners, arose in the twentieth century.

The big post-Revolution innovation in marine insurance was the establishment of joint-stock corporations dedicated to underwriting. As usual, Chestnut Street was not only in the vanguard, but on point. Philadelphia's first incorporated marine insurance company, the ICNA, should have been called the Phoenix because it arose out of the ashes of a failed tontine scheme. In November 1792 the ICNA, though still unchartered, offered its shares to the public. By December 1 forty thousand of the $10 shares had been taken up by subscribers making a $4 per share cash down payment.

Private underwriters struggled mightily against formal incorporation of the ICNA because they feared, correctly as it turned out, that chartered insurers would be their undoing. The ICNA offered policies similar to those offered by private underwriters. Worse, it had a price advantage because it sold to policyholders directly, not through brokers. Moreover, market participants immediately recognized that the corporation was less likely to default than private underwriters. After the company finally formally incorporated in 1794, it attracted yet more investors. Soon after, a rival company, the Insurance Company of the State of Pennsylvania (ICPA), also incorporated.

The new corporate insurers battled against syndicates of individuals for supremacy of the trade. It was a pitched battle, but longevity and stability gave the corporations the upper hand, as the following letter, written in 1799, attests:

> We went to the different Insurance Offices, to make the Necessary enquiry relative to the insurance you wished to have affected on the Ship Arrel; where we saw that Mr. Buckley's Insurance was done at 18 P Ct., out and home with liberty to touch for refreshments or trade to any place or ports in their Way, going & coming &c. for which premium either office will do this, on same conditions as that of Mr. Buckley's. The Out of Door underwriters (good Men) offer to do it at 17 1/2 P Ct. You have a credit of 16 months for the premiums, for which we shall have to give our note with an approved endorser. . . . Both the Insurance Offices are good; in this case we would prefer either. It being of a long duration before the Voyage is completed, *Deaths* and other *accidents* may (and does too often) happen to Individuals. [Emphasis in original.]

Note that the individual underwriters, the "Out of Door" men, understood their disadvantage and tried to compensate for it by charging a lower premium. Such tactics fell short, however, because individuals simply were not as efficient as large corporations. As early as 1704, shippers lamented that "Ensurers fail much." Marine insurance corporations, by contrast, rarely succumbed to bankruptcy. And they never died.[11]

Incorporated companies also enjoyed economies of scale that made them more efficient than individual underwriters. One area where they enjoyed a scale advantage was investments. Philadelphia's incorporated marine insurers invested their assets in government bonds, ground rents, corporate equities and bonds, personal bonds and mortgages, and special marine lending contracts known as bottomry and respondentia bonds, capital market instruments that dated from at least twelfth-century Italy. Their assets differed from those of commercial banks in that they tended to have longer maturities and higher face values. For instance, marine insurers, unlike banks, could purchase real estate for speculative purposes. (Legally, banks could only own real estate needed for the transaction of their businesses or taken to satisfy a defaulted loan.) Insurers also had little need to keep cash on hand. Instead, they maintained accounts with the city's leading commercial banks. Those banks sometimes granted insurers short-term loans so that they could pay claims due. An insurer with a formal line of credit with a bank need not have held any cash whatsoever.

Incorporated companies could also spend more funds investigating dubious claims and fighting fraudulent ones in court. Moral hazard was rife in marine insurance. Individual underwriters often found it cheaper to simply pay claims rather than to investigate them carefully or to fight them vigorously in court. With their larger capital cushion, corporate insurers could take more risks fighting fishy claims. Moreover, shysters understood all this and hence were more likely to seek insurance from private underwriters rather than corporate ones.

Also, it was easier for a few corporations to cabal to fix prices or terms than it was for scores of private underwriters to do so. The presence of private underwriters, however, prevented the corporations from carrying the practice to extremes. Indeed, in the first decade of its existence, the ICNA received $6,037,456.17 in premiums but paid out $5,500,887.57 in claims, leaving only 8.89 percent for expenses. The company's profits came almost wholly from the investment earnings of its capital, contingency fund, and premiums. Unfortunately for the company's stockholders, the depredations of the French and British in the 1790s depleted the company's capital. The company's stock price, detailed in figure 6.2, tells of its difficulties.[12]

Sensing opportunity, new entrants appeared. In 1803 the Union Insurance Company formed. It incorporated the following year, as did the Phoenix Insurance Company. Soon thereafter, in March 1804, the Delaware

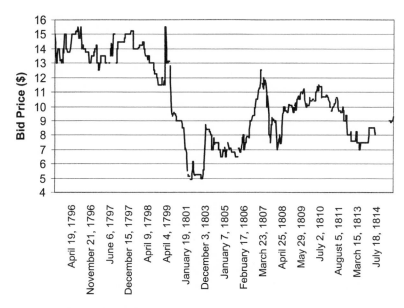

Figure 6.2: Stock Price of the ICNA, 1795–1815
Source: Richard Sylla, Jack Wilson, and Robert E. Wright, "Database of Early U.S. Securities Prices," ICPSR, Ann Arbor, Michigan.

Insurance Company and the Philadelphia Insurance Company received legislative approval. Growth in the number of companies and total capital invested in chartered marine insurers continued apace. By the War of 1812, Pennsylvania boasted nine marine insurers with over $4 million in capital.

British insurers also tried to enter the Philadelphia market by establishing offices in the city. Given the profound anti-British feelings of the time, however, the foreign offices had a tough go of it. As noted above, domestic insurers in 1810 managed to induce the legislature to pass a law effectively barring foreign offices from writing business in the Commonwealth.

Due to the advantages of incorporated insurers, individual underwriters slowly reinvested their at-risk capital in shares of incorporated marine insurers. Wartime conditions experienced throughout the 1790s and first decade and a half of the nineteenth century sped the transition. Brokers did not disappear because applicants found their knowledge of the insurance market of value, especially as the number of corporate insurers grew. Often, though, insurance brokers found that to make a decent living, they had to add claims adjusting and/or securities dealing to their repertoire.

In 1808 some marine insurers began to look for other markets. The Marine and Fire Association (which in 1809 incorporated as the Marine Insurance Company), for instance, insured inland navigation on canals and rivers and even wrote policies covering wagon transport overland. Soon the Lancaster and Susquehanna Insurance Company, which had an office in Philadelphia by 1808, was doing likewise. The Jefferson administration's trade restrictions, economic warfare measures aimed at Britain and France, brought the city's legal (and hence insurable) international trade to a near standstill, and thereby helped to spur the movement. Not all marine insurers jumped on the bandwagon, however. Some were content to keep their capitals invested and act simply like an investment or mutual fund.

Some established but relatively inefficient companies, like the United States Insurance Company (USIC), took a bath during the embargo. Due to Philadelphia's declining importance in trade, of which more later, they never quite recovered. Its capital impaired, the USIC suspended operations temporarily in 1824. Only after the legislature officially reduced the par value of its shares to $25 each did its stock price begin to rebound. The company remained profitable until the recession that began in the late 1830s injured its balance sheet and induced a rash of claims. As figure 6.3 shows, it slipped beneath the waves in January 1844.

After the War of 1812, incorporated insurers completed their triumph over the individual underwriters. But at the same time, Philadelphians noted that New York had overtaken their beloved city as the nation's most important port and that Baltimore was gaining fast. The completion of New York's Grand Canal, better known to history as the Erie Canal, sealed Philadelphia's fate.

Marine insurers therefore turned increasingly to inland and coastal insurance. The steamboats that plied the Delaware needed insurance, as did coal boats and barges on Pennsylvania's canals, and the many ships that skirted the coast from Boston to the Carolinas. Increasingly, insurers realized that overland freight needed to be insured too. In 1831, when the American Insurance Company of Philadelphia obtained its charter, railways were all the rage. Accordingly, the new company obtained the right to insure rail freightage. Partly for that reason, its IPO subscription filled quickly. The Philadelphia Fire and Inland Navigation Company went one better, combining in 1835 fire and inland marine insurance in one company, a hybrid with no known precedent on either side of the Atlantic.

Though Philadelphia's share of transatlantic trade was slipping, there was still business to write, especially after the marine insurers convinced the legislature to bar foreign and out-of-state companies from establishing agencies in the state. Pennsylvanians could and did continue to obtain marine insurance elsewhere but without the convenience of treating with a lo-

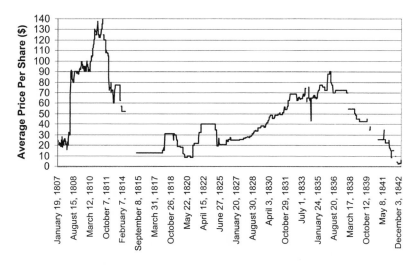

Figure 6.3: United States Insurance Company Stock Price, 1807–43
Source: Richard Sylla, Jack Wilson, and Robert E. Wright, "Database of Early U.S. Securities Prices," ICPSR, Ann Arbor, Michigan.

cal office. Except for the threat of war with France in early 1835, the first three-quarters of the 1830s were a propitious period for Philadelphia marine insurers. When the French finally agreed to pay old "spoilation" claims dating from the Napoleonic period, the industry experienced a mini-boom punctuated with huge special dividends of upward of 40 percent.

The Panic of 1837 and the years of recession that followed it, however, were not kind to marine insurers. But in 1838 conditions were good enough, and the future depths of the recession obscure enough, that a new marine insurer, the Washington Insurance Company, could form and an existing company, the Spring Garden Insurance Company, could obtain the right to issue marine and inland policies. The following year, the Washington petitioned for and received the power to insure its policyholders against fire.

Beginning late in 1839, marine insurers began to feel the pinch of recession. Three problems hit them simultaneously. First, premium revenues plummeted because trade volumes were low. Second, asset values plummeted as interest rates soared. Third, increased moral hazard led to increased claims. Because of the anemic premium receipts, insurers did not have the cash on hand to pay the unexpectedly large volume of claims, so they had to sell some of their assets into a depressed market to raise the necessary funds. By January 1841, at least eight Philadelphia marine insurers had stopped paying dividends. One of those companies, the ICPA, retired some of its stock and sliced the par value of the rest in half. Soon after, other companies also recognized their losses and reduced their official capitals. In October 1842, the Atlantic Insurance Company decided to voluntarily liquidate due to two shocks—a tax on dividends implemented in January 1841 and the death of its leader, political economist Condy Raguet, in March. The company paid all of its IOUs and returned stockholders the par value of their stock plus six dollars per share.

Other companies continued paying dividends, although they avoided insolvency only by rather unrealistically valuing their real estate at its purchase price and their mortgages at par (value lent). But stockholders knew that the companies should have "marked to market," that is, reported the current market value of their assets, not what they paid for the securities years before. Stockholders were not content with fake dividends or deceptive accounting, and one by one they forced managers to undertake controlled liquidations.

The core problem was that the volume of trade was simply too small to support so much capital. By 1840 New York insurers held scale advantages that Philadelphia companies could only dream of. To make it easier for Philadelphia shippers to insure in New York without the aid of a Philadelphia-based agent, Manhattan insurers innovated, offering to insure ships for an entire year rather than for particular voyages, as had been the custom for over a century.

The troubles of joint-stock marine insurers led to experimentation into mutual forms of insurance. But those efforts were no more successful in marine insurance than they had been in life or fire insurance. There were two basic types of mutual insurance—assessment and provisional premium. Under the assessment model, members essentially contracted to insure each other, making pro rata payments when group members presented valid claims. In the provisional premium model (called a "participating" policy in life insurance, as we have seen), policyholders paid to the mutual company conservatively large premiums, a portion of which was returned to the insured should expenses and claims prove better than expected. By the end of 1843, Philadelphia boasted two mutual marine insurers, one a pure mutual and new entrant, the other a partially mutualized stock company. The ICPA tried a different exit strategy—to fire insurance. The directors believed that Philadelphia's fire insurers had fared far better than its marine insurers. As we have seen, they were right.

✓⊘ So in insurance as in commercial banking, Philadelphia led the charge to modernity only to lose out to New York in the 1830s and 1840s.

Philadelphia boasted of the nation's first and most important life, fire, and marine insurance companies. But by shielding Pennsylvania companies from out-of-state and foreign businesses, the Pennsylvania legislature actually weakened Philadelphia insurers by reducing the competitive pressures that would have ensured their continued efficiency. The decline of the port of Philadelphia doomed the city's marine insurers, but no fundamental economic reason existed that would have prevented its fire and life insurers from thriving had the legal climate been more conducive to competition and financial transparency. So innovation suffered and eventually transmogrified into stagnation and in some cases liquidation. As we learn in the next chapter, Philadelphia's thrift industry followed a similar, but ultimately not so depressing, trajectory.

7

BUILDING NEST EGGS
AND HOMES

Today literally hundreds of communities claim to be a "City of Homes." But that comfy appellation first fell to Philadelphia, the subject of Talcott Williams's 1893 book, *Philadelphia: A City of Homes*. In most large nineteenth-century U.S. cities, including New York, Chicago, and Boston, the "poorer sorts"—mechanics, small tradesmen, and laborers, that is, humble people with jobs but little in the way of disposable income—rented a "flat" in a house or a cluster of small rooms in a tenement building. In Philadelphia, by contrast, many of the working poor managed to purchase their own homes. By today's standards, the row houses that nineteenth-century Philadelphians purchased by the tens of thousands are not terribly appealing. The median dwelling was about 650 square feet, space enough for five ten-by-twelve-foot rooms, a back shed, and a privy. Often adding to the ambience was a sordid street in front, a fetid alley in back, and noisy neighbors on either side. But compared to a Manhattan tenement, even Philadelphia's diminutive bandbox houses were mansions. Best of all, the occupants owned them, and ownership brought pride, stability, and incentives to invest in the community.[1]

Philadelphia became the nation's original "City of Homes" for two simple reasons: supply and demand. On the supply side, the city boasted a highly competitive home construction industry that erected some fifty-two thousand new houses between 1790 and 1850. Thanks to the institution of ground rents (discussed at length in chapter 2), entry into the building trades was relatively easy. Fierce competition among contractors was, for course, a great boon to home buyers. On the demand side, early Philadelphians were not unusually industrious nor unusually interested in owning their own homes. When it came to home ownership, they fared better than their brethren mostly because, thanks to Chestnut Street, they found it easier (read cheaper) to save and to borrow.

✐ Houses didn't grow on trees. Not even the wooden ones. Footers needed to be dug, foundations laid, fireplaces mortared, walls erected, roofs shingled, and doors and windows hung. Then the finishing work began—the painting, wallpapering, flooring, and installing of sundry fixtures. No part of the home construction business was easy or cheap. The key question was: Could quality houses be built inexpensively enough to induce people to buy them? In Philadelphia the answer was an unequivocal "Yes!" The reason was competition—many small artisanal home construction firms thrived. The reason so many firms existed despite the cutthroat competition was simple—cheap financing through ground rents.[2]

A common strategy used by early Philadelphia home builders was to purchase empty lots on ground rent, to use subcontractors to help erect simple inexpensive homes, then to sell the lots and homes for a larger ground rent or a bundle of cash and assumption of the original ground rent. That cash, perhaps with the help of short-term bank loans, went to fund the next round of building. Little wonder, then, that nineteenth-century Philadelphians regularly argued that "Philadelphia was a city of homes, made so primarily by the ground-rent system." Thanks to the relatively cheap financing made possible by ground rents, and later by institutional mortgage lenders, Philadelphia's home construction industry was nimble, efficient, and even prolific. The careers of three home builders show how Philadelphia became the City of Homes.

John Munday began life sometime around 1760. By 1782 he had finished his apprenticeship as a house carpenter. For the rest of the decade, he kicked around from job to job, scraping by, hoping that the economy would improve. As we learned in chapter 5, it did, thanks largely to the adoption of the Constitution and Alexander Hamilton's fiscal and financial reforms. By 1792 building houses in Philadelphia on speculation was a booming industry. Though deeply in debt, Munday had the skills needed to capitalize on the rapid expansion in the city's housing stock. The old Quaker City spread in all three directions available to it—due west to the Schuylkill River, north toward the prosperous farms of upper Philadelphia County, and south toward the swampy confluence of the Schuylkill and Delaware rivers. One young Quakeress told her father that he "wou'd hardly know the upper ends of Market, Chestnut, Walnut, and Arch Streets, they are so built up with new houses." Growth in the Northern

Liberties, Southwark, and other early Philadelphia suburbs was no less remarkable.

Munday set to work, keeping three to six new houses in progress at any
one time. Some of his work was on contract to Philadelphia's rich upper
crust, the 10 percent or so of folks who owned fully half of the city's taxable
property. Contract work was good because it was in one sense a sure
thing—the rich merchant or wealthy banker paid for the lot and house up
front. The problem was that there were lots of carpenters like Munday out
there bidding on such jobs. Sometimes the lowest bidder discovered to his
chagrin that he had bid too low, that after he had paid for the building materials and his assistants' time, there was little or nothing left over. Almost as
bad, contractors sometimes did not earn as much profit as they probably
could have. In 1796, for example, Munday built Samuel Fisher "a large and
elegant house with stables" for $4,288. Fisher quickly resold the property
for $9,000. Nice work—Fisher's, that is—if you can get it.

A year earlier, in 1795, rapid price inflation—caused by a negative supply
shock (a Hessian fly infestation that destroyed a big chunk of the wheat
crop) and a positive demand shock (increased demand for flour from war-
torn France)—led many artisans like Munday to contract for too little
money. Munday survived the ensuing shakeout because most of his projects at that time were speculative affairs. In other words, he fronted the
money to buy the lot—usually on ground rent—and build the house. He
then marketed the house, hoping that he could sell it for a substantial profit.
In the inflationary environment of 1795, Munday did quite well. Those on
contract jobs, however, did not fare well.[3]

Munday apparently was unable to obtain bank loans with any regularity.
To raise short-term cash quickly, he sold his IOUs to "note shavers" but at
relatively steep discounts. (Rates as high as 2, 3, 4, even 5 percent *per month*
were not unknown.) He also found he could sometimes borrow long term
on the security of his lots, materials, and partly finished houses. Of course,
when he was seriously short of cash, he sold partially completed homes to
other builders or speculators. Occasionally he bartered his speculative
houses for merchandise, which he then turned over to his wife to retail for
cash, presumably because he believed that his wife could profitably retail
the goods.

As the 1790s boom wore on and then out, Munday's failures began to
outnumber and outweigh his successes. In 1798 Munday finally succumbed
to his creditors. He returned to the ranks of day laborers, his family eking
by on his wages and the proceeds of Elizabeth Munday's store. The restless
Munday later moved his family to a farm in nearby Chester County and set

himself up as a St. Croix merchant. A nasty fall from a horse, a stint in debtors' prison, and unsanitary conditions aboard a ship weakened Munday's "constitution." He died in 1803, not yet forty-five, and worth only about $100 free and clear. (Elizabeth ran a boardinghouse until her death in 1812.) Ultimately, in the business sense of the word, Munday had proved a "failure." But the scores of Philadelphia families who lived comfortably in the affordable homes that he built in the early 1790s would surely have argued otherwise.

So would have the hundreds of families who came to reside in the homes crafted by Moses Lancaster, a native of nearby Bucks County. A Quaker born of modest means in 1783, Lancaster lived to the ripe old age of ninety-six, one of the few Americans who could recall what they were doing when they first heard that Washington *and* Lincoln had died. He spent most of the time in between building houses. Unlike Munday, Lancaster found that he could easily obtain the loans that his growing business needed to survive by tapping the savings of fellow Quakers. Most readers probably think of the Quakers as a religious group. They were that, of course, but the infamously frequent and nosy Quaker meetings also served important economic functions—they created and disseminated information about the creditworthiness of members, reduced the costs of searching for a lender (or borrower) by bringing members together on a regular basis, and served as a relatively cheap and effective contract-enforcement system. Quakers were so good at greasing the wheels of credit that non-Quaker groups, including the Masons, essentially copied them. Much of the venom directed at both groups was pure envy, plain and simple.

Like Munday, Lancaster started his career as a lackey, a journeyman paid by the day or the job. Unlike Munday, Lancaster married into a little bit of money. And he had those Quaker connections. In a short time, Lancaster transformed himself into a "master," the quaint early nineteenth-century term for a general contractor. By 1807, with his wife busy pushing out the first of twelve children, Lancaster began to implement his grand plan, which was a rather sophisticated one at that. Lancaster bought a city lot on credit from a fellow Quaker. He quickly erected an apartment building on it, which he proceeded to lease. The rents from the lease soon paid off the mortgage. Rather than sell the property, however, Lancaster clung to it, mortgaging and subsequently redeeming it numerous times in the future. Within a few years, Lancaster's credit record was sterling; he could now borrow from anyone, not just Quakers, at low rates.

He'd need all of the credit that he could get. The 1810s witnessed a second housing boom in Philadelphia. Lancaster, who often had about a dozen houses under construction at any one time, concentrated his efforts in the Northern Liberties, that part of the expanding metropolis closest to his native Bucks County. His usual strategy was to buy big lots on ground rent, subdivide them, and apportion them to meet his cash needs. Some subdivisions he sold for cash or ground rent. Others he allowed subcontractors to develop as they saw fit, keeping a share of the profits for himself. The remainder he built up on his own account, using his apprentices for the grunt work and hiring journeymen and seasoned carpenters as needed. If his new houses met an unfavorable market, as many did during the 1819–22 recession, Lancaster leased them to the poorest rung of Philadelphians. When the market turned and the leases expired, Lancaster could then sell, and the tenants would find new accommodations yet further from the city's center.

The new housing market remained soft in the 1820s, so Lancaster diversified into the grain trade and, more sensibly, the lumber business. As his wealth and family grew, so, too, did the social distance between Lancaster and his employees. Early on several of his employees actually resided in Lancaster's home, sharing his modest furniture and food. By the 1830s they lived far from their "master" geographically, socially, and financially. Moses led his workers out of the desert of unemployment, but only he made it to the promised land of milk and honey. That is not to say that everything always went Lancaster's way. In fact, in 1829–30 Lancaster found himself trapped between a sharp housing recession and an even sharper widow brandishing a rather blunt business contract. The blunder eventually cost Lancaster eight of his rental houses and two undeveloped lots. But he still commanded a good-sized empire that in 1838 he consolidated into a floor-covering manufactory. The long recession that followed the Panic of 1837, however, put that ambitious venture in the red. In 1841 Lancaster retired to Bucks County, where he lived off financial investments, his children, and the charity of a carpenter's association for almost the next four decades.

Warner Myers was the youngest but most ambitious of our three contractors. Born to a poor Philadelphia family in 1793, Myers began his career as a housepainter, an unsuccessful yet resilient one at that. He emerged from bankruptcy in the early 1820s to forge a partnership with wealthy attorney Joseph Reed. Reed kept Myers well supplied with credit by lending his own resources and those of the American Fire Insurance Company, of which Reed was president. Myers and Reed's strategy was to build scads and scads of very cheap homes very far from the city's center, often well north of even the most sanguine maps of the era, and in more convenient but swampy areas overlooked by earlier builders. With Reed's financial help, Myers by the late 1820s had scores of homes in various phases of construction. Unskilled and semi-skilled laborers in Philadelphia's burgeoning factories—ropewalks, mills, glass manufactories, breweries, and the like—scooped up Myers's inconvenient distant hovels. Similarly, a little pumping and lots of fill, most of it refuse, increased demand for Myers's swamp houses. But Myers could not sell enough of them fast enough to keep his head above water. By the end of 1829, both he and Reed were bankrupt.

In 1840, after a decade of painting and rebuilding his twice-shattered reputation, Myers became a real estate broker. The third time was not a charm. As late as 1860, the only thing that kept the aged Myers from starvation was his paintbrush. But like Munday, Lancaster, and hundreds of contractors like them, Myers was not a bad businessman. He simply chose to enter a very competitive industry that weeded out inefficient producers as quickly as a pride of lionesses culled slow or infirm gazelles. The beneficiaries of that intense competition were consumers, working-class Philadelphians.

⟋ Most denizens of early America's other large cities (except for Baltimore, which also enjoyed ground rents) found it very difficult to save or cheaply borrow enough money to purchase their own homes. They usually found themselves trapped in a vicious cycle of high rents and low or no savings. Unable to break the cycle, they remained tenants throughout their lives. Philadelphians, by contrast, enjoyed wages almost as high as those paid for similar work in New York, but paid rents only 50 to 75 percent as high. In the first decades of the nineteenth century, Philadelphians could rent a small brick house for $40 to $80 per year, a sum that would command only a room or two in New York. (The more things change, the more they stay the same!) For $250 per year, a Philadelphia family could rent a large genteel structure near the commercial heart of the city. In New York $250 a year would fetch only a wooden house in an inconvenient location.

New York's large financial intermediaries invested in commercial paper (short-term business IOUs), government bonds, and relatively large, well-secured mortgages. No major intermediaries specialized in lending to the poor. The Bank for Savings *borrowed* large sums from New York's poor but left lending to them up to private individuals, many of whom were less than scrupulous and none of whom enjoyed the extensive scale economies needed to lend small sums profitably.[4]

Philadelphia's financial intermediaries were different. For starters, they had no qualms about investing in ground rents. In fact, most considered well-secured ground rents to be gilt-edged securities, which is to say valuable long-term investments. Corporate entities with unlimited legal lives, financial intermediaries were perfect investors in the perpetual obligations and they knew it. They purchased ground rents in prodigious quantities, fueling home production. Ground rents served to reconfirm the notion, discredited elsewhere, that mortgages were appropriate assets for financial intermediaries to hold. Pennsylvania's enormous success with "loan offices" in the colonial and confederation periods had given Philadelphia's finan-ciers reason to hope that banks could lend on mortgages and remain solvent. Although other states, including New York, had successful experiences with loan offices, the sentiment elsewhere was generally that mortgages were too illiquid, too difficult to sell if needed, for banks to invest heavily in them. Chestnut Street financiers proved them wrong.[5]

The key was the creation of an institution that would solve the investment "trilemma" (a dilemma with three problems instead of two) in a new way. Investors essentially trade off between three variables: risk, return, and liquidity. Risk is a bad thing; return and liquidity are good things. When risk increases, investors must receive a higher return and / or higher liquidity in compensation. When risk decreases, investors give up some return and / or liquidity in exchange. Holding risk constant, investors must choose some combination of return and liquidity—the higher the return, the lower the liquidity and vice versa. Within those general parameters, anything goes. Early commercial banks solved the trilemma by providing depositors with low-risk, low-return, but highly liquid investments like banknotes and checkable deposits. In other words, depositors received zero interest but could get their money back on demand. Other trilemma solutions are possible, however. For instance, a bank could provide depositors with low-risk, high-return, but illiquid investments. That was the solution chosen by another of Chestnut Street's innovations, the savings bank. Economic theory proved the intrinsic value of such an investment. But philanthropy, not economic theory, drove the decision to offer the poor a high-return, illiquid investment vehicle.

After the War of 1812, the spirit of "Howard" suffused the upper echelons of American society. Howard was a Cardington squire who turned to philanthropy after the unexpected death of his kind and gentle wife. He went to great lengths to alleviate the suffering of prisoners in England and across Europe. Legend has it that "for seventeen years he wandered about visiting almost every jail and hospital in Great Britain and Europe." He died in January 1790, aged sixty-four years, while attending to a sick lady in Cherson, Russia. Such a fitting end cemented the philanthropist's fame.[6]

Howard's legend smoldered in America for almost three decades before a Jewish-American playwright turned journalist, Mordecai Manuel Noah, exposed it to enough air to set it ablaze. In a series of brilliant essays on "domestic economy," a double entendre referring both to "home economics" and the national macroeconomy, Noah cast himself as Howard and loosed himself upon the evils facing the nation. Through Noah's pen, Howard arose from the dead to chastise Americans for a wide variety of sins, ranging from overeating to overdressing to gambling to not saving enough. With the country mired in its first nationwide recession in 1819, Noah's "Essays of Howard," a compilation of his newspaper musings, made a big splash.[7]

Howard's explicit endorsement of a new institution, the savings bank, gave the emerging thrift industry a big boost. "There are few institutions more charitable in design, and useful in operation," he argued, "than a well conducted *Savings Bank*." Noah was a New Yorker, but Wall Street still lagged behind the Chestnut Street curve. The philanthropic spirit suffused the City of Brotherly Love long before Noah penned his first Howard essay. In 1816 Philadelphians like political economist Condy Raguet and merchant George Billington combined forces with British precedent to create a savings bank, the venerable Philadelphia Savings Fund Society (PSFS).[8]

The Philadelphia Savings Fund Society began business as an unchartered mutual association in November 1816. The first depositor was one of Condy Raguet's servants, a black man. To encourage deposits from other working persons, the PSFS offered evening hours. The Society stressed that it could offer high returns with low risk, an apparent contradiction, but an achievable combination because its deposits were illiquid. In other words, depositors could not withdraw their money on demand or draw a check against it, as they could with commercial bank deposits. In some savings banks, notice of several weeks had to be given. In others, withdrawals could only be made certain periods each year. The delay served two purposes. First, it allowed the savings bank itself to remain fully invested in fairly illiquid securities. Second, it dissuaded people from dissaving by encouraging them to think of their deposits as long-term investments, not just a place to stash cash to fund a binge.[9]

The early savings banks were essentially mutual funds. They received deposits, which they reinvested in mortgages, ground rents, government and corporate securities, and loans collateralized by investment grade bonds. Table 7.1 details the asset allocation of the PSFS. Note that the institution invested the vast bulk of its assets in mortgages, real estate, and ground rents. Many of those mortgages were "originated" by "conveyancers," that is, real estate brokers who specialized in screening borrowers and introducing them, for a fee, to lenders.

After 1821 the Commercial Bank of Philadelphia served as the PSFS's

Table 7.1: Assets of the Philadelphia Savings Fund Society, 1820–41 (in $000)

Date (Jan. 1)	U.S. bonds	PA bonds	Philadelphia city bonds	RR and canal bonds	Mortgages	Real estate	Ground rents	Loans	Cash	Total
1820	22.4	0	3.2	0	35.0	0	0	0	5.8	66.4
1826	83.5	0	87.5	0	204.5	36.4	1.2	149.4	2.4	564.9
1831	30.0	246.5	88.6	0	436.2	10.0	10.0	88.5	1.2	911.0
1836	0	338.6	40.8	23.0	893.5	35.1	10.0	147.3	4.7	1,493.0
1841	0	177.3	50.8	71.3	927.7	32.0	32.4	0	29.5	1,321.0

Source: James Willcox, *A History of the Philadelphia Savings Fund Society, 1816–1916* (Philadelphia: J. B. Lippincott, 1916).

custodian bank, receiving its deposits and paying its checks. The savings bank's expenses, therefore, were quite low. Savings banks elsewhere, including Baltimore, followed suit, making similar arrangements with local commercial banks.[10]

While commercial banks aroused the ire of many politicians, savings banks routinely found praise, and not only from Noah. The reason for the differential treatment stems from three facts. First, early savings banks were "friendly" mutual firms (i.e., owned by their depositors), not "greedy" joint-stock corporations. Second, savings banks attracted the savings of a wide variety of the "poorer sorts," which was thought to increase "economy" and decrease "pauperism." Third, aggregate deposits grew quickly, adding significantly to the pool of liquid capital available to fund business investment and home acquisition.

By 1836 Philadelphia teemed with savings banks. In addition to the PSFS, the following institutions invested the savings of the city's poor and middling classes, mostly in loans to the same groups: Broad Street Savings Institution; Central Savings Institution; Divitial Institution of North America & Six Per Cent Savings Bank; Girard Beneficial Association and Savings Institution; Kensington Savings Institution; the Manufacturing & Mechanics Beneficial Savings Institution of Northern Liberties; Mechanics and Tradesmen's Loan Company & Savings Institution; the Northern Liberties, Kensington, and Spring Garden Saving Fund Society; Northern Liberties Savings Institution; Penn Township Saving Institution; Philadelphia City Savings Institution; Philadelphia Loan Company & Savings Institution; Schuylkill Savings Institution of Philadelphia; Southern Savings Institution; and Western Savings Institution.

Despite the competition, in terms of both number of depositors and total deposits, the PSFS's growth, as detailed in table 7.2, was rapid until the

Table 7.2: Liabilities of the Philadelphia Savings Fund Society, 1820–41

Date (Jan. 1)	Deposits (in $000)	Contingency fund in $000)	Total (in $000)	Number of depositors
1820	64.3	2.2	66.5	665
1826	593.6	1.2	564.9	3,353
1831	903.5	7.5	911	6,077
1836	1,446.5	46.6	1,493.1	9,600
1841	1,196.7	124.4	1,321	7,912

Source: James Wilcox, *A History of the Philadelphia Savings Fund Society, 1816–1916* (Philadelphia: J.B. Lippincott, 1916).

Panic of 1837. The contingency fund was simply accrued profits not paid to depositors as dividends. It served the same economic function as capital stock in a joint-stock company, that is, as a buffer against losses. Most profits, of course, were paid out as dividends to depositors. By 1826, for example, the PSFS's contingency fund was only $1,200, but it had by that date paid out over $72,000 to depositors.

Finding the right mix between dividends and contingency was crucial to business, especially as competition stiffened in the late 1820s and early 1830s. If a savings bank retained too much of its profits, its dividends would be low relative to other savings outlets, including other savings banks. On the other hand, if it paid out too much in dividends, potential depositors might fear for the future safety of the bank and switch funds accordingly. Or, worse yet, the savings bank might not have a sufficient buffer to save it during a sharp downturn, like that experienced in the late 1830s.

Some savings banks actually went under as a result of the economic dislocations of the late 1830s and early 1840s. In New Orleans, for instance, that recession forced the New Orleans Savings Bank into liquidation, though as late as February 18, 1836, the trustees exclaimed "that the Savings Bank is in a prosperous and improving condition and accomplishing the philanthropic objects contemplated by the Legislatures in its incorporation." The Philadelphia banks held firm, though, probably because Philadelphia's deeper securities market provided them with a better safety cushion than that available to the New Orleans Savings Bank, which as it grew found itself forced to purchase riskier assets than it would have liked. (It still managed to repay its depositors, with 8 percent interest, by the end of 1855. Safe. Sound. Very illiquid.)[11]

Early U.S. commercial banks were not elitist cliques, as some historians have claimed. But neither did they have much to do with what Howard would have called the "industrious poor." Savings banks, on the other hand, tried to cater to *only* the working poor. Depositors in early U.S. savings banks included "mechanics, tradesmen, laborers, servants, and others living upon wages or labor," like boot cleaners, coachmen, cartmen, chambermaids, nurses, students, waiters, draymen, painters, sash makers, bakers, shoemakers, clerks, barkeepers, printers, ship carpenters, bricklayers, sailors, coach makers, turners, plasterers, joiners, millwrights, storekeepers, porters, farmers, schoolmasters, gardeners, stevedores, upholsters, and other members of the "frugal poor."

⌇◯ But Chestnut Street did not stop there. In 1831 a new institution dedicated to making home mortgages, the Oxford Provident Building Association, appeared in the Frankford section of Philadelphia County. Roughly equivalent to ground rents in terms of economic efficiency, building and loans like the Oxford grew slowly at first. After the legislature outlawed new ground rents in 1854, however, the associations blossomed.[12]

The Oxford arose from the experiences of three English émigrés, calico manufacturer Samuel Pilling, bleacher and dyer Jeremiah Horrocks, and doctor Henry Taylor. The trio drew upon vague recollections of similar associations in Britain, but, quite sensibly, they also consulted Jesse Y. Castor, a local attorney. With Castor's advice, the Oxford issued shares with a par value of $500 each, which cost $5 down and $3 a month thereafter. The Oxford's treasurer collected the down payments and installments, lending out portions to the stockholders who bid the most for them.

Like modern credit unions, building and loans were clubby, almost mutual aid societies. Instead of relying on professional bankers to ration loans and monitor borrowers, the members kept tabs on each other. Only stockholders could borrow, and only up to the par value of the shares they held, up to a maximum of five shares or $2,500. Moreover, borrowers could only use the loans "to build or purchase dwelling houses," so fellow shareholders could easily discern if the funds were being put to proper use. The associations were, in short, cash equivalents of "barn raisings." Instead of the whole community turning out to put up a house, they lent the funds necessary to purchase the requisite building materials and the services of skilled workers.

That made good economic sense and appeared to work. The first home funded by the Oxford, for instance, survived over a century due to the excellent "character of the materials and labor put into it." The Oxford made relatively few loans in its first decade; it was so tiny that it held its meetings in a local tavern. But the association began to attract significant attention.

In 1836 a group in Brooklyn, New York, formed a building and loan modeled after the Oxford. Milestown, Pennsylvania, followed suit in 1838. By the mid-1840s, several additional building and loan associations cropped up in nearby Germantown, Kensington, and even Frankford itself, suggesting that the Oxford was not large enough to meet burgeoning demand. That made sense given the local, clubby nature of the associations.

But small, local, and clubby did not necessarily mean inefficient or ineffective. In fact, by the Civil War, the building and loan industry had spread throughout most of the Mid-Atlantic and New England states. By the end of the century, building and loans had spread across the nation, from sea to shining sea. Building and loans evolved little over the course of the nineteenth century. As late as the Great Depression, they retained many of the same features as the Oxford. In fact, readers may recall that in *It's a Wonderful Life,* the holiday film classic, protagonist George Bailey runs the local building and loan association. In a moving scene masterfully portrayed by actor Jimmy Stewart, Bailey fends off a Depression-era bank run with the cash from his honeymoon fund and a stirring speech that succinctly captures the essence of the building and loan. Here is a transcript of the beginning of the scene:

(INTERIOR OUTER OFFICE—BUILDING AND LOAN—DAY. MEDIUM CLOSE SHOT— *More people have crowded around the counter. Their muttering stops and they stand silent and grim. There is panic in their faces.*)

GEORGE. Now, just remember that this thing isn't as black as it appears.

(*As George speaks, sirens are heard passing in the street below. The crowd turns to the windows, then back to George.*)

GEORGE. I have some news for you, folks. I've just talked to old man Potter, and he's guaranteed cash payments at the bank. The bank's going to reopen next week.

ED. But, George, I got my money here.

CHARLIE. Did he guarantee this place?

GEORGE. Well, no, Charlie. I didn't even ask him. We don't need Potter over here.

(*Mary and Ernie have come into the room during this scene. Mary stands watching silently.*)

CHARLIE. I'll take mine now.

GEORGE. No, but you . . . you . . . you're thinking of this place all wrong. As if I had the money back in a safe. The money's not here. Your money's in Joe's house . . . (*to one of the men*) right next to yours. And in the Kennedy house, and Mrs. Macklin's house, and a hundred others. Why, you're lending them the money to build, and then, they're going to pay it back to you as best they can. Now what are you going to do? Foreclose on them?

Unfortunately, most Depression-era building and loan associations did not have Jimmy Stewart and Donna Reed on their side. Many went under; survivors morphed into savings and loan associations. They, too, served their communities well—until the 1980s, that is. But that is another story.[13]

✑ All those homes needed water, preferably of the running, indoor kind. Stagnant pools and wells, combined with Philadelphia's relatively high population density, led to unhealthy conditions, including several devastating yellow fever epidemics in the 1790s. Philadelphia city government responded by building a municipal water system. But just as houses didn't grow on trees, city water systems didn't create themselves. To build the system, the city would have to tax and, ultimately, to borrow.

Philadelphia's first attempt to sell municipal bonds did not go well. In 1799 it offered fifteen hundred bonds of $100 each with a 6 percent coupon, payable semi-annually, plus a free water hookup, a $5 annual value. The last perk pointed to the backing of the bond issue, rents from the city's municipal water system. The city had a tough go of it, however, because the market was too smart to take the bait. Most potential investors realized that the city remained uncommitted to collecting the water rents due it. In fact, lackadaisical tax collection was what led it to test the capital markets in the first place. Not until it shored up its collection system in 1807 was the city able to reliably raise large sums in the capital market. The city serviced the debt well, allowing it in the early 1820s to refinance $535,000 worth of its outstanding bonds at 5 percent.[14]

With the help of $600,000 of investor money, some good engineers, and the Schuylkill River, Philadelphia's municipal water system became the envy of America—indeed, the world. In addition to visiting the two U.S. bank buildings, the U.S. Mint, and Girard College, tourists also invariably took in the waterworks. The steam engines that pumped the water out of the river into the piping system were particular favorites, though visitors also commented on the handsome buildings housing the pumps. "No stranger should visit Philadelphia without seeing the water-works," one British traveler confidently told his readers in 1833. Meanwhile, Manhattan's water system was run by a private corporation, the Manhattan Company, that used most of its capital to carry on banking activities throughout the Empire State. The Manhattan Company's wooden pipes and mule-driven pumps were a far cry shy of Philadelphia's water system.[15]

Chestnut Street roundly defeated Wall Street—this time. But in the next round, the struggle to control the vast trades of the Atlantic Ocean and the trans-Appalachian West, the outcome would be quite different. And in an era when control of trade routes meant control of trade deposits, and control of trade deposits attracted talented young financiers, Manhattan began to challenge Philadelphia for financial supremacy. The political decision not to recharter the Bank of the United States would tip the balance in favor of Wall Street.

8

TRANSPORTATION ELATION

In 1818 British traveler Henry Fearon called Baltimore "a commercial city of great importance." "Though not at present of the first rank," he added, the city was "rising with a rapidity almost unparalleled." Indeed, its population nearly doubled between 1810 and 1820. Fearon was not the only foreigner to gush over the rapidity of its growth. British traveler Basil Hall noted in 1829 that he heard "Mr. Carroll say that Baltimore, which now contains seventy thousand inhabitants, was a village of only seven houses, within his memory!" New York, too, was growing like gangbusters. Philly also swelled but not as quickly. And its trade was slipping fast. "On approaching Philadelphia," James Flint noted in 1818, "I felt disappointed in seeing the shipping so very inferior to that at New York." Geography was the clear culprit. Philadelphians had long understood that their city's natural economic hinterland, basically the Delaware River's drainage basin, was rather small. And it wasn't about to get any bigger.[1]

Through the usual combination of fate, luck, and intrigue that makes history so interesting, the Commonwealth of Pennsylvania was composed of not one but four distinct economic zones. In the eastern part of the state, as well as the eastern portions of Delaware and Maryland, all rivers led to the Delaware and hence to Philadelphia. Capturing the trade of that region was relatively easy because all that businesses needed to bring goods to market were small boats, even mere rafts, that, if necessary, could be sold as firewood upon arrival in Philadelphia. The resources of Pennsylvania's vast center, however, drained into the Susquehanna River and hence the Chesapeake Bay and Baltimore. Moreover, thanks to the Appalachian Mountains and the Ohio River, the western part of the state was economically closer to New Orleans than the Quaker City. Finally, the state's northwestern corner accessed the vast inland sea known as the Great Lakes and hence was linked economically more to Chicago and Montreal than to the City of Brotherly Love. Such were the cards that nature dealt Philadelphia.[2]

As early as 1771, Philadelphians realized that "Baltimore town in Maryland" had begun to carry off "almost the whole trade of Frederick, York, Bedford, and Cumberland," Pennsylvania's most important frontier counties. In 1788 French traveler Jean-Pierre Brissot de Warville also noted that Baltimore had drawn off "a great deal of the trade of Philadelphia." It simply made economic sense: Baltimore was closer to those counties in terms of time, distance, and overall cost of transport. But Philadelphians were not about to allow mere natural obstacles to impede the progress of their city or to limit the size of their purses. Artificial rivers could be cut, roads laid, mountains leveled or tunneled through, beasts and machines made to serve their human masters. If the Ohio River basin could be linked to the Susquehanna watershed, and the Susquehanna to the Delaware basin, Philadelphia could control the trade of almost the entire state—and perhaps beyond into central New York. And if it could make it to Lake Erie, boosters claimed, Philadelphia could take commercial control of the continent's rich center. Even more sanguine observers noted that only seventy-five miles of overland portage separated the Quaker City from the Pacific Ocean and the riches of the Orient.[3]

Philadelphia investors were therefore quick to invest in "internal improvement" concerns, companies incorporated to build turnpikes, canals, and, later, railroads. Alas, they could not prevent the inevitable—the trade of the continent flowed to New York via the Grand Canal (Erie Canal), and the trade of their own state flowed to Baltimore and New Orleans via mighty rivers. One of the three legs upholding Chestnut Street's financial ascendancy, deposits linked to its mercantile trade, atrophied and eventually snapped. But investors' efforts were not entirely in vain as the improvements they funded laid the basic groundwork for Philadelphia's antebellum industrial revolution, a topic we will return to in chapter 11.

↶ In 1792 the aptly named Philadelphia and Lancaster Turnpike became the first turnpike company chartered in the United States. Privately owned toll roads, turnpikes became extremely important components of southeastern Pennsylvania's economy in the first few decades of the nation's existence. Corporations built and ran turnpikes because roads typically required a large initial investment to clear the right of way (or to improve an existing thoroughfare) and frequent maintenance to keep the road passable. Ruts caused by wagon wheels ripped up formerly smooth road surfaces in the wet season unless roads were carefully graded, crowned, and covered with crushed gravel. The turnpike companies kept their roads in just enough repair to keep people traveling them—and paying tolls. That was far superior to local government roads, which were repaired when local farmers felt like repairing them. In fact, most tolls were collected in the wet season (November through April), when government roads were often impassable.[4]

Indeed, some turnpike companies took over and improved poorly maintained government roads. The Germantown and Perkiomen Pike, for instance, fixed up and then maintained a road initially built and maintained by local governments. The company found the thoroughfare in "wretched condition," a dangerous hindrance to travel. Some 240 investors, including twenty women, purchased shares in the company. Their monies transformed the road, like all of Pennsylvania's early turnpikes, into a stone-paved thoroughfare capable of handling heavy wagons, even during the wet season. Due to the improvements, the volume of traffic over the route increased rapidly; stores, taverns, and inns soon lined both sides.

Governments also found it difficult to erect and maintain bridges, even small ones. So again the market took over. Toll bridges owned and operated by private individuals became common in the 1780s. Larger bridges, owned and operated by joint-stock companies, appeared in the 1790s. Almost all were made of stone. Although they were more expensive to build than wooden structures, stone arches were much cheaper to maintain and hence were more economically efficient—and profitable. Some public-spirited people may have invested in bridges, turnpikes, and other internal improvements out of a sense of community duty. But most investors were rational calculators of self-interest whose concerns were, as an anonymous author put it in 1811, "confined to the mere rate per cent. or dividend which an investment will yield at the time it is made." Although some turnpikes and bridges proved poor investments, many provided steady dividends for dozens of years. The Cheltenham and Willow Grove Turnpike, for example, returned on average over 5 percent per year for decades. Corporate toll bridges regularly paid 6 percent dividends.[5]

Regardless of the motivations of their investors, early turnpikes and bridges tied Pennsylvania together politically, socially, and to some extent economically. Joshua Gilpin's 1809 travel journal highlights their importance:

Septr. 14th, We left Philadelphia on a tour to the Western parts of Pennsylvania: after crossing the Schuylkill permanent Bridge, we took the
Lancaster turnpike and soon rose by an easy ascent to the height of the
hills which skirt the western bank of the Schuylkill. . . . [T]his Turnpike
is very rough, the carriage upon it from the interior being very great. . . .
At the 60 mile stone, & 2 M. from Lancaster we cross the Conestogo
river, which is about 100 yards wide, over a handsome bridge of 7 stone
arches, the arches lined with marble—this bridge was built by Jacob Wit-
mer . . . at his own expense, under the privilege of a perpetual toll.

Like Gilpin, many thousands of individuals used the state's toll roads and
bridges to travel throughout the commonwealth for business, pleasure,
and / or politics. Numerous private taverns and inns provided thirsty, hungry, and weary travels with succor. Stagecoach lines varied in quality but
also in price, and, of course, travelers could use their own horses and car-
riages if they wished. No mode of travel was fast by today's standards, but
that did not deter early Americans from visiting distant relatives, business
partners, or coreligionists.[6]

The early turnpikes did less to link Pennsylvania's three major regions
economically, however. By 1800 over a thousand large Conestoga wagons,
each capable of carrying over ten thousand pounds of goods if drawn by six
sturdy horses, shuffled between Philadelphia and the inland towns over the
state's increasingly dense network of "Roman-quality" roads. By the 1820s
Pennsylvania boasted over two thousand miles of quality turnpike mileage
and hundreds of solid stone bridges. Even the mighty Susquehanna and
Delaware rivers had been bridged, the former in five places and the latter at
three. (According to one admittedly biased contemporary, Pennsylvania
boasted the nation's largest, strongest, and most beautiful bridges.)

But turnpikes decreased the cost of transportation by only 50 percent,
that is, from outrageously expensive to darn costly. Even on a good paved
road, overland transportation cost around $.20 per ton mile, versus about
$.05 via rail, $.02 via canal, and less than a penny per ton mile for descend-
ing river transport. Only high-value, low-volume items—like people, manufactured goods such as Reading's famous hats, and butter—could bear
the cost of wagon transport and tolls. It simply did not pay to ship most
goods overland, at least not very far. Most iron produced more than a score
or so miles of Philadelphia, for example, either shipped by water (to
Philadelphia or Baltimore) or by wagon to local market towns like Lancaster, Reading, and York. Only very high prices in Philadelphia, or very

low prices in the local markets, could induce iron producers to ship iron overland to the Quaker City. Similarly, relative prices had to be sky high to draw stone, plaster, lime, bricks, stones, hay, or salt to Philadelphia by wagon. The turnpikes were important, but they were no panacea, and everybody knew it.

✑ Philadelphia also got an early jump on the railroad craze that would soon sweep the nation, especially that part of it north of the Rappahannock. The movement began and ended in depression. The Panic of 1819 prostrated the nation's economy, and the Quaker City was especially hard hit. By September unemployment and other forms of suffering were acute enough that a minor incident, the inability of a stunt parachutist to inflate the balloon that was supposed to take him aloft, touched off a riot. The mob, upset at paying an *entire* dollar for nothing more than a few drinks, grew restless. When a security guard, in full view of the crowd, clubbed a young boy off a fence, the powder keg erupted. When it was all over, Vauxhall Gardens "were all reduced to ruins" and its pavilion to embers. As the recession deepened, social tensions grew and the number of paupers, mendicants, beggars, and thieves swelled. Fearful of the future, people cut back. Everyone from barbers to grocers to lawyers to merchants felt the pinch. Trade so diminished that Peter Grotjan, editor of the *Philadelphia Public Sale Report,* suspended his commentaries on price movements because there was simply nothing to report.[7]

By 1821 Philadelphians were so desperate to stimulate trade that they quickly jumped on John Stevens's plan to connect Harrisburg and Pittsburgh by rail. The state legislature thought it best if the new invention connected Philadelphia to Columbia, on the Susquehanna River, first. In 1823 the company and legislature agreed to the new plan. By then, however, Philadelphia's merchants had lost interest and Stevens was nearing retirement age. The company could not even raise enough money to build a mile of test track. It quickly expired. Had the railroad succeeded at such an early date, it may have muted the effect of the Grand Canal and placed Pennsylvania well ahead of the Empire State technologically.[8]

But it was not to be. Not until 1831 was the next east–west Pennsylvania railroad company, a short road between Carlisle and Harrisburg, incorporated, and this one, too, lapsed due to lack of investor interest. The Philadelphia, Germantown, and Norristown line fared better. According to the *Philadelphia Post* of March 26, 1831, "rail road fever" was all the "rage" in the city. The subscription books for the company's IPO were supposed to open at 9 a.m., but before daylight a crowd besieged the City Hotel. According to the newspaper report, "Hundreds struggled for hours to get near the door." The doorkeepers were no dummies—they provided admittance to the highest bidders. Similar scenes also occurred in Germantown and Norristown, where subscription books were also opened. But anyone conversant with the geography of southeastern Pennsylvania will immediately realize that a line from Philadelphia to Norristown, profitable though it may have been, was not a major undertaking. In fact, it survives as the R6 line of Philadelphia's regional commuter rail system. Nor was it a big technical breakthrough—for the first few years, horses served as the "engine," as they did on the West Chester line (now the R5 line), and other early short roads.

Pennsylvania eventually did get a few long roads designed for steam engines under construction, just in time for them to get waylaid by the recession of 1837–43.[9] The rest of the 1840s brought better times and the 1850s better still. By 1850 Pennsylvania boasted 981 miles of completed railroad track. Just nine years later, 2,971 miles of completed track crisscrossed the Keystone State, making it second only to Ohio in total track mileage.

Many of those miles, however, fed Baltimore or Pittsburgh (and hence New Orleans), not Philadelphia. Moreover, Pennsylvania's early railroads were not terribly efficient. Building, maintaining, and operating a railroad was far from easy, requiring skills that few early railroad managers possessed. The result at first was high costs and, unsurprisingly, relatively low profitability. That forced railroad managers to sell bonds or preferred stock, an equity-bond hybrid security. But Pennsylvania investors wanted only so many railroad securities, inducing some companies to try to sell bonds to Boston and New York investors. Some companies, including the Philadelphia & Reading Railroad, also sold bonds denominated in pound sterling in the London capital market.

Table 8.1 shows just how important debt had become to Pennsylvania railroads by the eve of the Civil War. The high degree of leverage (borrowing) caused governance problems. "The great difficulty," wrote industry analyst F. H. Stow in 1859, "appears to be how and in what manner [management's] affairs are susceptible of reconstruction, so as to meet the conflicting interests and views of the several kinds of creditors." Basically, bondholders just wanted the interest due them to be paid punctually, so they urged managers to undertake safe and steady investments. Stockholders, on the other hand, sought bigger dividends and hence desired to undertake riskier projects. Managers desired to grow, whether the growth was profitable or not, in order to capture bigger salaries. Stow thought the answer was to convert bonds into common shares. "The affairs of a company," he explained, "are then subject to the control of but one interest."

Table 8.1: Capitalization and Debt of Pennsylvania Railroads, 1859

Name of Railroad	Capitalization ($)	Total Debt ($)
Pittsburgh, Fort Wayne, and Chicago	5,259,040	8,142,722
Cumberland Valley	472,000	803,212
North Pennsylvania	3,086,710	3,106,106
Philadelphia and Reading	11,737,041	13,151,843
Pennsylvania	13,240,225	16,571,054
Sunbury and Erie	3,903,843	836,591
Philadelphia, Wilmington, and Baltimore	5,600,000	2,749,341
Lehigh Valley	1,794,500	1,500,000
Cleveland and Pittsburgh	3,942,369	5,572,147
Cleveland and Mahoning	580,000	1,363,500
Harrisburg and Lancaster	1,056,450	459,872
Alleghany Valley	1,661,050	328,567
Philadelphia and Trenton	1,000,000	500,000
Pittsburgh and Connellsville	3,207,850	—
Erie and Northeast	600,000	100,000
Hempfield	—	—
Williamsport and Elmira	1,500,000	2,429,034
Pittsburgh and Steubenville	1,202,784	800,000
Catawissa, Williamsport, and Erie Railroad	1,700,000	2,373,152
Chartiers Valley Railroad	—	—
Delaware and Hudson Canal Company and Railroad	7,500,000	1,222,717
Philadelphia, Germantown and Norristown	1,208,500	479,520
Lackawanna and Bloomsburg	—	—
Indianapolis, Pittsburgh and Cleveland	835,971	1,045,919

Source: F. H. Stow, *The Capitalist's Guide and Railway Annual for 1859* (New York: Samuel Callahan, 1859).

According to Stow, in 1859 six Pennsylvania railroads were overleveraged and badly in need of reorganization and debt conversion. He blamed the stockholders themselves for the sorry state of affairs at those roads. "The stockholders, after an election," he complained, "do not meet often enough to inform themselves of the acts of their directors." "Frequent stockholders' meetings are necessary in order to secure an interchange of opinions and views respecting past and future management," he argued, adding that "if unsuccessful the opportunity will then be afforded to hold the officers to a strict accountability." The sheer size of the railroads, however, made stockholder monitoring difficult. By 1859 consolidation had produced several long interstate lines, like the Pittsburgh, Fort Wayne, and Chicago Railroad, which stretched some 470 miles. Not until after the Civil War would railroad industry management fully utilize the potential of the new technology.

For some classes of goods, Pennsylvania's railroads were more economically efficient than New York's Grand Canal. But for other goods, nonperishables with high bulk to value, the canal remained superior. Moreover, New York also built railroads with western links, including the Erie and the New York Central. Philadelphia's railroad ventures were not fruitless endeavors, but they did not supersede the Grand Canal or return the Quaker City to the top of the trade rankings.[10]

✒ Ironically as it turned out, Pennsylvania had also been an early entrant into the canal game. In 1791 its legislature incorporated two canal companies, one charged with connecting the Schuylkill and Susquehanna rivers, the other with linking the Delaware to the upper Schuylkill. Both companies met with unanticipated engineering difficulties. Equally troubling, during the heady 1790s most investors looked to "the allurements of external commerce" rather than "the moderate and progressive, though certain and permanent advantages of internal commerce." So when the canals ran short of cash, which they quickly did, they bogged down.

Though difficult to believe, the early canal companies couldn't even sell most of their lottery tickets! Philadelphians *loved* their lotteries, but their eagerness to gamble turned out to be a mixed blessing for the canal companies. As a rule, Quakers opposed gambling, but a clever bit of categorical legerdemain exempted lotteries from the long list of activities they sought to prohibit. In short, if a lottery's profits funded a good public purpose, Friends let it slide as a sort of voluntary tax or charitable contribution. By the 1750s lotteries were frequent affairs in Pennsylvania, used mostly to fund churches and schools, but also public works like lighthouses, forts, and street-paving projects. (Up to 1833, church lotteries alone supplied some half a million tickets and $3 million in prize money to the market.)[11]

As the Revolution approached, Philadelphians also embraced lotteries designed to encourage the domestic manufacture of critical war materials like steel and textiles. After the Revolution, Quakers no longer controlled the state government, so the floodgates opened further. Between 1796 and 1808, the state legislature gave the go-ahead to seventy-eight different lotteries. Moreover, some Pennsylvanians were audacious enough to run lotteries without obtaining prior legislative sanction. Certain "foreign" lotteries were also authorized to sell tickets in Philadelphia, and many others simply sold their tickets without any explicit approval to do so. By 1833, when the state legislature banned all lottery activity in the commonwealth, *several hundred* out-of-state lotteries had entered the Philly market. According to one observer, the "flaring and intrusive signs" of Philadelphia's lottery brokers met "the eye at every turn." Sounds like hyperbole, but other sources claim that the city was home to some four hundred lottery offices by the early 1830s.

Clearly, rampant competition caused the early canal lottery tickets to get lost in the shuffle. The company sold only $60,000 of the $400,000 allowed by law. It's one thing when your bonds don't satisfy investors, quite another when your lottery tickets can't even satisfy gambling junkies! One thing seems certain: Philadelphians simply did not care if the artificial waterways were completed or not. But interest in the unfinished ditches revived briefly during Jefferson's trade war with Britain in the latter half of the 1800s. In 1811 the two original canal companies merged under the title of the Union Canal Company of Pennsylvania. The officers of the new company— Philadelphia bigwigs like Charles Paleske, George Simpson, and Joseph Watson—argued that "the desired communication between the [Great] lakes and the atlantic [*sic*] can be effected in Pennsylvania with less delay than any other route, and at less expense." Philadelphia merchant and former BUS director Samuel Breck made much the same claim in 1818 when he argued in favor of "the superior situation of Philadelphia, geographically considered, for the attraction of the great and increasing trade of the countries bordering on the Susquehanna, the Lakes, and the Western rivers." They were all quite wrong.

The charter of the Union Canal Company allowed the company to "raise by way of loan from any individuals, bodies politic or corporate, on such terms and conditions as they may think fit, such sums of money as they may, from time to time, find expedient for the completion of the objects aforesaid, upon the credit of the capital stock and incorporation; including the nett [*sic*] proceeds and avails of the lotteries hereby authorised and the tolls and profits of the same; and for the fulfillment of the terms and conditions of any such loan to mortgage any part, of the whole, of their property, tolls, profits, or estates." In other words, the Union Canal could sell bonds and lottery tickets. Early on it had difficulty disposing of the former. In 1811, for example, it tried to sell $100,000 of its bonds but found few buyers because of the "unprecedented pecuniary embarrassments" that prevailed due to the federal government's trade war against Britain. The company also had a load of existing debt and no clear way to service it, save its lotteries. Given the lackadaisical demand for its predecessors' tickets, it is little wonder that investors put little faith in them. But this time, things were different, largely because the company decided to circumvent the glutted Philadelphia market and sell its tickets throughout the country via agents. Between 1811 and 1833, the Union Canal awarded prizes in excess of $33 million. Unfortunately for the company's stockholders, and ultimately Chestnut Street's financiers, recurrent accounting "irregularities"—many of its agents apparently had sticky fingers—meant that the company netted only 5 to 10 percent on the schemes instead of the full 15 percent designed.

The will to complete the much-needed water connections remained weak until the success of New York's Grand Canal made completion imperative. "Whenever we hear of the New York canal," a Pennsylvanian noted in 1818, "a kind of tremor seizes our frames." Once Philadelphia's dire predicament became clear, Chestnut Street led the way, helping Pennsylvania's canal companies to sell their stocks and bonds. By the 1820s it also helped canal companies to devise and market new hybrid securities. In 1821, for instance, the Lehigh Coal and Navigation Company issued preferred shares, half-bond, half-equity securities that paid fixed dividends before common stockholders received a cent. In 1823 the Schuylkill Navigation Company sold Stephen Girard $230,850 of convertible securities, essentially bonds that Girard could convert into common shares should he see fit. The bonds were backed by a first mortgage on the company's real estate, so Girard was covered whether the company went bankrupt, limped along just enough to make its bond payments, or if its business and stock soared.[12]

Despite Chestnut Street's innovative financing, Pennsylvania could not catch New York's Grand Canal. Its failure was not due to lack of effort on the part of the state government, which often borrowed to help fund "public improvements," including turnpikes, canals, and railroads. "The progressive spirit and well known resources of Pennsylvania," noted one observer, "rendered it for her a matter of little difficulty to borrow all needed funds upon favorable terms." Table 8.2 lists the terms and purposes of the state's many bond issues. The state also purchased over $354,000 of turnpike shares and some $6,000 of bridge shares, not to mention direct investment of over $100,000 in the maintenance of common roads, navigable creeks and rivers, and piers and wharves.[13]

All that money served Pennsylvania well. But the network of improvements did not establish inexpensive, convenient connections between the state's three major watersheds and Lake Erie. Philly got its flour, wood,

Table 8.2: Pennsylvania Bond Issues, 1821–53

Loan date	Coupon (%)	Purpose	Reimbursable	Outstanding on December 1, 1853 ($)
2/4/21	6	Turnpikes, bridges	1841	630
4/1/26	5	Public improvements	1846	7,074
4/9/27	5	Public improvements	1850	26,827
3/24/28	5	Public improvements	1853	1,786,331
12/18/28	5	Public improvements	1854	706,851
4/22/29	5	Public improvements	1854	1,920,898
12/7/29	5	Public improvements	Bank charter loan	50,000
3/13/30	5	Public improvements	1858	3,843,256
3/21/31	5	Public improvements	1856	2,309,236
3/28/31	5	Eastern Penitentiary	1861	79,900
3/30/31	5	Public improvements	1856	279,103
3/30/32	5	Public improvements	1860	2,158,830
4/5/32	5	Public improvements	1860	294,172
2/16/33	5	Public improvements	1858	2,458,014
3/1/33	4.5	Union Canal Co.	1863	188,200
3/27/33	5	Public improvements	1858	500,732
4/5/34	5	Public improvements	1862	2,071,645
4/13/35	5	Public improvements	1865	920,428
1/26/39	5	Public improvements	1859	1,093,598
2/9/39	5	Public improvements	1864	1,186,867
3/16/39	5	Franklin R.R. Co.	1864	89,852
3/27/39	5	To pay other loans	1868	465,168
6/7/39	5	Pennsylvania and Ohio Canal Co.	1859	47,798
6/27/39	5	To pay other loans	1864	1,098,769
7/19/39	5	Public improvements	1868	2,017,270
1/23/40	5	To pay interest and temporary loan	1865	753,912
4/3/40	5	Interest and public improvements	1864	733,957
6/11/40	5	Interest and public improvement	1870	1,838,878
1/16/41	6	To pay interest	1846	3,128
3/4/41	6	Pennsylvania Insane Asylum	1847	500
5/4/41	0	Treasury purposes and public improvements	1846	528,351
5/5/41	5	To pay interest	Bank charter loan	390,009
5/6/41	6	To pay loan of 1821	1841	3,959

continued

Table 8.2 (*Continued*)

Loan date	Coupon (%)	Purpose	Reimbursable	Outstanding on December 1, 1853 ($)
7/27/42	6	For interest due August 1842	1843	6,103
3/7/43	6	For interest due February and August 1843	1846	9,275
4/29/44	5	Funding of interest certificates	1849	3,221
5/31/44	5	For interest due February and August 1844	1846	11,788
4/16/45	5	Interest certificates funded	1855	4,121,953
1/22/47	5	Charter loan renewed	Bank charter loan	24,000
4/11/48	6	Relief notes funded	1853	149,838
4/10/49	6	To avoid Schuylkill incline plane	1879	400,000
4/2/52	4.5–5	For completion of North Branch extension	1882	850,000
5/4/52	4–5	For redemption of PA 6s, interest certificates	1877	5,000,000
4/19/53	5	For redemption of State stocks due	1878	125,000
Total				40,555,315

Sources: *Public Works of Pennsylvania: Cost, Revenue and Expenditure Up to November 30, 1853* (Harrisburg, PA: A. Boyd Hamilton, 1853); "A Brief Review of the Financial History of Pennsylvania," in *Report of the Auditor General on the Finances of the Commonwealth of Pennsylvania* (Harrisburg: Lane S. Hart, 1881), 266–316.

coal, marble, and iron on the cheap, but much of the trade of the central and western parts of the state ended up with merchants in Baltimore and New Orleans. And via its magnificent Grand Canal, Manhattan economically drained the entire Great Lakes basin. The liquid wealth of the nation therefore poured into the financial institutions of Wall Street, not Chestnut Street. Transportation proved to be the beginning of the end for the Quaker City's financial district, and many an observer knew it. As table 8.3 suggests, the state made a furious attempt to catch up, especially in the early 1830s. By the Civil War, the state of Pennsylvania had invested $41.6 million ($14.40 per capita) in transportation improvements, most of it in canals.

Alas, it was too little, too late. Why did both Pennsylvania's private and public transportation efforts fall short? Undoubtedly, many factors were at play, but the main one, in my estimation, was a lack of vision. Philadelphia's merchants, especially the Quaker ones, enjoyed a reputation for business

Table 8.3: Pennsylvania Internal Improvement Projects, 1830–34

Improvement	Year Begun	Total Cost ($)	Total Revenue ($)	Total Expenditure ($)
Columbia and Philadelphia Railway	1833	5,277,278	9,020,278	5,860,291
Eastern Division of Canal	1830	1,737,285	2,932,571	862,938
Juniata Division of Canal	1830	3,575,966	1,496,430	1,950,688
Allegheny Portage Railway	1834	2,708,672	3,520,408	4,010,789
Western Division of Canal	1830	3,173,432	2,812,312	1,340,535
Delaware Division of Canal	1830	1,454,937	2,746,650	1,223,301
Susquehanna Division of Canal	1830	897,161	475,255	605,990
North Branch Division of Canal	1830	1,598,379	1,374,259	799,775
West Branch Division of Canal	1830	1,832,583	573,388	815,319
French Creek Division of Canal	1831	817,780	5,820	143,912
Beaver Division of Canal	1834	519,365	38,312	210,360
Unfinished improvements	—	8,695,045		
Total		32,287,883	24,995,683	17,823,898

Sources: *Public Works of Pennsylvania: Cost, Revenue and Expenditure Up to November 30, 1853* (Harrisburg, PA: A. Boyd Hamilton, 1853); "A Brief Review of the Financial History of Pennsylvania," in *Report of the Auditor General on the Finances of the Commonwealth of Pennsylvania* (Harrisburg, PA: Lane S. Hart, 1881), 266.

conservatism. According to one traveler, John Melish, Philadelphians were "industrious and sober, and, though sufficiently commercial, they do not conduct their business in the same *dashing* style which is done by some commercial cities; but confine themselves within bounds, and secure what they gain." Their conservative ways certainly did not prevent them from creating innovative new financial institutions. But it likely prevented them from launching a bold plan on the scale of New York's Grand Canal. Their efforts, though strenuous, remained piecemeal. And the pieces weren't good enough, especially given that another of Philadelphia's traditional assets, its financiers, were also slipping away.[14]

9

PHILADELPHIA'S FINEST

Philadelphia did not need a modern police force until after the Civil War, so the title of this chapter does not refer to its cops. Rather, the title refers to its financiers. Fine as they were, they were only mortal. With each passing year, a little bit more of Chestnut Street's tremendous pool of human capital drained away. In the first decades of the nineteenth century, Robert Morris, Thomas Willing, and dozens of other financiers whose careers spanned the late colonial, Revolutionary, confederation, and early national periods all succumbed to the inevitable. An epoch ended when the youngest of that august generation, naturalized American Stephen Girard, died the day after Christmas, 1831. (Albert Gallatin lived until 1849, but he had long since left Pennsylvania for Pennsylvania Avenue and then Wall Street. Moreover, he never really had been part of the Chestnut Street crowd.) Though Chestnut Street still possessed many fine young financiers, the true innovators—the men whose financial genius had been forged in the crucible of empire, war, and state building—were gone forever.

The financial exploits of Morris, Willing, Girard, and merchant-financier William Bingham have been recounted elsewhere. The lives and careers of Philadelphia's second tier of financiers usually have not. Men like securities dealer Clement Biddle, broker Andrew Summers, bank cashier George Simpson, and bank director Samuel Breck are virtually unknown, even to historians of the period. Their stories are so long, and so interesting. They deserve a book of their own. But to give readers a feel for the timbre of such men, the life and career of one of them, Michael Hillegas, will be summarized. A music retailer, ironmonger, merchant, land speculator, and politician, Hillegas also found time to serve as the first treasurer of the United States.[1]

Hillegas was not Philadelphia's most important financial innovator by any stretch of the imagination. In fact, he was just one of many important Philly financiers. Thanks to its relative freedom from religious persecution, government regulation, and oppression, the Quaker City brimmed with financial talent. As the decades rolled by the old stalwarts died, one by one. Sometimes a younger man or a newcomer filled the void. Increasingly, however, the passing of a financier such as Hillegas marked a diminution of Philadelphia's human capital base and a step closer to the ascendance of Wall Street.

Michael Hillegas Sr. was born in Alsace. Alternatively described as German or French, the "Hilde-gras" family was actually both, but Hillegas's immediate ancestors were culturally German. A Protestant, Hillegas fled Alsace for the Palatinate because of religious persecution, then left Europe for America before 1724. Eager to put religious bigotry and poverty behind him, he set up shop in Philadelphia and became a leading trader and citizen, amassing considerable real property in the city and Northern Liberties. Deeds and mortgages indicated he was a potter, innkeeper, and storekeeper. Hillegas Sr. died in 1750 survived only by his son and namesake, his wife, and two daughters. Though possessed of considerable property, he had not bothered to write a will. Had more than one son survived infancy, that might have caused problems.[2]

Michael Hillegas, the financier, was only twenty-one years old at his father's death, but he was well equipped to assume the family business. In July 1750 the Philadelphia County Orphans' Court assigned Hillegas half of his father's estate and gave one-quarter to each of his sisters. (Hillegas's mom agreed to receive a £100 annuity and use of the family home for life.) The healthy inheritance greatly aided Hillegas's future prosperity in business and land speculation.

Hillegas soon fashioned himself into a merchant by becoming a part owner of several ships. He also purchased a wharf near the public landings in the Northern Liberties. The wharf generated a healthy income stream throughout Hillegas's career. At his store near Front and Second streets, Hillegas sold copper stills, sundry types of cast-iron stoves, and musical instruments. A lover of the music of George Frideric Handel, Hillegas was something of a musician himself, specializing in the flute and the violin. The merchant mixed his love of music and his religious convictions with his business, selling instructional pamphlets and chamber organs "suitable for a gentleman in his house, or a country church." Later he added a huge array of musical instruments and accessories to his inventory.

As his profits accrued over the years, Hillegas also added to his impressive hardware and stove inventory. By 1769 he served as the Philadelphia sales agent of Henry Stiegel, ironmaster of Elizabeth Furnace. Stiegel probably supplied Hillegas with some of his ironwares, and Hillegas gladly took custom orders in Philadelphia and forwarded them to the Lancaster furnace "with dispatch." The connection interested Hillegas in iron manufacture, a venture he embarked upon as the Revolution erupted. Hillegas also sold paper, linseed oil, shingles, some dry goods, and spices. His expertise in fine paper proved instrumental in his treasury career.

An extremely tough dealer and a good retail salesperson, Hillegas in 1760 chastised Stiegel for offering £18 for a violin, case, and bow. Hillegas reminded the ironmaster that the price was £19, a "really excessively Cheap" price given that the violin was Italian, and as "Loud" and "Bold" as he had ever heard. Hillegas offered a cheap, though "Sweet" domestic model to Stiegel if he still balked at the price of the import. Stiegel bought the Italian instrument at full price. Hillegas acted tough on the purchasing end of his business too, informing London merchant John Johnson that if he did not give him low prices on musical instruments, he would lose the Philadelphian's "custom," the customary way of saying "business" at that time.

During the Revolutionary War, Hillegas invested in at least one successful "Adventure to France" and repeatedly asked to be included to the tune of £400 or £500 in other ventures. Hillegas also continued to sell his musical wares when he could, a trade he seems to have practiced until his death, but it appears he concentrated his wartime business concerns in manufacturing and land speculation. Undoubtedly influenced by his ironware trade and his association with Stiegel, Hillegas joined the iron manufacturing business in early 1774.

Established on a small branch of Pequea Creek, a tributary of the Susquehanna River in Lancaster County, around 1755, the Martic Forge and Furnace suffered a shaky existence. Servants and slaves, the company's main source of labor, too often absconded for the concern to be profitable. The owners put the manufactory, its buildings, and its lands up for auction in 1764. Unable to unload the entire concern, the owners split it into shares for easier sale but again failed to attract purchasers. The sheriff finally interceded in 1768. He slowly sold it off by shares in 1769 and 1770. Hillegas purchased a one-eighth share in the forge in 1774 for £625. He took advantage of the continued difficulty of the forge and the financial problems of the war to make a further purchase, a quarter share for £375, in 1777.

Unlike very wealthy merchants like Thomas Willing, however, Hillegas did not possess sufficient capital to exploit every opportunity the war offered. In 1780, for example, in the midst of extensive land speculations in Bedford County, Hillegas turned down an offer to buy a one-sixteenth interest in the Hibernia Furnace, complaining that he was "a little distressed for Money" and seeking to divest. His ownership of the Martic Forge was mostly to blame. Soon after Hillegas bought in, the company found itself embroiled in a dispute over timber rights. Thoroughly soured on the endeavor, Hillegas sold his remaining interests to ironmasters George Ege and Robert Coleman in 1793 for £1,400. (Although it appears Hillegas made a profit on the purchase and resale of the forge shares, Hillegas's net gain or loss cannot be determined because payments he made over the years to keep the forge running are not known.)

Overall, it is clear that Hillegas "amassed a considerable fortune" over his career. In 1756 tax assessors rated Hillegas's property in Mulberry Ward at £90, a level exceeded by only ten of his five hundred closest neighbors. By 1767 his assessment had increased to £154, a sum that included his home, his plantation at Point-No-Point, 10 acres of land in Creesham, a vacant lot, two ground rents paid to him, and leases from a property in Mulberry Ward and four properties in the East Northern Liberties district. The assessor subtracted £11 10s. for ground rents that Hillegas paid to William Abbott. He also noted that Hillegas's property was "Incumbred," a nearly illiterate way of saying that Hillegas had mortgaged it to secure a loan. In 1769 Hillegas's assessment dropped to £140, but it rebounded to £161 in 1774. Both figures were well over the average assessments of others involved in the Revolutionary movement (in 1769, £79), including merchants (£77), Anglicans (£84), Quakers (£118), or Whigs (in 1769, £48 10s.; in 1774, £63). Only eventual Tories (in 1769, £147; in 1774, £178) were as rich as Hillegas on average.

Though true Hillegas inherited substantial real property from his father, it is clear that he increased his legacy over the years. His half of his father's estate included two brick tenements on the east side of Second Street between Mulberry and Sassafras; seven other lots, mostly in the Northern Liberties; a lot on the Delaware; a 10-acre tract in Germantown; a 100-acre tract in Philadelphia County; a 68-acre tract in Bucks County; and a lot in Lancaster borough. Most of those properties Hillegas held for years and even decades, then sold at an opportune time and propitious price. Some of the estate, however, most notably the 100-acre tract in Philadelphia County, Hillegas sold off immediately. The young man was probably pressed for cash, because he sold the tract for £80—£4 less than his father had paid for it just two years before.

Hillegas was even shrewder on his own account. He purchased outright at least eleven lots in Philadelphia County between 1768 and 1798. He paid some $10,000 for 84 acres of tracts and over 26,000 square feet of lots, mostly in the Northern Liberties. Six of those purchases Hillegas made at sheriff's sales between 1773 and 1775. The merchant also made eleven purchases on ground rent, again mostly in the Northern Liberties. All told, he paid an annual ground rent of around $400 for over 40,000 square feet.

Between 1751 and 1793, Hillegas sold at least ten tracts and lots in Philadelphia County totaling 124 acres and 22,498 square feet, respectively, for around $7,500. In the last few years of his life, he sold four lots, totaling over 10,000 square feet, for $20,976.50. He also sold by ground rent at least eight lots, around 10,000 square feet, to artisans in the Northern Liberties. Those sales, in sum, produced an annual revenue of over $200.

Hillegas entered into at least three contracts with other Northern Liberties landowners designed to aid the development of the district. Two involved the creation of new streets, and one granted land for a cemetery. Hillegas and other area landowners voluntarily ceded some land for the cemetery and roads because improved access to the lands greatly increased the value of their remaining lots and the cemetery created a sense of community.

In 1764 Hillegas and fellow Philadelphia merchant Jacob Winey purchased 600 acres of land in Coventry Township, Chester County, for £4 per acre. By 1768 the partnership sold at least two pieces of that tract, totaling 154 acres, for £5 per acre. Hillegas also speculated successfully in western Pennsylvania lands. For example, in 1760 he sold, for £117, a Lancaster borough lot that his father had bought for £70 in 1751. He also lent £111 to John Specker of Tulpehocken Township in early 1752 on security of Specker's dwelling, stillhouse, and four acres of land. Specker's debt probably arose when he purchased the liquor-making apparatus from Hillegas's store.

Hillegas made hefty profits speculating in Bedford County lands during the Revolution. He took control of twenty-one tracts, ranging from 202 to 337 acres each, in Bedford County in the fall of 1776. In March through May of 1780, he bought 650 acres of land on Dunnings Creek for £1,550. The next month Hillegas sold the entire tract to a French merchant named Lazarus De Francy for £2,112 10s., a quick and hefty profit. Also in 1780 in Bedford County, he sold 6,769 acres to his future boss, Robert Morris, for £25,387, or £3 15s. per acre. Hillegas had paid only about £2 10s. per acre for the tracts just a few months before. Despite his success in Bedford during the war, Hillegas made only one other purchase in the county, a 362-acre tract he acquired in 1788 for about £6 and back taxes. Hillegas owned land in other states, too, including Virginia and Ohio. In 1768 Hillegas even joined eight others as agents in the sale of land in Nova Scotia, a scheme that Benjamin Franklin aided.

Not all of Hillegas's speculations succeeded, of course. He lost out when he failed to make local tax payments or when ownership of the land came into question, an all-too-common occurrence in eighteenth-century Pennsylvania. Other endeavors cost yet more dearly. In early 1792 Hillegas, Jacob Weiss, William Henry, and Charles Cist formed the Lehigh Coal Company to exploit an anthracite coal discovery on Summit Hill. Hillegas served as the company's secretary-treasurer. Composed of forty shares priced at $200 each, ten of which notorious speculator John Nicholson purchased, the unchartered company foundered because the owners fought with one another instead of managing the details of a new industry. The cost of extracting and transporting the coal to potential customers proved prohibitive in an age of relatively ample timber supplies and tricky river navigation. Limited demand posed yet another problem: Pennsylvanian ironmakers did not use coal until well into the nineteenth century. Coal, when it was wanted at all, sold for only $3 a ton at Wilkes-Barre in 1790. The coal venture was premature but not illusory. After the canals and railroads reduced transportation costs, and people learned how to efficiently burn the new fuel, demand soared and the Lehigh Valley became a significant coal-producing region.[3]

✐ A self-proclaimed "poor Slave to his Country," Hillegas joined public life more from a sense of duty than from a desire to further his own interests. Active in religious, philanthropic, and political life, the young nation bestowed upon him one of its highest positions of trust, and he would not disappoint it. Baptized into the Reformed Church, Hillegas joined the Anglican Church after his marriage to Henrietta Boude in 1753. He served as a vestryman in Christ Church in 1772 and 1773. He sat on a few committees dealing with settlement of accounts and other legal and financial issues, but attended only a third of the dozen and a half meetings held during his tenure. During the Revolution, the church invested Thomas Turner's £500 bequest with Hillegas. He returned the principal in 1779 with interest and a "gratuity" of £100. He later served as a church trustee, returning the titles of the real property in his charge to the church in 1800.

His philanthropy extended beyond the church and showed his deep sentiments for the community at large and his German brethren in particular. In 1761, for example, Hillegas helped to manage two lotteries, one for creating a public school in Germantown and another for the Philadelphia Academy. That year he also helped to adjust the accounts of Joanna Christiana Lutsen, an insolvent innholder; debtor Philip Kerner, stocking weaver; and Adam Probst, another German American. He administered the estate of Christian Steer of Pottstown and the estate of Cain Connolly in 1765 and 1768, respectively. In 1779 he administered the estate of Adam Van Hart of Bucks County. From 1773 until 1776, Hillegas served as one of the auditors of the property of Joseph Richardson, an insolvent debtor and notorious counterfeiter.

Hillegas aided humanitarian causes too. In 1765 he served as one of five treasurers to receive donations for the poor of the suburbs of Philadelphia. A Mason, Hillegas was also active in the Library Company in the early 1770s. In 1780 he became treasurer of Pennsylvania Hospital. That same year he donated £68 to help feed the Continental army.

Though his humanitarian concern was here clearly tinged with self-interest, Hillegas also sought ways of protecting homes from the ravages of fire. He even wrote Benjamin Franklin in London to inquire about the cost and feasibility of sheathing roofs in copper. The extravagant notion was probably tied to Hillegas's financial interests in mining, the metal trade, and fire insurance. (Hillegas held a directorship in the Philadelphia Contributionship from 1772 through 1776 and insisted that his ground-rent tenants buy fire insurance as early as 1756.)

Despite his extensive nongovernmental services, elective office and assembly commissions constituted the bulk of Hillegas's public duties. He served as Philadelphia County assessor and then commissioner in the late 1750s and early 1760s, dutifully attending every meeting. After the Revolution, Hillegas served as a Philadelphia County justice of the peace, an alderman, and an associate justice of the Mayor's Court of the City of Philadelphia. Before, during, and after his long legislative career, the assembly selected Hillegas as commissioner to implement a wide variety of laws. In 1765 he became a Skippack Bridge commissioner, empowered to receive subscriptions for the bridge's construction. Later the assembly selected Hillegas as one of three commissioners charged with settling the tangled affairs of the Skippack Bridge Lottery. In 1773 Hillegas sold tickets in the Wilmington Lottery, designed to raise money for "certain pious uses" in Delaware and to fund the construction of two small Anglican chapels in the Northern Liberties of Philadelphia. Hillegas also served as a state lottery manager in 1784 and appears to have been involved in the York, Heidelberg & Lebanon Lottery. The assembly selected him as State House trustee, Province Island commissioner, Delaware navigation commissioner, Mud Island commissioner, Revolutionary War documents compiler, and barracks tract sale commissioner. Perhaps because he owned land at Point-No-Point, Hillegas served as Delaware River clearance commissioner with particular alacrity. Hillegas's knowledge of paper, and his intimate knowledge of the assembly library, probably earned him the documents compiler appointment.

Though an Anglican, Hillegas launched his decade-long assembly career in the fall of 1765 on the Quaker Party's Philadelphia County ticket. In his first term, Hillegas seemed to shadow Thomas Willing, a member of the opposing Proprietary Party. One chronicler called Hillegas's assembly career "very busy and aggressive." He certainly was busy, serving, over his career, on an average of 19.5 committees per term, approximately eleven more assignments than the average assemblyman obtained. Though many of his assignments were mere errands, Hillegas also served on important committees such as the Committee of Grievances and the General Loan Office Account Settlement and Minutes Revision committees. Many of his assignments dealt with economic issues, including supply bills during the 1765, 1771, and 1772 terms; tax reform bills, including the major efforts of 1771 and 1773; manufacturing concerns, including the investigation of the public usefulness of three inventions; and various internal improvement committees charged with building, repairing, or clearing various rivers, dams, islands, barracks, ports, sewers, highways, and fortifications. (Hillegas had gained experience with such endeavors as a Philadelphia County commissioner.) He was also appointed to committees dealing with church lotteries, poor relief reform, and various humanitarian efforts, including the inspection of Pennsylvania Hospital.

In the decade leading to the Revolution, the assembly often turned to Hillegas when it needed financial counsel, like estimating the public debt, raising funds by lottery or paper money, ascertaining the best method for authenticating contracts, recovering money due from public servants, creating mechanisms for troop supply, and implementing the House's 1773 salary raise. He also helped the assembly to make economic decisions concerning the price of bread and the regulation of flour, timber, leather, fish packing, fisheries, inns, peddlers, and—due to his connection to the Contributionship—chimney sweeps. Hillegas also served on committees dealing with issues of law and order, like attempts to discourage frontier rioting and the firing of guns on New Year's Day. Finally, he was often charged with collecting the fines that legislators incurred for nonattendance and breaches of House rules. During his illustrious legislative career, Hillegas helped to write sixty-two pieces of legislation, or 5.6 per term, forty-five of which became law, a 73 percent success rate.

Aside from his regular House salary, Hillegas received at least £121 for his service on standing committees and £322 for "extra" services. Those payments show that he was very active "outside the bar." The financier also received payments or reimbursements of £4,951 for advances he made for "Repairs at the Province-Island Deep Water Island, sundry Indian Expences, Firewood for the Assembly, Orders of the Committee of Safety, and Orders of Assembly and Committee of Assembly for Drums, Colours, &c." He made about £20 superintending various colonial emissions of bills of credit.

All that activity paled in comparison to Hillegas's duties in the early stages of the Revolution. As armed conflict neared, the assembly increasingly called on Hillegas to help superintend the province's finances and make important diplomatic and military decisions. In July 1774 and again in October, for example, the House authorized Hillegas and three others to draw on the provincial treasurer for the pay and support of the rangers then protecting the frontier from Indian attacks. Shortly thereafter, Hillegas sat on a committee charged with instructing Pennsylvania's delegates to Congress and answering Governor Penn's message on Indian affairs. He also sat on a committee that responded to the governor's rejection of a budget bill. In October 1774 the House asked Hillegas to entertain and support an Indian chief during his visit to Philadelphia. The following March the assembly empowered Hillegas to draw on the provincial treasurer for up to £100 to pay the expenses of the Indians then in town. Also in March 1775 the House instructed Hillegas and two others to prepare a bill for the emission of £6,000 of bills of credit for the use of the Philadelphia port wardens. In June Hillegas joined with Thomas Willing, Benjamin Franklin, and others to sign a joint promissory note to procure a £6,000 advance from Pennsylvania treasurer Owen Jones. Also in June the assembly appointed Hillegas treasurer of an emission of bills of credit, requiring him to post a £10,000 performance bond. In late June Hillegas joined the Committee of Safety, a rebel body, as its treasurer. The Continental Congress selected Hillegas and fellow Philadelphian George Clymer as joint Continental treasurers in July 1775.

Though a "moderate" on the independence issue, Hillegas easily won reelection to the House in October 1775, receiving only eleven fewer votes than front-runner John Dickinson. That same month he rejoined the Committee of Safety for a nine-month stint. In March 1776 the assembly asked Hillegas and three others for estimates of the cost of paying and feeding fifteen hundred soldiers. The answer, £64,789 per month, made half of the assembly balk at the notion of raising troops for an entire year, but Speaker

John Morton cast the deciding vote in favor of the exertion. Probably because of this experience, the assembly selected Hillegas as one of three men to decide which army supply contracts to take up for the provisioning of the state's soldiers.

In November 1775 the assembly appointed Hillegas treasurer of an emission of £80,000 in bills of credit. Hillegas held the bills to meet drafts drawn by various officials, including battalion commanders, barrack commissioners, the army paymaster, and the Committee of Safety. He received additional funds from county treasurers, various fines, and certain prize cases, receivables traditionally under the purview of the provincial treasurer. In other words, Hillegas became Pennsylvania's de facto treasurer although Owen Jones still claimed the de jure title. When Jones resigned under pressure in late May 1776, the assembly immediately elected Hillegas the province's lawful treasurer.

The Continental Congress and the Pennsylvania legislature probably selected Hillegas as treasurer for several reasons. Seemingly foremost, he had much experience in public finance. However, because many others—like Thomas Willing, Robert Morris, and George Clymer—were more famous for their financial exploits, or just as experienced in public finance, still other explanations must be sought. Hillegas, it will be recalled, had a good knowledge of paper products and markets, a crucial component of bills-of-credit production. That was important because it was clear that rogues and the British would attempt to counterfeit rebel currency en masse and that a paper shortage could impede the war effort. Perhaps most importantly, Hillegas at this time was pro–fiat paper money. His acceptance of bills of credit was probably based on his personal experience and financial interests. Unlike many of those opposed to fiat currency, Hillegas was neither a large net creditor nor reliant on foreign trade for his livelihood. Moreover, like many Pennsylvanians, he harbored fond memories of the efficacy of the General Loan Office. Finally, Hillegas's residence near Chestnut Street undoubtedly aided his candidacy.

As state treasurer, Hillegas performed many of the same duties required of him as treasurer of the bills-of-credit emissions, but he was also charged with exchanging pre-1773 bills of credit for more recent emissions. "It is hoped no Lover of his Country will neglect it," Hillegas's first advertisement read. In his second advertisement, the treasurer noted that the new emission contained more small bills so the exchange process would alleviate the dire "Want of Change in Circulation."

As Continental treasurer, Hillegas's biggest chore was to receive, store, and disburse Congress's money. Additional duties broke up the monotony of keeping the new nation's extensive books. For example, for a time Congress also charged Hillegas with trying to coax Americans into lending money to the rebel government in exchange for interest-bearing debt certificates. Hillegas also oversaw the printing of Continental bills of credit and Congress's paper securities, for which he received $500 in bonuses. Congress also empowered Hillegas to employ persons to help him to sign the thousands of bills, notes, and certificates he caused to be printed. Hillegas chose his son Samuel as one of the signers. In May 1777 Congress also authorized him to sign U.S. lottery notes, the interest-bearing promissory notes given in lieu of cash prizes. Especially when the treasury was low, Hillegas took special pains to promptly pay the paper, copperplate, and other suppliers who kept the Continental presses churning. Unfortunately, as more Continentals entered circulation and loan-office interest obligations accumulated, the purchasing power of each dollar decreased as the public rightfully questioned Congress's ability to redeem its currency and make its interest payments.

As both provincial and Continental treasurer, Hillegas fought hard to maintain the value of America's "SACRED" fiat currency and negotiable securities. He sent a one William McCreery to meet Benjamin Franklin in Paris with the "Expectation" of McCreery's selling Continental Loan Office certificates in France. During the occupation of Philadelphia, Hillegas sought ways of preventing counterfeiting of bills of credit. He also wrote a crucially important and somewhat ironic letter to Franklin concerning the differences between general price inflation and depreciation of bills of credit. "I must acknowledge that the high prices things have borne here pleads undoubtedly strong that the Money has depreciated," the treasurer began, "but give me leave at the same time to observe that this has not been altogether occasioned by the Quantity of Money which has been issued with us." This was much the same pro–paper money argument Franklin himself had used when trying to gain repeal of the Currency Act of 1764. But the treasurer took the analysis further. "A Scarcity of foreign Articles," Hillegas explained, combined with "the Traders . . . secreting the Goods we really had," exacerbated the price increases. That spirit of avarice "soon got among the Farmers," who raised their prices too. Hillegas was hopeful because it appeared that "taxes have already commenced in most if not all the States." Also, the treasurer reminded Franklin that "the Money which has been issued, . . . is good, because the Estates of America are & will be a sufficient security for the redemption of all the Money that has been issued and even much more." Once trade picked up, he argued, the burden of debt would be a light one. It was this realization of the latent economic power of

America, and his belief in the power of Christ, that saw Hillegas through the darkest of the Revolution's many dark days.

Hillegas fled from Philadelphia to Baltimore with both the Continental and Pennsylvania treasuries during the invasion scare of December 1776. Though his dual offices were functionally very similar, the assembly now saw the potential conflict of interest facing Hillegas, so it quickly accepted David Rittenhouse's January 1777 offer to serve as the state treasurer. (Rittenhouse, readers may recall, was later the first director of the U.S. Mint.) The House took Hillegas's account books and pressed for the settlement of accounts and the return of funds. Hillegas remained in Baltimore in the spring and summer of 1777, overseeing the printing of Continentals and Loan Office certificates. Though Congress wished him to return to Philadelphia, Hillegas removed his family and the treasury, for safety's sake, to Reading, and later York, Pennsylvania, in early autumn 1777. The assembly and Congress also retreated inland after the British moved into Philadelphia in the fall of 1777. The British turned Hillegas's house into a makeshift hospital during their short occupation of the city. Hillegas returned to Philadelphia under armed convoy in late July 1778 shortly after the British evacuation.

That August Congress relieved Hillegas, who was hard-pressed under the weight of his many duties, of his Loan Office responsibilities. Hillegas still found his hands full, however. When in funds, he juggled payments between various states' bills of credit and Continentals, attempting to pay in the currency particular creditors valued most highly. When out of cash, as in the summer of 1780, the treasurer put off creditors as best he could. He even had to turn friends away and quickly rebuffed those who tried to coax him into bending the rules in special cases, as when he told Samuel Purviance, an old friend, that he could not divert money from the lottery account to meet a bill due to him.

A faction in Congress clearly mistrusted those in direct control of the purse strings. Though Congress allowed Hillegas to continue as sole treasurer after the resignation of George Clymer in early 1776, it clung steadfastly to the Board of Treasury, its awkward, inefficient, multifarious oversight committee. Hillegas, a staunch advocate of efficient administration, struggled against Congress's bureaucratic safeguards the best he could, but he had to comply with many unnecessary requests, including sending two sets of proof sheets of Continentals to each state. When he had no specie to meet obligations specifically contracted to be paid in coin, Hillegas quickly suggested payment in bills of exchange on Europe, but the Treasury Board allowed Congress's credit to suffer rather than consider the request in due time. The board grew increasingly intrusive in 1780, launching an investigation that occasioned much bureaucratic infighting. It chastised Hillegas for advancing small sums "to clerks in the offices when in great distress" and $100 to the doorkeeper of Congress, because he was under general congressional orders not to make such disbursements. Some also complained that Hillegas failed to discharge two men from his staff although the Treasury Board had ordered him to do so. Subsequent investigations cleared Hillegas and the treasury of wrongdoing. By exposing the committee's pettiness and inefficiencies, the episode somewhat ironically helped lead to the dismantling of the Board of Treasury. Robert Morris headed its replacement, the Office of the Superintendent of Finance. Congress unanimously chose Hillegas to remain at the helm of the treasury during that crucial 1781 reorganization.

Though his role changed and he had to start a new set of books, Hillegas welcomed Morris's regime. In the late 1770s, the value of Pennsylvania's and Congress's fiat money continued to sink vis-à-vis specie. By 1781 the complex maze of depreciation schedules confused even Hillegas at times. Realizing the need for institutional solutions, Hillegas joined the fiscal reform movement. He purchased one of the initial shares in the Bank of North of America, for instance, and, as U.S. treasurer, received the large shipment of government specie carried overland from Boston that constituted much of that bank's initial capital. He negotiated a $100,000 loan on behalf of the national government on the bank's first day of business, January 7, 1782, and dealt frequently with the bank on the nation's account thereafter.

Hillegas worked closely with Morris to try to redeem Congress's broken credit. The financiers met to discuss means of making interest payments on loan office certificates, eventually deciding to issue "indents," additional IOUs. Morris was an imposing figure in a powerful position, however, and much of the time he simply bid Hillegas to implement his policies. In early 1782, for example, the superintendent instructed Hillegas to turn over his excess paper supplies to three of Morris's new bills-of-exchange printers. He also bade Hillegas to advertise and sell excess Continental cannons and instructed him to safeguard uncurrent paper money rather than to destroy it. Though Hillegas continued to receive taxes due from the states, Morris kept tight control of other receivables and most disbursements and often denied Hillegas or his clerks funds that the treasurer needed to pay creditors.

Morris felt that he had to ration disbursements carefully so that the nation's most important creditors would receive at least partial payments. But even this expedient was insufficient to maintain Congress's liquidity. Morris

therefore began to issue cashlike promissory notes of various denominations and due dates. He instructed Hillegas, Cashier of the Superintendent
John Swanwick, and Paymaster General John Pierce to do likewise. Hillegas's notes—bearer instruments like Morris's but issued exclusively for
army subsistence—were not used in the southern states. Because the national government accepted them at par from its debtors, Hillegas's notes
circulated somewhat broadly in the lower Mid-Atlantic states, especially in
and around Philadelphia and southern New Jersey.

The Peace of Paris greatly relieved the nation's financial woes, but the
subsequent removal of the capital to New York City brought Hillegas some
personal pain and almost prematurely ended his treasury career. Hillegas
cared deeply for his family. A striking example of this occurred in 1792 when
he delayed settling accounts with Pennsylvania's comptroller general of accounts, John Nicholson, because "the Indisposition & low situation of Mrs.
Hillegas" prevented his "going out to any distance from home, not knowing but her death may happen while out." She died soon after; Hillegas later
joined his beloved Henrietta in the burial ground of Christ Church. The
musician's fatherly affections also waxed strong as his tender 1786 missive
beseeching his "Dear Children" to live happy and sober lives demonstrates.
The merchant named at least two of his ships for his daughters. Finally, Hillegas admitted that his desire to provide for his children inspired his successful land speculations. Those vital family values and his relatively meager salary as treasurer explain Hillegas's reluctance to follow Congress to
New York. Congress was in no mood for sentiment, however, and career
politicians like Rufus King, Timothy Pickering, and Elbridge Gerry stood
poised to sweep the Philadelphian from office. Luckily for Hillegas's career,
fellow Pennsylvanian Charles Thomson, the so-called "prime minister" of
Congress, stalled legislative action while prompting Hillegas to arrange his
"private affairs" and move to the new capital by October "to administer the
duties of . . . [the] office [of] Treasurer." Thomson pointed out that Congress's lengthy indulgence showed that it needed his experience. Hillegas
agreed, moved to New York alone, and remained the nation's treasurer until the new government took effect in 1789. Desiring a fresh start with fresh
faces, George Washington and Alexander Hamilton decided against retaining the officers and staff of the old treasury. The change did not disturb Hillegas as it allowed him to return to Philadelphia. Besides, he had ardently
supported the formation of the new government.

⌐○ In fact, Hillegas was one of the first patriots to argue, clearly but privately, for the efficacy of a strong national government designed to create

and foster a free market economy through uniform commercial regulations. Not overtly a strong party man, Hillegas was a Federalist, unafraid to aid the cause of national unity. According to Alexander Hamilton, Hillegas left important papers relating to Republican senator William Maclay's politically motivated investigation of $7,000 of warrants granted to Federalist Baron von Steuben locked and taped in his private desk in New York. Maclay expressed "great Surprize That Mr. Hillegas should lock public Papers belonging to the Treasury in his private desk," but he could do little about it. His attack fizzled.

Though a staid financier, Hillegas was not opposed to socializing. In 1783 Philadelphia farmer and politician Jacob Hiltzheimer noted that "the bottles and glasses were not idle" when Hillegas visited friends. In 1795 Hillegas joined Hiltzheimer, Thomas Mifflin, Edward Shippen, and other hoary inhabitants of the City of Brotherly Love in a quarterly dining club. Hillegas was also a member of the Fishing Company of Fort St. David and the American Philosophical Society. He also enjoyed corresponding with Philadelphia printer-entrepreneur Mathew Carey about his museum. The Commonwealth of Massachusetts, however, shattered the fraternity and serenity of Hillegas's final years.

In early 1800 Hillegas found himself indebted to Massachusetts for over $15,000. The cause of this debt is not clear today and, indeed, was not entirely clear at the time because it involved complex accounting issues and entries made over a decade before. Hillegas may have owed the money to the estate of his dear friend John Hancock; Hancock's widow was certainly involved in the affair. But if the debt was a public one, many believed that "the United States ought to pay it," not Hillegas. There were many ways that Hillegas, as treasurer, could have run afoul of Massachusetts. For example, as treasurer he sued the state over the "illegal seizure" of the schooner *Hodgson*. He also received at least $1.75 million worth of warrants drawn in his favor by Nathaniel Appleton, commissioner of the Continental loan office for Massachusetts, for which Hillegas explicitly was "to be accountable."

Whatever the cause of the debt, Massachusetts ignored pleas to "do an act of humanity" for "an old revolutionary character" and insisted that U.S. Attorney General Charles Lee "take the most direct measures the law will allow of to obtain the money." Hillegas did not have the necessary cash on hand, so he signed a bond pledging repayment in three annual installments, with interest. To secure the bond, he mortgaged two of his most valuable properties, his Second Street store and his Northern Liberties water lot and wharf, with its many "Dwelling Houses Shops and Stores," in early May

1800. Because "frequent visitations of the fever" depressed the Philadelphia real estate market, Hillegas found himself unable to sell lesser properties to pay the first installment on the bond. Hounded by Massachusetts officials, trustees sold Hillegas's Second Street property to Philadelphia merchant Joseph Clark in return for Clark's payment of the principal of the bond. Hillegas paid the almost $1,800 in interest without sacrificing further real property.

Hillegas drew up his last will on September 25, 1804, just four days before his death. After leaving special legacies to his son Samuel and his housekeeper, Hillegas divided his estate into five equal parts, one-fifth for each of his four surviving children and one-fifth to be shared equally by Samuel's children. In other words, Hillegas divided his estate more or less equally among the surviving members of his immediate family and his grandchildren. Hillegas's estate was a large and complex one. It was not settled until December 14, 1850, after it had distributed at least $111,156 to his heirs.

⟋◯ Hillegas alone would not a financial dynamo make. But in the first few decades after the Revolution, Chestnut Street was home to dozens of financiers of similar capabilities and a few of superior qualities besides. Obviously, Hillegas's death in 1804 did not bring the end of Chestnut Street's dominance in the 1830s. The eventual death of all of Philadelphia's early financial innovators, though, did play a big part in Wall Street's ascendance.

One wonders, too, if the relative decline of Quakerism played a role. Especially after the Hicksite division split the sect, Quaker influence in the region waned. Foreign observers like Joseph John Gurney thought the Quakers "may perhaps have been one cause of the quiet, orderly habits for which the more respectable classes" of Philadelphians had "been so long remarkable." But they make no mention of the early freedom that the Quakers had brought to the shores of the Delaware. Without a clear lead in that intangible but crucial resource, Philadelphia began to lose new human capital to Manhattan. Moreover, because of the decline in her trade, Philadelphia also began to lose a very tangible resource, her trade deposits.[4]

10

WALL STREET ASCENDANT

As Philadelphia's finest passed to eternity and as its trade fled to New York, Baltimore, and New Orleans, Chestnut Street's lifeblood—deposits—also began to dry up. Increasingly, Americans had credits in, or had to make payments to, Manhattan, not the Quaker metropolis. So the nation's banks, which numbered nearly four hundred by 1830, kept their big deposit balances in Wall Street, not Chestnut Street, institutions. Manhattan's banks lent those deposits to New York's merchants, giving them a further advantage over Philadelphia's merchants. And they also lent them—overnight with strong collateral—to securities brokers, dealers, stockjobbers, and anyone else who wanted to play in the securities markets. So New York's stock market was soon awash in liquidity (a good thing for investors) and hence attracted yet more investment funds.

In short, New York bootstrapped itself into a virtuous cycle. Wall Street financed the creation of a very long but strategically located ditch. It also lent to the merchants who transformed that ditch into the nation's most important interior commercial artery. In return, Wall Street was entrusted with a big chunk of the nation's cash, which it used to make its stock exchange yet more attractive to investors. Wall Street's financiers then turned those investment flows into additional projects, including extensions of the canal system, railroads, steamship lines, and the cotton and cotton goods trades. All that trade brought yet more deposits to Wall Street's banks, giving the positive feedback cycle yet another spin.

Like any good predator, the hungry sharks of Wall Street smelled blood in the water; they did not wait long to strike. In retrospect, Chestnut Street didn't have a chance. In the early 1830s, however, it looked like a long, pitched battle for financial dominance might ensue. But the Wall Street shark, now a card shark, had an ace up its sleeve, the ace of government. When it deftly played that card, Chestnut Street folded. This chapter relates how Wall Street dealt itself such a killer card.

⌒ Wall Street, the physical place, has a hoary history that need not concern us here. Suffice it to say that by the 1820s Wall Street was the center of much of New York's financial activity. Auctioneers, banks, brokers, coffeehouses, insurance companies, and mercantile countinghouses, with the occasional high-end bookseller or tailor nestled in between, lined both its north and south sides. Some financial firms were not located right on the street, but all looked to it when a financial deal had to be made on the quick. According to one contemporary, "The whole money-dealing of New York is here [Wall Street] brought into a very narrow compass of ground, and is in consequence transacted with peculiar quickness and facility." As any good trader will tell you, the speed of execution is a major consideration when choosing where to place an order.[1]

Wall Street followed Chestnut Street closely in the early years. Soon after a new institution appeared in Philadelphia, an eerily similar-looking one cropped up in Manhattan. The Bank of New York formed soon after the Bank of North America's monopoly ended with the Revolutionary War. New York brokers signed the Buttonwood Agreement, which created a proto–New York Stock Exchange, shortly after Philadelphia brokers formed a proto-exchange. The Bank for Savings popped up shortly after the Philadelphia Savings Fund Society organized. Ditto with all three major types of insurance, building and loans, and other financial innovations. Save for ground rents, which New York never adopted, the general rule was: Where Chestnut Street led, Wall Street followed.

In the 1820s, as New York waxed and Philly waned, many wondered why Wall Street should continue to play second fiddle to Chestnut Street. The answer was clear: Chestnut Street possessed a mutually reinforcing *network* of financial institutions that made it strong. And the center of that network, its server if you will, was the headquarters of the second Bank of the United States. In a fit of ignorance, politicians had allowed the charter of the first Bank of the United States, Hamilton's brainchild, to expire in 1811. During the War of 1812, the government learned what a valuable institution the BUS had been. So in 1816 it chartered a similar institution but with three and a half times the capital—$35 million, a truly enormous sum for the day.

The Second Bank, as it came to be called, got off to a rocky start. If it didn't outright *cause* the Panic of 1819, it certainly exacerbated the recession that followed it, and in the process created a large number of enemies. But as prosperity returned in the 1820s, many forgave the bank. Indeed, under the able guidance of Philadelphia banker Nicholas Biddle, many eventually came to see the Second Bank as a great good. Biddle and his bank were widely believed to have prevented Britain's 1825 financial crisis from spreading to America. As the first shock waves reached our shores, interest rates soared. According to one source, lenders discounted "solid" notes at 18 to 24 percent. No word what they charged for "shaky" ones, if they dealt with them at all. Like any good central banker, Biddle saw the poison of financial contagion approaching and scotched it with the proper antidote—confidence backed with cash. It worked. While John Bull lay prostrate, Uncle Sam surged onward, and westward. As the prosperity of the late 1820s turned into the economic ebullience of the early 1830s, Biddle took on what late twentieth-century Americans would recognize as a Greenspan-esque glow.[2]

The problem was that the stronger Biddle and his bank became, the more envious Wall Street's leading lights became. The most damnable thing about the Second Bank, from Wall Street's perspective, was its extensive system of branches. Baltimore, Boston, Buffalo, Burlington, Charleston, Cincinnati, Fayetteville, Hartford, Lexington, Louisville, Mobile, Nashville, Natchez, New Orleans, Norfolk, Pittsburgh, Portland, Portsmouth, Providence, St. Louis, Savannah, Utica, Washington, D.C.—all had branches of the Second Bank and hence fell under the sway of Biddle and Chestnut Street. Moreover, most were significant establishments, not rinky-dink offices. The Second Bank branch at Buffalo, for instance, did what one contemporary called "a very large, safe and profitable business, furnishing exchange on all parts of the United States at a very low rate, affording great benefits to the travelers and merchants by freely giving its own notes for all others eastern or western, discounting very readily paper at four months as well as that at shorter dates." With such powerful advertising and pull in virtually all of the nation's most important commercial centers, spread over twenty states and the capitol district, it is little wonder that most observers—outside of Manhattan, of course—still considered Chestnut Street the nation's financial heart.[3]

When the Second Bank was founded in 1816, Philadelphia was not a bad choice for headquarters. Morris, Hillegas, and a few others had died, but many of its top financiers—including Thomas Willing, who had ably led the first Bank of the United States for over a decade—were still alive. Moreover, the trade war between Philly, Baltimore, and New York was as yet unsettled. As we have seen, all that had changed by 1830. Wall Street financiers realized that the Second Bank was the third and final leg of the "stool" that propped up Chestnut Street's continued financial dominance. Break that leg, and Chestnut Street would fall.

But how to break it? Any economic attempts to snap it would likely backfire. No one institution had the strength to take on the Second Bank. It was simply too big and geographically diversified. A simultaneous attack by many institutions might have worked but was impossible to coordinate or monitor. The only thing that could destroy the SBUS, Wall Street financiers soon realized, was the same thing that created it, the federal government.

But would the government again be dull and venal enough to destroy its central bank? Especially with Nicholas Biddle, the most storied banker in U.S. history to that time, firmly at the helm? Clearly, Wall Streeters reasoned, the government would need both a push and a pull, something to repel it away from the Second Bank and to draw it to Wall Street. That key insight led to the creation of a double-pronged strategy that eventually ensured that the coveted ace of government ended up in Wall Street's hand. Chestnut Street even helped out a bit, of course unwittingly.

⮴ The man most directly responsible for dealing the ace of government to Wall Street was Martin Van Buren. Born in Kinderhook, near Albany, New York, in December 1782 to tavern keepers of obvious Dutch extraction, Van Buren had little formal schooling but much day-to-day experience interacting with the sundry characters who slept, ate, and most importantly drank in his parents' house. His political training began in earnest at age fourteen when he apprenticed to Francis Silvester, a local lawyer of the Federalist persuasion. Perhaps due to his humble roots, Van Buren disdained Federalism, opting instead to join Thomas Jefferson's Republican (later Democratic) Party.[4]

The young Van Buren campaigned actively for Jefferson and Aaron Burr in 1800 and was for several years thereafter a devout Burrite in his state politics. By 1803, however, Van Buren switched his allegiance to the Republican faction of George and DeWitt Clinton. It would not be the last time that Van Buren smelled a loser early enough to distance himself from the stench. His abandonment of Burr was vindicated in July 1804 when the vice president murdered former treasury secretary Alexander Hamilton on the dueling grounds at Weehawken, New Jersey. Soon thereafter Burr found himself implicated in a plot to form a new nation west of the Appalachians, a little scheme that placed him in the same league of iniquity as King George III (for Republicans) and Napoléon Bonaparte (for Federalists).

Van Buren married Hannah Hoes, his cousin, in 1807. She bore him four children, none of whom inherited any untoward genetic diseases. If anything, the union aided Van Buren's career, which proceeded apace. In the decade following his marriage, Van Buren catapulted himself from pettifogger to judge to state senator to state attorney general. In 1816 he entered a lucrative law partnership with Benjamin F. Butler, one of the state's leading attorneys. But soon thereafter several disasters struck: His wife died of tuberculosis; new governor DeWitt Clinton, an enemy ever since Van Buren abandoned him after his failed presidential bid in 1812, deposed him from office; and Van Buren's stance against the Grand Canal won him nothing but derision.

Down but not out, Van Buren decided to establish his own political faction, the Bucktails. In 1820 the Bucktails gained control of the state legislature and voted Van Buren into the U.S. Senate. The following year Van Buren's faction controlled a convention that created a much more liberal state constitution. Conveniently, it also cut Clinton's gubernatorial term short. In 1822 the Bucktail candidate defeated Clinton for the new governorship. The coup was now complete. Moreover, Van Buren's initial skepticism of the Grand Canal was forgiven and forgotten.

Episodes such as those led Van Buren's friends to dub him "the Little Magician." His enemies thought "the Sly Fox" a more fitting sobriquet. Both friend and foe agreed on one thing: politically speaking, Van Buren could get things done. During the 1820s he expanded the Bucktail faction into the nation's first true party machine, the fabled "Albany Regency." Headed by Van Buren, Butler, William Marcy, and Silas Wright (no relation), the Regency controlled the state through a network of party newspapers and political appointees. The blatant politicking sickened many members of the Revolutionary generation, but to his dying day (July 24, 1862), Van Buren vigorously defended his actions and argued that political parties were beneficial.

In the 1824 presidential election, the Regency backed Treasury Secretary William Crawford, who came in a distant third behind Andrew Jackson and John Quincy Adams. But Crawford won enough electors to throw the election into Congress. Due to a "corrupt bargain" that would make even Florida blush, the House of Representatives eventually gave Adams the nod. But from the get-go it was clear that, like his dad, Adams would be a one-termer. Shrewdly, Van Buren switched allegiance to Jackson. He campaigned for "Old Hickory" and, more importantly, used his power in the Senate to forge a coalition that assured Jackson of victory in 1828. Riding high, Van Buren also got himself elected governor of New York in 1828. He stayed in that position just long enough to pass a banking law called the Safety Fund, of which more anon. He then joined the Jackson administration as secretary of state.

But the sly Little Magician was far from done. It appeared likely that Jackson would win reelection in 1832. But who would succeed him in 1836? Jackson's vice president, South Carolinian John Calhoun, was the odds-on favorite. He had already served as James Monroe's secretary of war (1817–25) and as Adams's vice president (1825–29). Moreover, he was a Southerner. Save for the Adamses, the South had a lock on the presidency. By this time, however, Jackson and Calhoun shared very different ideologies. Jackson was an ardent nationalist who vowed to "die in the last ditch" before seeing the Union disbanded. Calhoun, on the other hand, believed in "nullification," a sort of state-level judicial review, acceptance of which would have weakened both the Union and the U.S. Constitution significantly. Moreover, Calhoun was a slaveholder with an aristocratic bearing. Jackson, like Van Buren, was more down-to-earth.[5]

Despite his humble origins, Van Buren played Calhoun for a fool. By the time it was all over, Jackson was threatening to march to South Carolina to hang his vice president! Needless to say, Van Buren, not Calhoun, joined Jackson on the presidential ticket in 1832. As planned, Van Buren won election to the presidency in 1836, but despite his pro-slavery pronouncements, he ran badly in the South and barely won. As the economy turned sour in 1837, his popularity dropped further, rendering him America's third one-term president. It was a fitting end. Van Buren was largely responsible for fomenting the panic and recession. The story of how Van Buren destroyed Chestnut Street and in the process almost ruined the American economy is a long and somewhat complicated one, but one well worth telling—and, I hope, reading.

⌒◯ During his brief stint as governor of New York, Van Buren basically did one thing—drastically revise New York's banking system. The existing system was hardly broken. Except for a few small banks upstate and Jacob Barker's private bank, New York banks were sound and well regarded. They were not solid and highly regarded enough, however, to take the place of the Second Bank. Van Buren aimed to change that. His plan began to unfold in the mid-1820s, when New York decided it needed to compile, codify, and revise its laws. One of three important jurists assigned to the project was Benjamin F. Butler, Van Buren's erstwhile law partner. Butler convinced his colleagues that New York needed very strict banking laws so that people would have complete confidence in all of its banks. When it came to banking, New York's Revised Statutes, as they were called, were very strict, too strict as it turned out. Nobody wanted to form a new bank under such onerous regulations.[6]

That posed a huge problem for Wall Street, especially as many of the state's existing banks were coming up for recharter. Without further legal reforms, those banks would have to wind up their affairs, flee to another state, or reincorporate and suffer under the restrictive new regulations. So a crisis atmosphere greeted Van Buren as he was sworn into office. That was perfect for the Little Magician because crisis meant quick action. In the legislative melee that ensued, Van Buren—with help from his Albany Regency, of course—was able to foist off on New Yorkers a bank reform package that created a deposit insurance scheme. Known as the Safety Fund, the reforms looked great—on the surface. Each bank had to pay a tax of 3 percent of its capital into a special account. Should a bank fail, the account would make depositors and note holders whole. To make sure that banks did not fail, the tax would also pay the salaries and expenses of government bank examiners.[7]

Now, anyone who suffered through the Savings and Loan Crisis of the 1980s will upon reflection realize that the Safety Fund was neither safe nor a fund. We learned then that deposit insurance gives banks an incentive to take on added risks and that government examiners are not terribly motivated, or good. Worse, while sufficient to handle a few failures, the insurance was wholly inadequate to stem the tide of a systemic shock wave. U.S. taxpayers footed most of the bill for the S&L debacle.

The more things change, the more they stay the same. The Safety Fund itself eventually suffered losses and ran out of funds. Government bank examiners could sometimes see trouble brewing at a bank, but they were powerless to stop it from going under. And when panic struck in 1837, they were completely overwhelmed. New York by then realized its mistake and passed a free banking law that was much superior to the Safety Fund. Van Buren's reform was allowed to slowly fade away. Before its oblivion, however, it fulfilled its primary political objective, that of serving as an apparently viable alternative to the Second Bank.

Astute observers immediately grasped the Safety Fund's weaknesses. One called the Safety Fund "a modern invention of very questionable value." Downstate banks were particularly outraged because they felt that a flat tax on capital that did not account for a bank's riskiness or the volume of notes that it circulated was patently unfair. City banks, after all, tended to be sound, even conservative, institutions with relatively few notes outstanding. Country banks, by contrast, were subject to much less monitoring and hence tended to issue more notes and take greater risks. In protest, the city banks stopped making loans in an attempt to pressure Albany into revoking or at least revising the Safety Fund. Equally ironically, just as New York's economy began to go down the toilet—excuse me, the outhouse hole—Biddle stepped in, promising to lend to any solid New York person, business, or bank in need of aid. Manhattan's banks relented and began to lend once more. Of course, Biddle at that time had no idea that the Safety Fund would eventually rise up to smite him, and the Manhattan banks had no clue that the Safety Fund would soon help to crown Wall Street. In order to work his magic, the Sly Fox from Kinderhook kept his cards close to his vest, very close, indeed.

Despite the obviously earnest objections of Manhattan banks against the Safety Fund, most Americans fell for Van Buren's propaganda hook, line, and sinker. They believed that the fund made New York's banks safer and more powerful than even the Second Bank. So when the Bank War, as the struggle for recharter of the Second Bank came to be called, began, there was what appeared to be a viable alternative available. And it centered on New York.

ᴄᴏ Hubris. If one had to describe Philadelphia financiers in the mid-1830s, that single word would suffice. They seemed to think that Chestnut Street would always rule the nation's financial system. After all, it always had. They held an ace, Nicholas Biddle and his Second Bank. They knew that the ace of government existed, but they thought that it was still in the deck, undealt. Even if it appeared in Wall Street's hands, maybe it would not be played. Or maybe, just maybe, the Biddle ace would trump it. Like I said, hubris.[8]

To be fair, Chestnut Street financiers had reason to be sanguine. Their fearless leader, Nicholas Biddle, was a dashing figure. Born in 1786, Biddle missed the Revolution and the framing of the Constitution. Hamilton's financial revolution also came too soon after his birth to form an impression upon his mind. The financing of the Quasi-War with France in the late 1790s and of the Louisiana Purchase in 1803 were more familiar, but still foggy. The defining moment of his early life was the destruction of the BUS and the financial chaos that followed. The War of 1812, oft known at the time as the Second War of Independence, and the recession that followed the Panic of 1819 were the crucibles that formed this financier. From those experiences, which in many ways were reminiscent of the first Revolution and ensuing economic stagnation, he came away with one fundamental, overriding idea: the United States needed a strong central bank and an intelligent central banker.

Biddle became that banker, and his bank became that bank. Under Biddle, the Second Bank fine-tuned the U.S. economy to maximize its growth. For starters, Biddle and his bank kept state banks in line by returning their notes to them for redemption in specie. Always fearful that an agent of the Second Bank would appear with a wheelbarrow full of their notes, state banks took care not to issue too many. That kept inflation in check. In addition, the Second Bank bought and sold inland exchange on the cheap. That made it easier for people and businesses to remit funds from one part of the country to the other, which of course was a great boon to domestic trade. Finally, as mentioned above, the Second Bank acted to stabilize the domestic economy when the business cycle or international events buffeted it.

For all those reasons, Biddle, like a general in battle, evinced, even exuded, a contagious courage that provided Philadelphia's financiers with a certain esprit de corps. Unfortunately for Chestnut Street, its opponents on Wall Street were allied with an even more courageous and formidable general, a bona fide general.

Andrew Jackson was by all accounts a fearsome creature. His courage knew no bounds. Neither did his temper. Combined, the two allowed Old Hickory to fight and win numerous duels against his personal enemies, skirmishes against the "savage" Indians, and titanic, history-changing battles against Britain's best troops. His courage and temper also allowed him to survive a gunshot wound to the chest, a shattered arm, several mutinies, and an assassination attempt. With a little help from a whispering little magical fox, they also gave him the fortitude to crush the nation's largest and most important financial institution.

Jackson entered office with an intense hatred of the Second Bank, indeed of all banks. Twice Jackson had found himself near bankruptcy, owing large debts to seemingly voracious bankers. Worse, Jackson had witnessed how the Second Bank, under the inebriated leadership of William Jones, had economically injured millions of Americans by causing, and then exacerbating, the Panic of 1819. Like any good general, Jackson bided his time, waiting for the opportune moment to demolish his enemy. Like any good politician, Jackson did not want to alienate any voters until he absolutely had to. He knew that he was immensely popular, but he knew, too, that the American electorate was fickle. One wrong wiggle and he could end up a one-term worm. The Second Bank's charter automatically ceased in 1836. For its life to continue, Jackson would have to sign a bill extending its life. Unlike previous presidents, Jackson had no qualms about using his veto powers. If reelected in 1832, he, and he alone, could squelch the "many-headed hydra." All he had to do was wait while his veto speechwriters sharpened their quill pens.[9]

Jackson explicitly warned Biddle not to make the Second Bank an election issue in the 1832 presidential campaign. Knowing that a second term for Jackson would certainly spell the end of his institution, Biddle disregarded Jackson's warning and went on the offensive. In 1832 his lobbyists pushed through Congress a bill rechartering the Second Bank: 28 to 20 in the Senate, 107 to 86 in the House. As Biddle expected, Jackson vetoed it. What Biddle did not expect was that Jackson's veto message would eloquently attack the Second Bank as a tool of evil aristocrats and leechlike financiers. It played both the monopoly card and the class card, a card rarely seen in American politics before or since. But there it was in black-and-white: Jackson accused Congress of passing legislation aimed at making "the rich richer and the potent more powerful." Appalled, Biddle called the veto message "a manifesto of anarchy." He thought it so insane that he paid to have it widely reprinted! The veto, and the veto message, became the focal point of the 1832 presidential campaign. Despite the most strenuous exertions on the part of the SBUS and its friends, Chestnut Street lost. Big-time. Voters put Jackson back in the White House and put enough of his friends in the federal legislature that there was no chance of overriding his veto, which required a two-thirds vote of both houses of Congress.

Why did Jackson win? For starters, state bankers were ambivalent about the Second Bank, as if it were a father figure in some Freudian financial epic. They disliked the Second Bank's power, but they knew that they needed its discipline. The oldest and strongest among them, the Wall Street banks, were prepared to go Oedipal on the Second Bank. So, rather ironically, many state banks campaigned for Jackson, the bank hater. They knew that as a federal official, Jackson could destroy only federally chartered banks, and there was only one of those.

Jackson's supporters knew that if put to a plebiscite, the charter of the Second Bank would have passed, probably easily. In fact, almost two hundred pro-bank memorials came into Congress, compared to only eight anti-bank memorials. So the Jacksonians attacked Biddle and his bank with every bit of vituperation that they could muster. The charge that most resonated with Americans was that the Second Bank was a "monopoly." To this day, the "M" word injures our tongues and stings our ears. In the 1830s it was truly the kiss of death, probably as powerful as the race card was in the 1990s. Like the race card, the monopoly card evoked our most primitive emotions regarding justice and fair play, or rather the lack thereof.

Moreover, the question put to the American people in 1832 was not "The

Second Bank, yea or nay?" Rather, it was "The Second Bank or Andrew Jackson?" That was a much more difficult question. Ultimately, more Americans adored the strong, earthy Jackson than admired the haughty Biddle or his Second Bank. The United States has never suffered a military coup because Americans vote their heroes into office without a shot being fired. Today that means we end up with professional wrestlers and silver-screen action heroes heading some of our most important states; a *sitting* president, festooned in a military flight jacket, landing on aircraft carriers and swooping into hostile cities for a little Thanksgiving turkey; and presidential candidates touting their stunning victories over a handful of ill-equipped ethnic insurgents. Back in the day, that meant that we ended up with bona fide military heroes in the Oval Office—men like JFK, Ike, Teddy, Grant, Harrison, Washington, and, of course, the "Old Hero" himself, Andy J.

So if Jackson said that the Second Bank was a mighty beast that shat on the Constitution and usurped the liberty of the people, and was not the beneficent central bank, the macroeconomic stabilizer and optimizer, that most people thought it was, well, then, what to do but vote Democratic? Besides, the Safety Fund looked all right, or at least less imposing. Finally, there were other reasons to keep Jackson in office, like those crazy South Carolinians who threatened secession every time the tariff went up a few (dozen) points.

With Jackson in for another four years and his ire aroused, the Second Bank was clearly doomed. Some patriots, political economists, and financiers tried to make the best of a bad situation by cajoling Jackson into backing a new central bank, a smallish one located only in Washington, D.C. "What alternative is there?" they asked rhetorically. The government couldn't trust its banking to just anyone. Some even suggested, citing the experience gained during the War of 1812, that the national treasury "could not go on for a single year without the Bank."

Enter Van Buren, Jackson's new vice president. He reminded Jackson that New York had in place a fabulous new Safety Fund. What could be safer (sounding) than that? Jackson was wary. They were still banks, after all, and he hated banks. The Second Bank was still around for four more years. That gave Jackson some time to experiment, to play around with federal deposits. In September 1833 he ordered his new treasury secretary, William Duane, to stop depositing the government's tax receipts in the Second Bank and to start placing them in state banks around the country, especially in New York. The effect of that course would be the slow removal of the government's deposits from the Second Bank as its checking account balance dwindled to zero.

Duane was no friend of the bank, but he genuinely feared that removal of the deposits would wreak havoc on the economy, particularly in "the cottage of the farmer." So he bravely refused Jackson's orders, perhaps the only man to ever do so and escape with his life. Though he did not hang Duane, Jackson promptly cashiered him, replacing him with Roger B. Taney, a puppet who would do Jackson's bidding. (Later, as Chief Justice of the U.S. Supreme Court, this same puppet would allow his slaveholding puppet masters to move the nation a step, a big step, closer to Civil War with his decision in the *Dred Scott* case.) The new depository banks—derisively known as "pet banks" in the same vein as the expression "teacher's pet"—proved equal to the task, but barely. As early as November 1833, petty squabbles among Manhattan pet banks—the Manhattan Company, the Bank of America, and the Mechanics Bank—were responsible for creating "intolerable" pressure on the Wall Street money market. Stocks plummeted as interest rates spiked upward. The Second Bank branch in New York managed to diffuse the situation quickly, but what the outcome would have been without its assistance was unclear.

Despite the awkwardness of the pet bank system, Taney decided to accelerate the process by breaking the earlier promise to slowly withdraw the government's deposits from the Second Bank. He did so by issuing sight drafts on the Second Bank to the tune of $2.3 million. Not all of the drafts were immediately presented for payment, but Biddle and the Second Bank were understandably shaken. After consulting with the board, Biddle responded the only way he could, by protecting his bank. That meant restricting bank loans and redeeming state bank notes for specie faster and more vigorously than ever. The Second Bank reduced its loans by some $5.5 million in just two months, a significant curtailment certain to have a profoundly negative effect on the national economy. If a sharp recession that would send voters scurrying to elect a pro-bank House in 1834 ensued, Biddle reasoned, so be it. Van Buren saw this coming, so he whispered instructions to the Safety Fund banks lined up along the northern border of Pennsylvania to flood the Keystone State with their notes, many of which were of small denomination and hence very costly to collect and redeem. The fox was sly, but he was no financier. His ploy failed; the economy sank into recession.

Biddle's attempt to influence the electorate also failed, however. Some voters were peeved that Biddle apparently manipulated the health of the national economy for personal gain. Perhaps Jackson had been right that the Second Bank was too powerful? Nay, responded anti-Jackson politicians and bank advocates: "King Andrew" was the power-hungry fiend upon which to cast blame. After all, Jackson had been the one who ordered the reckless yanking of $10 million out of the Second Bank. The public blinked. It was not clear whom to believe.

On top of all this, Pennsylvania exacerbated the dire economic situation by publishing a list of foreign holders of its bonds. According to one legislator, the publication "was a violation of an implied contract of secrecy, such as exists in all commercial and financial matters between parties that deal together" and "contributed to discredit our stocks." Indeed, the prices of Pennsylvania's bonds fell precipitously relative to those of New York and Ohio in the latter part of 1833. That meant that interest rates in Pennsylvania increased, the precise opposite of the correct policy response. Whether this strange policy was designed to deepen the recession, and hence the reaction against the Second Bank, I have not been able to ascertain. If it was, the effect was perverse because the recession and high interest rates severely injured Pennsylvania's banks. That allowed, in 1834, a desperate pro-SBUS faction in the state assembly to pressure Pennsylvania's banks to publish uniform balance sheets each week. The faction wanted to force the state banks to publish their decrepit financial conditions so that the public would see how shaky they were and hence how necessary the Second Bank was. Weekly publication was necessary because it was too easy to hide weaknesses when making quarterly or less frequent reports. For example, the Girard Bank frequently "improved" its balance sheet by hiring temporary short-term deposits a few days before it had to make its annual report to the legislature each November. Frequent reports made such shenanigans more difficult, if not impossible, to implement and also allowed the market to identify seasonal or "accidental" (random) fluctuations in each bank's condition.[10]

Opponents of the Second Bank, which included many of the state banks, fought against the publication of the balance sheets, calling legislative action in the matter an illegal intrusion into personal privacy, inexpedient, and "calculated to do mischief" by affecting each bank's "general credit." That was rather ironic given that the much-touted Safety Fund required such reports. The proponents of balance-sheet publication noted that "secrecy"—what we would today call individual privacy—was an important part of banking, but that any interested party should be able to access the *general* financial condition of any money-issuing corporation. They were, in short, arguing for what we today call "transparency," not the "invasion" of the privacy of individual account holders. The political machinations involving the Second Bank issue aside, the proponents of balance-sheet publication were essentially correct and eventually won the cause. More frequent publication of bank balance sheets helped market participants to determine the creditworthiness of each bank more easily and cheaply. Unfortunately, after the Second Bank left the scene, transparency was not quite enough.

By February 1834 many businesses had gone belly-up, but no banks of any significance had failed. The Second Bank had adjusted to removal of the federal deposits; its vaults brimmed with gold and silver. Biddle, fearing a political backlash if he kept the monetary noose about the nation's neck tight, ordered the branches to begin expanding loans slowly. In late March the Bank of Maryland folded, through no fault of the Second Bank. But that domino touched no others. The economy improved, just long enough to bring Van Buren into the White House. But within months of the sly magician's inauguration, a steep and prolonged economic contraction began. With a little help from Nicholas Biddle, the Panic of 1837 and its aftermath brought the nation's banking system to its knees.

After many banks suspended specie payments, most Jacksonians were completely fed up with banking. So they began a campaign to jettison the pet banks and to keep the government's deposits with the government itself, in the so-called Independent Treasury or subtreasury system. Whatever you call it, the plan was simplicity itself. Instead of depositing their receipts in a bank, tax collectors were instructed to hold on to them and pay them out when the treasury secretary ordered them to. The system was economically inefficient, but it worked at a functional level. As federal deposits drained away from many of the pet banks, Biddle saw a chance to wreak revenge on Wall Street. Without hesitation, he took it.[11]

Instead of winding up the Second Bank's affairs, Biddle decided to carry on under a Pennsylvania charter. The bank paid a high price for its new charter—$2 million in cash and promises to purchase large sums of stock of favored internal improvement companies, to establish a branch in Pennsylvania's western wilderness, and to make large low-interest loans to the state government on demand. Those concessions, which Biddle calculated were worth almost $6 million all told, were large enough to allow the state to eliminate an unpopular personal property tax enacted in 1831. Biddle considered the price tag "onerous," but he urged stockholders to accept it because the bank, rechristened the United States Bank of Pennsylvania, obtained a thirty-year charter. It maintained agents in other states, especially in the South, which desperately needed financial intermediation, but all of its branches outside of Pennsylvania had to close. Nonetheless, Biddle felt certain that the institution would return the nation's financial capital to its rightful place, Chestnut Street.

✎ Almost every great war ends with a desperate counterattack by the losing side: Waterloo; banzai and kamikaze attacks; the Battle of the Bulge; Chestnut Street's raid on Wall Street in 1839, which we might term the Bulge of the Biddle. Biddle's plan of battle was simple and indubitably devastating. Which side it would devastate, however, was an open question. Biddle's soldiers were IOUs known as "postnotes." They were simply banknotes issued by the United States Bank that could not be redeemed for specie for six months. When priced to yield 1 or 2 percent per month, investors from Boston to Baltimore gorged themselves on the notes, giving up, say, $80 worth of banknotes today in the hopes of receiving $100 in half a year.[12]

Biddle collected the banknotes, and collected them, and collected them. Meanwhile, the United States Bank also sold foreign bills of exchange for specie. Allegedly, it then shipped the specie to Europe to pay the bills. Everyone realized that that would have been a losing operation. The bank responded to the effect that the public should not look a gift horse in the mouth. Why would the bank, many wondered, be so kind to the same public that had allowed its federal charter to lapse? Something evil was afoot, and Wall Street bankers knew it. In a desperate attempt to retain adequate specie reserves, they began restricting new loans and calling in old ones. They were just in time. In late August 1839, the United States Bank sprang, redeeming $1.25 million of New York banknotes for specie in the space of just a few days. The United States Bank hoped to give the coup de grace to Wall Street's banks on the twenty-seventh by presenting, without warning, large checks near the end of the day. It had notaries standing by, ready to attest to each bank's failure to pay. That would have touched off a more general run that might have ruined Wall Street. But it was not to be.

The United States Bank exhausted its resources in the failed run. One of its European bankers, Hottinguer & Co., began to protest its bills of exchange. The United States Bank quickly applied to the Bank of England for relief but to no avail. Other requests fell on deaf ears because London bankers concluded that the bank's activities were simply "monstrous." The bank's finances unraveled quickly; it stopped payment on October 9. If the run had succeeded, Biddle would have been a hero once more, at least on Chestnut Street. But in the end, he looked quite the fool for having borrowed of everybody at 15 to 20 percent "in order to lend again at 6 percent." The following poem, which appeared in *Niles' Register* on April 24, 1841, recounts Biddle's folly:

I had a mighty hobby-horse
His name was Nicky-Noddy.
His head was made of *paper rags*—
Of cotton bales his body;
I saddled him, and bridled him,
And drove him to Gotham town,
There came a "breeze" from *Hottinguer's*
And blew my hobby down!

Technically, the United States Bank clung to its corporate life until February 4, 1841. It was clear to all, however, that the threat it posed to Wall Street died in the autumn of 1839. By the end of that year, Wall Street stood in uncontested control of the nation's financial system. One indication of that fact was that the *New York Herald* took considerable pains—and precious space—to rip on Philadelphia's financiers. It called Episcopalian lawyer Thomas Dunlap a "man with no great deal of capacity." Cheyney Hickman, it chided, "never goes to any church, but often to the exchange." The former currier and leather dealer, the *Herald* asserted, had "the most unmeaning countenance that ever was created by the Almighty." Lutheran Dutchman John Bohlen the paper labeled "a shrewd, cunning man." John A. Brown, the eldest son of Alexander Brown of international investment banking fame, was "industrious to a fault." Quaker Caleb Cope, nephew of Thomas P. Cope, was "too venturous in business [and] apt to trade beyond his means," the New York paper opined. Richard Alsop, an Episcopalian who "made a great deal of money in the South American and Canton trade," was also "very apt to go beyond what prudence would dictate."

And the *Herald* was just getting warmed up. Matthew Newkirk, it snidely remarked, "came a poor boy from New Jersey." "It is very doubtful," the paper asserted, "if he is as wealthy as imagined." Former Pennsylvania governor John Andrew Schultz the *Herald* called "a mild, amiable man, with little or no capacity" and a thick "German accent." He attained election to the board of the Pennsylvania Bank only "to propitiate the German interest in Pennsylvania." The *Herald* called the son of Richard B. Jones of Merion Township "a gay boy," though admittedly it may not have meant that in the modern sense, especially given that it went out of its way to note that the boy's father was "fond of beautiful women." John Kirkbridge was a Quaker, but, according to the paper, he had "very little to say." He was "hardly known even in his own neighborhood," it claimed. George Sheaff was "of exceedingly moderate capacity," the paper intimated, even for an old German Lutheran.

To be fair, the *Herald* spoke highly of Philadelphia financiers Richard Price, Ambrose White, and Manuel Eyre. But the unprecedented attack on the rest of the Chestnut Street establishment heralded, if you will excuse the pun, the new era. And in the new era, New York grew ever stronger. The Civil War gave it another boost, as did the great industrial merger movement of the 1890s. By 1910 its three major exchanges handled over 90 percent of the trading in stocks and bonds. Philadelphia in that year had a market share of just over 5 percent.[13]

The ultimate fate of the Second Bank, ignominious failure, further cemented Wall Street's new position atop the nation's financial system. The strain of the concessions, risky cotton deals that turned sour, the deepening recession that gripped the national economy, and the failed counterattack on Wall Street had plunged it into bankruptcy. Biddle was largely to blame; without board approval, he directed some $16 million into risky cotton speculations and the ill-fated run was largely his idea. When Biddle died in February 1844, aged just fifty-eight years, his longtime friend Thomas P. Cope wrote in his diary: "Gen. Jackson excepted, no man known to me has inflicted so deep a wound on the credit & character of the country." Cope was right, but luckily neither man lethally wounded the financial system or the economy, both of which staggered to their feet in the mid-1840s, stronger than ever. Fittingly, that was far too late to save Van Buren's aspirations for a second term.[14]

~11

LEGACY OF GROWTH

Doomsayers had claimed that if Philadelphia lost the race to the Great Lakes, it would "dwindle into a small town," the melancholy fate that had earlier befallen Annapolis, Maryland; Gloucester, Massachusetts; and Perth Amboy, New Jersey. The Quaker City did lose the race, causing her importance as an international port to shrink from 20 percent of U.S. imports (by value) in the 1790s to a mere 5.5 percent by the 1850s. Soon after the completion of the Delaware and Raritan Canal in 1834, it simply became cheaper for Philadelphia wholesalers to import foreign goods via Manhattan.[1]

Unlike other commercial "has-beens," however, Philadelphia thrived rather than shriveled. It did so by industrializing, by transforming itself from an American London into "the Manchester of America." One moving force behind that profound transition was Chestnut Street, which remained the center of Philadelphia's financial district as well as its most "fashionable" street. Its hotels, like the Girard House, still attracted Europe's well-heeled tourists. Its rows of mature trees, fancy shops, and handsome buildings still drew Philadelphia's finest for their daily "promenade." Most importantly for our story here, Chestnut Street's financial institutions still attracted both buyers and sellers of IOUs. Despite its demise as the nation's financial leader, Chestnut Street still existed and was large and smart enough to finance good projects.

Thanks to Philly's numerous artisans, engineers, and mechanics, there were plenty of good, cash-hungry industrial projects for Chestnut Street to nurture. According to British traveler Henry Fearon, Philadelphia was still the "best poor man's country." Philadelphia's skilled artisans and semi-skilled mechanics, he argued, "receive higher wages, and are more independent of their masters, [and] live better . . . than men following like occupations in England." Philadelphia still had its freedom, too: "Men are here independent of each other," Fearon wrote, noting that "this will show itself even in an hour's walk through the streets of Philadelphia."[2]

In short, Philadelphia's legendary freedom and finance were still abundant. The only difference was that after the death of the Second Bank, both turned inward. Intense focus on the regional economy, rather than international trade, drove Philadelphia's growth in the antebellum period, the decades leading up to the Civil War. This chapter describes how Chestnut Street financed the Delaware Valley's miraculous transformation from export-oriented agriculture and import-oriented commerce to domestically oriented agriculture and industry. 'Tis a fascinating tale, with Chestnut Street smack-dab in the midst of the action.

✐ The fact that Chestnut Street played an important role in industrialization will probably come as a surprise to readers who have elsewhere encountered nineteenth-century Philadelphia or the U.S. industrial revolution more generally. For reasons too complex and sordid to discuss here, historians of industrialization have generally avoided the issue of external finance, the sale of IOUs by businesses. It turns out that most firms sold significant amounts of IOUs to finance their activities. Corporate finance is the easiest to document; it might have been the most important type of business finance.[3]

It is a fact that most early Philadelphia businesses were unincorporated. But the same holds true today. When we think of businesses today, we tend to think first about big corporations and largely forget about all the little guys (and gals). There is good reason for this—though far fewer in number than proprietorships and partnerships, corporations today create most of our economic output. Was the same true in antebellum Philadelphia? In some sectors, yes, early corporations did dominate.[4]

Early Pennsylvania was home to a large number of business corporations, over six hundred by 1837, in fact. The vast bulk of those corporations were banks, bridges, canals, coal mines, insurers, manufacturers, railroads, and turnpikes, but a few corporate theaters, ice houses, and for-profit libraries also existed. Most of those corporations were located in eastern Pennsylvania; almost all relied on Philadelphia investors for at least a part of their capital. After 1837 the pace of incorporation quickened statewide. By the Civil War, Pennsylvania had incorporated 2,320 companies. Even distant enterprises headquartered in Pittsburgh sought capital investment from Chestnut Street.

Corporate finance took three primary forms: equity, negotiable debt, and bank debt. Equity simply meant ownership and was represented by shares. Save for a handful of mutuals, like savings banks, Pennsylvania corporations raised their initial capital by selling shares of themselves in initial public offerings (IPOs). Early on, the process consisted of little more than advertising the sale, opening subscription books, and taking down names and collecting down payments. (Subscribers generally paid for their shares over time, as the corporation needed cash.) Later, as the number of corporations swelled, some companies found it difficult to sell themselves like that on their own. Increasingly, specialized intermediaries known as investment banks facilitated IPOs by widely advertising the shares and by placing their imprimatur, their stamp of approval, on the offering. By the Civil War, Pennsylvania corporations raised approximately $500 million via IPOs.

It should come as little surprise to readers to learn that Chestnut Street was home to America's first investment bankers, who emerged during the War of 1812 to help sell U.S. government bonds. Those investment bankers later turned their expertise to the corporate securities market. In addition to helping to facilitate sales of equity, investment bankers became increasingly important in the placement of corporate bonds, long-term IOUs that made fixed interest payments until the principal came due ten, twenty, even thirty years hence. Corporate managers liked to sell bonds because any profits earned above and beyond the interest payment, which was usually 5 or 6 percent of the nominal sum borrowed, accrued to the corporation. That made them look good. Moreover, bondholders, unlike stockholders, had very little say in management so long as the interest payments on their bonds were made punctually. In the period under study, Pennsylvania corporations raised about $500 million from the sale of long-term negotiable bonds.[5]

Railroads were especially large issuers of corporate bonds. But Pennsylvania's canal companies also borrowed on bond, as did the occasional large manufacturing concern. The latter often found it more convenient to borrow by mortgaging their premises and equipment. Railroads took the mortgage concept a step further by developing, with the help of Chestnut Street financial alchemists, the mortgage bond. Like conventional mortgages, mortgage bonds pledged specific physical property to the lender in the case of default. Unlike conventional mortgages, mortgage bonds were easily negotiable, that is, salable to other investors via the secondary securities market.

Philadelphia's stock exchange was a fairly insignificant institution until the 1830s and not terribly important thereafter. It is important to note, however, that the exchange was but a small part of Philadelphia's securities *market,* which by 1830 boasted over a hundred different regularly traded securities. Investors could buy or sell corporate equities or bonds (government bonds too) on the exchange or in the broader market. All told, the volume of trading was impressive by nineteenth-century standards. Transactions costs (brokerage fees, bid-ask spreads, etc.) were low, generally less than 1 percent for brokered orders, and prices were competitive with those available elsewhere. Assured that they could easily and inexpensively sell should the need arise, and as we learn below generally protected by limited liability, investors had no problem buying up corporate securities.

The investing "class," as it were, was geographically and occupationally diverse. In addition to institutional investors like savings banks and charitable organizations, large-scale capitalists, and powerful merchants and manufacturers, many an attorney, doctor, and substantial farmer owned corporate securities. Widows from the middling sorts on up usually owned portfolios of securities, and even artisans, grocers, and other retailers were known to enjoy investment portfolios (though relatively modest ones). Not everyone was a shareholder or a bondholder, but as the century progressed, increasing numbers owned a stake in American big business, if only indirectly through their savings account or life insurance policy.

For shorter-term loans, corporations usually obtained bank loans. Banks liked to lend to corporations because they were relatively safe and because they usually borrowed big chunks of cash. Bankers realized that it was cheaper to lend $10,000 to a corporation than to lend $100 to a hundred small businesses. The volume of corporate borrowing from banks is not known with any degree of precision. Extant bank records suggest that corporations used banks mostly to safe-keep cash. Then as now, corporate treasurers deposited cash receipts into banks, drawing on those deposits with checks as necessary. Unlike smaller firms, corporations often found it possible to obtain an automatic line of credit with their respective banks. Only in the case of a temporary shortfall did they borrow. The relative dearth of corporate bank borrowing explains why creditworthy small businesses still found it to possible to borrow from banks.

⟲ Hitherto, those few business historians who have taken the trouble to think about business finance have paid far too much attention to commercial banks and stock exchanges. They can hardly be blamed; those two institutions were by far the "sexiest" and most controversial financial institutions in antebellum America. But they were not the most important, at least not in Philadelphia. The money market, where short-term business IOUs traded, was far more important. Yet it is also the least-studied early financial market. Why? For starters, many money market transactions were technically illegal because of the high interest rates that lenders often extracted from borrowers. Despite that fact, the markets were politically uncontroversial. Oh, occasionally a politician would rail against "usurers" and declaim against "grinding the faces of the poor." But politicians knew that they could not have stomped out the money market even if they had wanted to. It was populated by numerous small, unchartered, nimble firms. Moreover, most politicians were attorneys, and many of the firms that lent in the money market either hired attorneys or *were* attorneys. In short, politicians were not about to try to eradicate the money market, and participants in the market had good reasons to leave only ambiguous records of their activities. It therefore took years of tedious archival research to tease out the outlines of the early money market. It was well worth the effort, though. Here is the skinny.

When Philadelphia businesspeople needed cash, they would first troll the city, searching out their debtors in the hopes for collecting some or all of their outstanding debts, their accounts receivable. In early August 1808, for instance, four dry-goods merchants appeared in the shop of Philadelphia tailors Wilkins and Atkinson. The artisans paid "cash on account," that is, made partial payments of outstanding balances, to three of the merchants and paid off all of a trifling debt of just shy of £2 owed to William Biddle. But not all debtors were as obliging as Wilkins and Atkinson. In fact, most were not! Account books reveal that it usually took customers anywhere from a year to eighteen months to pay off their tabs. Collection duty, then as now, was often a frustrating, unfruitful affair.[6]

The next stop for cash-hungry firms was usually one or more banks. The "established course" of the coal companies, for example, was to "draw at long periods for the full value of all the coal they ship as fast as it is shipped from Pottsville," then to discount the drafts at "one or other of the banks." Generally, banks offered the best interest rates in town. That was the good news. The bad news was that everybody hoped to get a nice, cheap bank loan. That meant that everybody applied. So the banks had the pick of the litter. If your credit was good, or you could post stocks and bonds as collateral, you might get lucky. If both you and your credit were poor, well, there was always a snowball's chance somebody might blink.[7]

If collections and bank applications failed, the third stop was the money market. There, loans were rationed on price rather than on quality. That meant that just about anyone could sell his IOUs, for a price roughly representing both the rental price of the money and the risk that the principal would not be repaid. Many contemporaries deprecated money market lenders as "note shavers" because they might pay, say, $85 for an IOU with a face value of $100 payable in six months. Such lending was so lucrative that at least one immigrant advice book suggested it as a viable way for newcomers to create a competence. The author claimed that note shaving was of "little general utility," but in fact the shavers performed important financial intermediation services.

The same could be said of pawnbrokers, the fourth and final stop for the truly desperate businessperson. Regardless of one's credit history, the pawnbroker would lend, albeit at high rates, on the security of physical goods like fine clothing, watches, jewelry, or other easily salable luxury items.

Most of the time, though, Philadelphia's numerous small entrepreneurs enjoyed credit good enough to use the money market to smooth their cash flows. They often used evidence of accounts receivable as collateral for the short-term loans. Until the 1850s, for instance, people who deposited specie at the U.S. Mint had to wait up to several months for their coin. Understandably, many found the wait inconvenient. Depositors therefore often sold their Mint receipts at a discount to lenders who gave them "prompt payment" in exchange for ownership of the claim against the Mint. Other evidence of accounts receivable could also be sold to money market brokers for immediate cash. If a businessperson had no accounts receivable, or at least none that could be assigned to others, he could always sign a promissory note, the nineteenth-century equivalent of a credit card loan.

To decrease the discount (interest charge), issuers of IOUs (borrowers) often sought cosigners or guarantors of the note, usually individuals or firms of high credit standing. Sometimes the guarantors provided their guarantees gratis; sometimes they sought a fee. Borrowers paid the fee if the guarantee reduced the interest charge by an amount greater than the fee, which in the 1830s generally stood at about 2.5 percent of the IOU. Borrowers also obtained guarantees by hypothecating securities (pledging assets), including life insurance policies and real estate, for repayment of the debt.[8]

Small brokers dominated the money market. As the following letter from 1790 suggests, the brokers were quite efficient at what they did, linking buyers to sellers of IOUs:

I shall send Potter up from Elkton with £750 currency to invest in bills. I don't wish you to run about Town in this business. The Brokers understand the matter & I will gladly pay their charge.[9]

Politicians couldn't have stopped such activity even if they had wanted to.

⤳ Most early Philadelphia firms were *not* corporations because most were not large enough to make incorporation necessary. Artisanal shops, professional offices, and even small manufacturers did not need to incur the costs of incorporating, which could be substantial. In short, most firms did not have to grow very large in order to reach a profitable scale. Good patent laws were a big help here. The ability to assign patent rights kept entry costs into manufacturing relatively low because it allowed investors to purchase the right to manufacture, use, and sell new inventions. The inventions of even the poorest, least entrepreneurial could therefore still find their way to market. William Woodworth's planing machine, perhaps the most important labor-saving invention of the early nineteenth century, proliferated in this way. Philadelphians Martha Inslee, Joseph Inslee, George McClelland, and Tobias Huber—four businesspeople of relatively modest means—purchased rights to the planing machine for $6,000, $2,000 of which they borrowed by mortgaging some of Martha's real property. The foursome then leased a building and a steam engine, purchased a supply of lumber, and began churning out floorboards for the City of Homes![10]

Some industries, however, required a certain amount of scale to be profitable. Chemical producers, for instance, were much more profitable when they could churn out huge volumes of one chemical rather than small batches of many different ones. In such industries, larger firms were more efficient, and large firms generally found incorporation worthwhile. The corporate form came with certain rights and privileges that made it easier to obtain external financing. Moreover, after a business attained a certain size, it became easier (though not easy) to govern as a corporation. A few companies became joint-stock companies but did not formally incorporate. The Society for Promoting the Manufacture of Sugar from the Sugar Maple Tree, for example, did not see fit to obtain a charter. Nevertheless, it issued shares via an IPO just like a corporation would. Similarly, the African Insurance Company never incorporated. Then again, its capital stock amounted to only $5,000. It disappeared after just a few years in business, possibly due to doubts about stockholder liability and possibly due to legal pressures.[11]

In some sectors, like financial intermediation, the corporate form was both legally necessary and economically superior to partnership. In other sectors, like commerce, incorporation was usually not the best call. In coal mining and textile production, the corporate form held advantages and disadvantages that left room for the continuance of sole proprietors and partnerships in some niches. In yet other businesses, including iron production and manufacturing, proprietors thought incorporation would have been propitious but did not bother to seek a charter because they believed that "applications for them would not be very favorably received by the legislature."[12]

The iron makers thought incorporation salubrious because it would have helped them to obtain relatively cheap equity financing. In America limited liability was the default. All corporate shareholders enjoyed it unless the corporate charter expressly stated otherwise. Evidence of that fact abounds. In 1792 James Sullivan noted that corporate creditors enjoyed "no remedy" against the "private estates" of stockholders. "This is an agreed point," he argued, "for the shares being transferable in their nature, it is *quite impossible to know who the proprietors are.*" Similarly, the first stockholders of the ICNA sought incorporation to ensure that their liability was limited. In 1842 a bill introduced into the state legislature would have made stockholders personally liable for all corporate debts, but it failed to pass.[13]

Limited liability essentially pushed the risk of corporate bankruptcy away from stockholders and onto other types of creditors, including bondholders and banks. Corporations in dire straits had to rely on the credit of their directors in their individual capacities in order to sell their IOUs. In other words, in order to obtain loans, the corporation's directors had to effectively cede their limited liability. But most of the time, creditors were unconcerned about stockholders' limited liability because they simply based their lending judgments on the corporation's balance sheet and cashflow projections.

All in all, limited liability increased the overall amount that investors would lend to corporations because it accorded with human nature, plain and simple. People don't mind taking a calculated risk, even big risks, with portions of their wealth. Consider, for example, the popularity of lottery schemes in Pennsylvania, then and now. What people hate is the possibility, however remote, of losing their all. So while most people will spend a buck, or a hundred, for an almost infinitesimal chance to win millions, most will not accept a dollar, or even a hundred, to face an infinitesimal chance of losing all of their wealth. By eliminating the latter possibility, limited liability made the purchase of corporate equity that much more attractive.[14]

Unfortunately, limited liability also impacted corporate governance, and largely negatively. Corporate governance was directly tied to a business's performance and early Americans knew it. By the 1830s, if not earlier, it was well understood that "a proprietor who resides on the spot, who sees with his own eyes, and makes his own bargains, must do business cheaper than a corporation which acts by Agents." Many people also realized, though, that given the proper incentives, agents or employees would work just as hard on behalf of stockholders as they would on their own private account. "Talent and integrity should be secured and paid for accordingly," one early pundit explained. In exchange for those payments, though, employees, particularly officers, had to bear in mind that their duties had to be performed "with a view to remunerate the stockholders annually for their investments, leaving all personal feeling or private money making considerations, by virtue of his position, aside."[15]

Though the underlying principals were clear, actual governance of a corporation was not an easy task. Holding size constant, however, it was certainly easier than governing an unincorporated business. For starters, a corporation was a single legal entity that could sue or be sued in its own name, alone. Corporations therefore enjoyed cheaper access to the court system than partnerships did. Moreover, corporations were bound by law to engage in certain activities and forbidden, again by force of law, from engaging in others. That limited the possibility of malfeasance by restricting the company to certain very specific activities. Unincorporated businesses could engage in any lawful practice, making it that much easier for active partners to swindle passive ones.

Corporate charters contained numerous provisions designed to reduce the likelihood of fraud by employees, officers, or directors. Like political charters or constitutions, they were chock-full of "checks and balances." First and foremost, stockholders had the right to vote for directors, to whom they delegated only limited powers, retaining for themselves the right to vote upon major policy decisions. Generally, shareholders could vote in person or by proxy, though some early charters stipulated that all votes had to be cast in person. In some companies, each share entitled a stockholder to one vote. In other companies, voting rights were capped. Stockholders in the Union Canal Company, for example, could cast one vote per share, but only up to twenty shares. Many companies imposed complex voting rules, some with caps, others without. For instance, the state charter of the United States Bank stipulated:

> The number of votes to which each stockholder shall be entitled in voting for directors shall be as follows: for one share and not more than two

shares, one vote; for every two shares above two and not exceeding ten shares, one vote; for every four shares above ten and not exceeding thirty, one vote; for every six shares above thirty, and not exceeding sixty, one vote; for every eight shares above sixty, and not exceeding one hundred, one vote; but no person, copartnership, or body politic, shall be entitled to a greater number than thirty votes.

Such rules were designed to prevent individuals or small cabals from seizing control of the company's assets. Stockholders served as election officials to ensure that company elections fairly represented their collective decisions.

Most early charters also rotated directors or imposed term limitations on all directors except the president. To prevent conflicts of interest, directors were usually forbidden from holding directorships in competing companies. The Union Canal Company went so far as to bar its president from engaging in "any kind of manufacturing, mercantile, or speculative concerns." It also forbade any director from owning "any real estate on the route of the Canal, previous to the same being fixed and declared, exceeding the value of one thousand dollars." Directors were also forbidden to "be directly or indirectly concerned" in any of the company's construction or maintenance contracts. The fear, of course, was that directors would try to enrich themselves by routing the canal near or through their personal lands or by steering lucrative contracts to themselves or their cronies. For similar reasons, elected officials and judges were generally not eligible for election to corporate directorships.[16]

Directors met periodically to pass decisions on routine business policies. Charters almost invariably noted the number necessary to form a quorum during such board meetings. That was to prevent a small group of directors from making important decisions. For a similar reason, the overall number of directors was also important. If too few, they could more easily form into what railroad industry analyst F. H. Stow ominously called "a clique." If too numerous, decision making often bogged down.[17]

Many corporate charters also stipulated the type of assets that each company could own. The goal here was also to prevent fraud. Banks, for instance, were not supposed to engage in real estate, commodities, or equity market speculations and hence were limited to owning "bills of exchange, gold and silver bullion," and bonds, except where other assets were seized as collateral for unpaid debts. Similarly, many early corporate charters held directors personally liable for material breaches of the charter. For example, if the liabilities of the state-chartered United States Bank exceeded twice its capital stock,

the directors under whose administration it shall happen, shall be liable
in their individual capacities, and an action of debt may in such case be
brought against them, or any of them, or any of their heirs, executors or
administrators, in any court having competent jurisdiction, by any creditor or creditors of such corporation.[18]

To ensure that directors did not exaggerate their company's profitability,
most charters prohibited them from paying unwarranted dividends. To
judge a company's worth, therefore, one need only look at its recent dividend history. No EBITDA (earnings before interest, taxes, depreciation,
and amortization) or other arcane measures of profitability then!

Each company president received a salary "allowed by the stockholders
at a general meeting." Other directors generally received no direct remu-
neration. High dividends and a high stock price would be their reward. Directors negotiated salaries and performance bonds with each officer. The
performance or surety bonding of employees and officers was ubiquitous,
but varied in amount from company to company and position to position,
depending on the magnitude of possible fraud. The Union Canal Company,
for example, made its treasurer secure a bond for $30,000, conditioned on
the treasurer's "faithful performance of the duties enjoined upon him."
That large sum was necessary because the treasurer's job was to "receive all
the monies belonging to the said company." To further safeguard itself, the
Union Canal Company, like most early nonbank corporations, forced its
treasurer to deposit company receipts "in any of the incorporated banks,"
where cash would be both physically safer and less susceptible to moral hazard because only the company's president *and* secretary could make withdrawals, and even then only by check and with the consent of the board.

Directors and officers were responsible to the stockholders and had to
provide them with corporate records at scheduled annual meetings as well
as at any stockholder-called emergency meetings. Moreover, charter provisions were not the only bar to fraud. Corporations also created by-laws,
specific rules and procedures designed to align the interests of stockholders, employees, officers, directors, and liability holders. As a final check,
many corporations periodically had to submit their balance sheets to the
state and, if required, to submit to legislative investigations into their operations. That was rarely necessary because early stockholders, who were
rather more active than twentieth-century stockholders, were more than
happy to conduct such investigations themselves. For example, when the
stockholders of the Philadelphia & Reading Railroad worried that the company had taken on too much debt, they hired independent consultants to

examine the company's assets and liabilities and to make suggestions about how to put the company on a more secure financial basis. The consultants, who of course hailed from Boston, suggested reducing the railroad's "floating debt" by offering bondholders a debt-to-equity conversion deal. The managers concurred and successfully paid off $1.1 million of debt with new stock certificates. "Larger business and higher prices" further ameliorated the company's situation.

Not all shareholders monitored their investments so closely, however. According to one critic, George Taylor, stockholders in coal companies were invariably either speculators ("day traders," in modern parlance) or capitalists investing their "small surplus funds." Neither group had the incentive to monitor operations a hundred miles away. The result was a relatively inefficient and unprofitable industry.[19]

Coal companies oft displayed "a large quantity of coal," claimed it was only the first of many such shipments, threw around some numbers, and published a circular, all with an eye toward puffing the stock "to par or higher, and then put off upon ignorant or unwary capitalists" who soon learned that they bought "a losing concern overwhelmed with debt." The price plummeted until the "stock-jobbers buy in again; then comes another grand display of coal works" and a continuance of the cycle *"ad infinitum."* Taylor went so far as to argue that the coal companies were really in the business of manipulating stock prices and that they cared not a whit whether the coal sales made a profit or not. Published stock prices indeed show that shares of the North American Coal and the Lehigh Coal and Navigation Company were volatile and cyclical. An episode in winter 1827 when Lehigh stock soared from $47 to $103, only to abruptly plummet to the $50 range in late spring, fits the pattern Taylor described. As figure 11.1 shows, later swings were less marked and part of a long trend to the upside. The big drop in the late 1830s was, of course, directly attributable to the economy-wide recession.

Likely, Taylor exaggerated. But the coal companies did suffer from a fundamental error in business judgment. They erroneously believed that to be successful they had to be highly vertically integrated, owning every step of production and distribution from "owning lands, working the Mines, owning and navigating boats, and ships, and owning wharves, and yards, at the place of consumption: and even owning retail carts and following the Coal into the cellar of the consumer." Under such a system, however, human capital and monitoring costs were simply too high. Indeed, the coal trade in England was carried on by five distinct types of companies, one that owned the coal lands, a second that mined the coal, a third that purchased the coal,

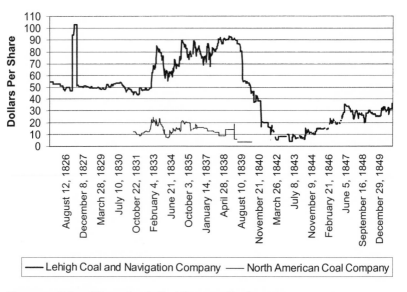

Figure 11.1: Price of Pennsylvania Coal Company Stocks, 1827–50
Source: Richard Sylla, Jack Wilson, and Robert E. Wright, "Database of Early U.S. Securities Prices," ICPSR, Ann Arbor, Michigan.

a fourth that shipped it to a major port, and a fifth that purchased it and exported it abroad. "It would be just as reasonable," argued Taylor, "for a manufacturer of cotton goods to say it was necessary for him to own cotton lands, raise his own cotton, own wharves, and ships to export his goods; and retail stores to retail them." Moreover, noted Taylor, "besides the impossibility of one person superintending establishments hundreds of miles apart; no one possesses the requisite skill, experience, and turn of character necessary, properly to direct and controul [sic] so many dissimilar pursuits."

ᴐ Despite their shortcomings, the coal companies did deliver considerable quantities of coal to Philadelphia. Those black rocks (and as late as the 1850s, wood) heated the City of Homes. Coal also fueled the steam engines that ran the railroads and steamships that, in turn, lowered transportation costs. Coal-powered steam engines—179 were in place by 1838—increased the efficiency of industries ranging from Chestnut Street's U.S. Mint to the chemical factories of the Northern Liberties. True, Manayunk's textile mills used water power. The canalization of the Schuylkill River made it so easy to tap the river's power to drive turbines that by 1832 fourteen factories lined the mill race. But most of the city's textile mills were not located along the river and hence also utilized steam engines.[20]

The people living in those homes and working in those industries needed more than just coal to keep them going. They also needed food and drink. The farmers in the countryside surrounding Philadelphia were more than happy to oblige. They provided the city slickers with fresh milk, eggs, butter, fruit, vegetables, fattened livestock, and bread flour. They also served up oats and hay for the city's many horses. Much of the money the farmers earned went right back to Philadelphia for cloth, farming implements, food utensils, and a host of other manufactured goods.

That immense flow of regional trade—some $16 million annually by the late 1830s—was made easier, and cheaper, by the turnpikes, bridges, canals, railroads, and other internal improvements that Chestnut Street had helped finance in the first decades of the nineteenth century and continued to fund through the antebellum period. The coal came in by rail and canal. Livestock came in "on the hoof." Less mobile farm products, like apples and tomatoes, came to market via the turnpikes on mammoth Conestoga wagons. Perishables—like milk, butter, and cheese—rushed in on smaller wagons. Manufactured goods went out by rail, canal, or turnpike, depending on their destination and their weight-to-value. Everything, except the livestock, traversed the region's many fine stone bridges.[21]

The manufacturing boom pushed Philadelphia's population ever higher, ever faster, up a whopping 58 percent over the 1840s, compared to the approximately 33 percent growth the city had experienced each decade in the 1810s, '20s, and '30s. Why the dramatically increased rate of growth? The city's manufacturers needed "hands" to run looms, to stoke steam engines, to pack and ship finished products, and to do innumerable other semiskilled and unskilled tasks. Importantly, thanks to Chestnut Street institutions, the manufacturers usually had the cash needed to pay those workers their fair due. The workers, in turn, had funds to buy food from the region's farmers and even to purchase manufactured goods themselves. As we've seen, many also earned enough to purchase or at least lease their own homes.

So while some of those newcomers were babies born to Philadelphians, most were adults. Some were immigrants from other states or foreign lands, but New York's increasingly dominant role in international trade gave her the lion's share of the latter. Most of Philly's new denizens were regional laborers whose exertions were no longer needed on the farm. The reason? Farms had become much more productive. Thanks to Chestnut Street and local banks, farmers could obtain the loans they needed to invest in fences, fertilizers, super seeds, stud fees, and other agricultural productivity boosters. Burgeoning demand from Philadelphia ensured that the farmers were able to sell the additional apples, cucumbers, and eggs that they were producing at a price good enough to allow them to repay their loans and also to compensate themselves for their added exertions.

Chestnut Street also ensured that the productivity of factory workers continued ever upward. By 1840 output per worker in Philadelphia averaged $1,044. The nationwide average was only $707. Part of the reason for the higher productivity of Philadelphia's workers was that the average capital employed per worker in the Quaker City was $668 versus the national average of $561. In 1840 Philadelphia's tanneries, distilleries, breweries, and potteries produced more hides, shots, beers, and pots than the national average. Overall, Philadelphia produced $86.47 of manufactured goods per capita, compared to only $20.97 nationally, $58.81 in New York, and $51.96 in Boston.

Output per worker soared because factory owners could borrow to procure additional machinery, to reorganize assembly stations, and to purchase raw materials en masse. That was not all. Once the extra goods began streaming out of the factory, the owners could borrow to advertise their products more widely and to extend credit to wholesalers or commissioned salespeople. The textile, publishing, chemical, and machine industries, as well as a number of smaller industries like chocolate factories, all boomed. Indeed, until the 1850s Philadelphia produced more textiles, by value, than New England's larger, more famous mills. By the 1850s Philadelphia factories churned out more sulfuric, nitric, and muriatic acids than any other city in the world. They also produced more medicinal chemicals than anywhere else, supplying almost all U.S. demand and eventually even much of the demand of Europe. Meanwhile, many of Philadelphia's earlier industries took advantage of the region's extensive and inexpensive transportation system to shift production to more rural, lower-cost areas throughout the Delaware Valley. Soap, glass, and papermakers, brewers and distillers, millers, brick makers, potters, and lime producers, for instance, migrated out of the city to the hinterland. It was the economically efficient thing to do, so the good firms that migrated had no problem obtaining financing for the move from Chestnut Street. By the Civil War, the Delaware Valley from Wilmington to Trenton was one long strip of factories, while mills, shops, forges, and other manufactories filled in the less arable plots throughout the region. Philadelphia's productivity played no small part in the eventual outcome of that titanic contest. In turn, the war spurred the further industrialization of the region.[22]

The transformation of the publishing industry in the first half of the nineteenth century is a good case study of Philadelphia's industrialization.

In 1800 the Quaker City's publishers were all tiny businesses, little more than printers really. A few journeymen and apprentices under the direction of a master printer, and perhaps a proprietor or two, carried out day-to-day activities that Benjamin Franklin would have easily recognized. By 1850 Franklin would hardly have recognized his former occupation. For starters, the size of the industry exploded. The number of titles published jumped 82 percent in the 1790s; the number of titles and volumes produced ascended ever upward in subsequent decades.[23]

Secondly, specialization sliced and diced the industry into numerous niches. Most importantly, the physical printing of books and book publishing—vetting and editing manuscripts and marketing finished books—divorced. Increasingly, publishers did not even sell their own books. Retail booksellers, from rural peddlers with carts to large urban bookstores, sprang up to serve that specialized function. Moreover, publishers began to specialize in the types of books they published. Some stuck with the Bible, sermons, and other religious works, perennial favorites in the early nineteenth century. Others published poetry or plays or novels. Some found almanacs and schoolbooks profitable. Printers and bookbinders also specialized, some crafting handsome, hand-sewn volumes flawlessly printed in elegant typeface. Others made cheaply typeset, glued books. Some printers churned out broadsides, newspapers, or tiny pamphlets that required no binding whatsoever.

Regardless of their niche, Philadelphia firms involved in the book trade found Chestnut Street's assistance of crucial importance. Like the building industry, Philadelphia's publishing industry was extremely competitive. In that environment, firms churned out low-cost products or they went bankrupt. Achieving low cost often meant producing in volume, forgive the pun. To make books in large quantities required publishers to pony up significant sums up front. They had to pay advances to authors, salaries to editors, and per book fees to printers. To fund book projects, early publishers tried to sell the books before they were written. The tactic sometimes worked but often it did not as book buyers feared that they would pay today for nothing tomorrow. The next step was to get people to promise to buy a book when it appeared. That worked better but threw the risk onto the publisher—not all of those who agreed to buy a book would actually do so. And, of course, those promises could not be used to pay start-up costs without some form of financing. At best, subscriptions gave authors, publishers, and financiers some idea how much demand for a particular book existed.

To spread risks and obtain some financing, early Philadelphia publishers sold shares of books to investors, usually other publishers. But the industry's intense competition made such risk and capital sharing difficult to sustain. Printer-bookseller William McCullough spelled this out in a depressing but eerily accurate little ditty:

> There is no faith in man's obdurate heart.
> It does not feel for man.
> The nat'ral bond.
> Of brotherhood sever'd.[24]

Where mutual assistance failed, Chestnut Street succeeded. Increasingly, large publishers like Mathew Carey borrowed frequently from the city's banks. Smaller players occasionally received bank loans but met most of their short-term borrowing needs in the money market and by borrowing from the big suppliers or retailers who could obtain bank loans. Longer-term capital came from inheritances and retained earnings (profits from previous years of business) but also from the sale of mortgages and bonds. Few publishers were yet incorporated, but all found easy access to inexpensive external finance necessary to maintain competitiveness. Loans gave publishers the edge they needed to publish more copies, to lower per unit costs, and to penetrate distant markets.

The situation in most of Philadelphia's other emerging industries was similar. Competition reigned supreme. Any edge that a firm could get, it had to take to stay alive. That spelled efficiency and a drive for constant improvement. Complacency in business was no longer an option, not in the City of Brotherly Love anyway.

Greased with Chestnut Street's loans, Philadelphia and the Delaware Valley in the 1830s entered a virtuous cycle of economic growth, population increase, productivity increase, and yet more economic growth. The cycle had many dimensions. Higher growth attracted emigrants. Those new folks increased the supply of the goods that they produced and simultaneously increased demand for the many goods that they consumed. They also bid up asset prices, particularly real estate values. That gave entrepreneurs more collateral on which to borrow, which, in turn, allowed them to undertake additional profitable projects. That meant higher growth and yet another spin of the cycle. So far from disintegrating into a Perth Amboy, Philadelphia continued to grow despite the loss of its international trade and its perch atop the financial system. Not until well into the twentieth century did the city's decline begin.

⌒○ A charitable interpretation, too charitable in my estimation, of Philadelphia's nineteenth-century economic history would argue that Philadelphians saw that the industrial revolution, and not finance and commerce, was the key to future economic growth. They also realized that nearby energy sources—coal deposits and the canalized Schuylkill River—provided them with a comparative, or perhaps even an absolute, advantage over most other regions in the United States when it came to making things. So they gave up Chestnut Street and Port Deposit to industrialize Manayunk, Frankford, and Trenton. (A bridge in Trenton long proclaimed, in ten-foot-high lights: "TR NTON MAKES, THE WO LD TA ES." Apparently, the city didn't have the funds to fix the missing *e, r,* or *k.*) While true that industrialization was the great growth stimulant of the second half of the nineteenth century, it must be recalled that New York also industrialized and did it while maintaining its status atop the commercial and financial world. In other words, it was possible to industrialize, trade, and finance all at once. Indeed, the three undoubtedly created synergies that led to still further industrialization, trade, and financial preeminence. That is why New York is now a world-class city and home to over 8 million people while Philadelphia is an economic and business backwater, home to about 1.5 million souls. Like Chestnut Street's financial institutions, Manayunk's mills and the Delaware Valley's other industries eventually lost their competitiveness and withered.[25]

Few vestiges of the city's past greatness still linger. The U.S. Mint survives, but it is arguably less important today than it was even in the 1790s. Ditto the Philadelphia Stock Exchange, which has done an admirable job of staving off extinction by nimbly responding to niche needs. Nevertheless, the NYSE has long since dwarfed it in size and importance. Most of the city's banks and other financial intermediaries have folded or been subsumed into larger, more efficient institutions. Even the venerable Philadelphia Savings Fund Society eventually succumbed and merged itself away. Vanguard, the mutual fund giant, inhabits Valley Forge, about twenty miles northeast of Chestnut Street. The big publishers are all gone, off to New York or oblivion. Late twentieth-century efforts to revive the Delaware River's shipbuilding industry were almost laughable. The region's pharmaceutical industry is still strong, but it, too, may give way to inexpensive imports from India. A mini–Silicon Valley has arisen of late along the Route 202 corridor in Chester County, and a few defense contractors are still about, hiding behind Americans' understandable reluctance to outsource critical weapons systems. But much of the region's economic activity is service oriented—education, tourism, health care. Philadelphia is not depressed, but neither is it elated.[26]

Wall Street remains the center of the nation's financial system, but there are cracks in its almost two-century-old edifice. Faint malodorous breezes during the 1990s stock market boom waxed in the early years of the third millennium into the stench of rot. Numerous scandals—fake accounting, pension fund frauds, IPO price manipulation, disingenuous stock analysts, piss-poor corporate governance, outrageous salaries for the head of the stock exchange, high-visibility insider trading scandals, even shenanigans by allegedly staid mutual funds—may portend the beginning of the end.

Finance, as we have seen, is a very competitive service industry. If the costs of geographical clustering outweigh the benefits, rapid decentralization will occur. If the costs of a *particular* geographical clustering outweigh the benefits, a quick shift to a new center—Chicago, San Francisco, Charlotte, Philadelphia—could take place, especially if the federal government gets involved. Continued scandals—combined with the maturation of the Internet, a shift in government policy, and perhaps another terrorist attack—could end Wall Street's hegemony. America has already changed its financial center once, from Philadelphia to New York in 1836. It could switch again. The transformation might injure the economy for a time. After all, the United States suffered a major recession the last time it underwent financial heart transplant surgery. But as long as the financial sector survives—and without major political upheaval it will—the nation's economy will continue to grow in real per capita terms.

NOTES

CHAPTER ONE

1. For Philadelphia's early physical layout, see Mary Schweitzer, "The Spatial Organization of Federalist Philadelphia," *Journal of Interdisciplinary History* 24 (1993): 31–59.

2. A good recent overview of the economic growth literature is Ross Levine, "More on Finance and Growth: More Finance, More Growth?" *Federal Reserve Bank of St. Louis Review* 85 (2003): 31–46.

3. For a description of America's role in the twentieth century, see Alfred Eckes Jr. and Thomas Zeiler, *Globalization and the American Century* (New York: Cambridge University Press, 2003).

4. A superb introduction to the colonial economy is John J. McCusker and Russell R. Menard, *The Economy of British America: 1607–1789* (Chapel Hill: University of North Carolina Press, 1985).

5. For more about the relationship between institutions and productivity, see William W. Lewis, *The Power of Productivity: Wealth, Poverty, and the Threat to Global Stability* (Chicago: University of Chicago Press, 2004). On average, slave labor was cost-efficient for individual slaveholders but inefficient for the entire economy because slavery created a number of large negative externalities, the cost of which slaveholders managed to impose on society. For a fuller explication of this point, see Robert E. Wright, "Bound and Unbound Labor: Socioeconomic Decision-Making," in *Against Slavery: Systems and Institutions of Immediacy,* ed. James Mueller (Philadelphia: University of Pennsylvania Press, forthcoming).

6. Robert E. Wright, *The Wealth of Nations Rediscovered: Integration and Expansion in American Financial Markets, 1780–1850* (New York: Cambridge University Press, 2002), 193–211.

7. Except where otherwise noted, this section is based on Robert E. Wright, "New Financial Services: Banks, Insurance, and Brokerage," in *Financial Revolution: The Financial Transition in Early America, 1750 to 1820,* ed. Cathy Matson and Richard Sylla (New York: Cambridge University Press, forthcoming).

8. Robert E. Wright, "Origins of Commercial Banking in the United States, 1781–1830," *EH.Net Encyclopedia,* http:// www.eh.net / encyclopedia / contents / wright.banking.commercial.origins.php.

9. Sharon Ann Murphy, "Life Insurance in the United States through World War I," *EH.Net Encyclopedia,* http:// www.eh.net / encyclopedia / murphy.life.insurance.us.php; Melissa Thomasson, "Health Insurance in the United States," *EH.Net Encyclopedia,* http:// www.eh.net / encyclopedia / thomasson.insurance.health.us.php.

10. This section is based on Frederic Mishkin, *The Economics of Money, Banking, and Financial Markets*, 7th ed. (New York: Pearson, 2004), 169–334.

11. This is simply to say that compared to most other places in the world, the United States possessed more liquid securities markets and more per capita banking capital. For more about America's financial rivals, see Larry Neal, *The Rise of Financial Capitalism: International Capital Markets in the Age of Reason* (New York: Cambridge University Press, 1990). The classic international comparison of financial sector depth is Raymond W. Goldsmith, *Comparative National Balance Sheets: A Study of Twenty Countries, 1688–1978* (Chicago: University of Chicago Press, 1985). A more recent comparison is Robert E. Wright, "Early U.S. Financial Development in Comparative Perspective: New Data, Old Comparisons," NBER Financial Markets Conference, Cambridge, MA, December 5, 2003.

12. Eckes and Zeiler, *Globalization and the American Century*, 199–201.

13. Charles Kindleberger, *Manias, Panics, and Crashes: A History of Financial Crisis*, 4th ed. (New York: John Wiley and Sons, 2000), 62–63, 177, 189–95; Edward Chancellor, *Devil Take the Hindmost: A History of Financial Speculation* (New York: Penguin, 1999), 191–232.

14. This section is based on a masterly history of the Federal Reserve: Allan Meltzer, *A History of the Federal Reserve*, vol. 1, *1913–1951* (Chicago: University of Chicago Press, 2003); and Mishkin, *Economics of Money*, 335–432.

15. Before that it was a different story. See Thomas E. Hall, *The Rotten Fruits of Economic Controls and the Rise from the Ashes, 1965–1989* (Lanham, MD: University Press of America, 2003).

16. For overviews of financial sector regulation, see Stuart Banner, *Anglo-American Securities Regulation: Cultural and Political Roots, 1680–1860* (New York: Cambridge University Press, 1998); David McCaffrey and David Hart, *Wall Street Polices Itself* (New York: Cambridge University Press, 1998); and Mark Stevens, *The Big Eight: An Incisive Look Behind the Pinstripe Curtain of Eight Accounting Firms* (New York: Collier, 1981).

17. On U.S. productivity, see Lewis, *Power of Productivity*, 80–104. On corporate finance, see John Micklethwait and Adrian Wooldridge, *The Company: A Short History of a Revolutionary Idea* (New York: Modern Library, 2003).

18. U.S. Census Bureau, *1997 Economic Census Summary: Finance and Insurance* (Washington, DC: U.S. Department of Commerce, 2001), http://www.census.gov/prod/ec97/97f52-sm.pdf; Robert E. Wright and George David Smith, *Mutually Beneficial: The Guardian and Life Insurance in America* (New York: New York University Press, 2004), 266–70, 401.

19. For a vivid description of the rise of virtual states and companies, see Richard Rosecrance, *The Rise of the Virtual State: Wealth and Power in the Coming Century* (New York: Basic Books, 1999).

20. A good history of early Wall Street is Walter Werner and Steven Smith, *Wall Street* (New York: Columbia University Press, 1991). Except where otherwise noted, this section is based on Wright, *Wealth of Nations Rediscovered*.

21. Bernard Bailyn et al., *The Great Republic: A History of the American People*, 4th ed. (Lexington, MA: D.C. Heath, 1992), 338.

22. Bray Hammond, *Banks and Politics in America: From the Revolution to the Civil War* (Princeton, NJ: Princeton University Press, 1957), 405–50.

CHAPTER TWO

1. McCusker and Menard, *Economy of British America*, 189, 193.

2. "An Act Appointing Wardens for the Port of Philadelphia, and for other Purposes therein mentioned," *Pennsylvania Statutes* (1772).

3. For a comparison of U.S. ports, see Robert Albion, *The Rise of New York Port, 1817–*

1860 (New York: Charles Scribner's Sons, 1939); and David Gilchrist, ed., *The Growth of the Seaport Cities, 1790–1825* (Charlottesville: University Press of Virginia, 1967).

4. For descriptions of the fever and its effects, see J. H. Powell, *Bring Out Your Dead: The Great Plague of Yellow Fever in Philadelphia in 1793* (Philadelphia: University of Pennsylvania Press, 1949).

5. On Baltimore's growth, see Edward Papenfuse, *In Pursuit of Profit: The Annapolis Merchants in the Era of the American Revolution, 1763–1805* (Baltimore: Johns Hopkins University Press, 1975). On the ways that slavery injured urban development, see John Majewski, *A House Dividing: Economic Development in Pennsylvania and Virginia Before the Civil War* (New York: Cambridge University Press, 2000). On the Chesapeake's international credit system, see Jacob Price, *Capital and Credit in British Overseas Trade: The View from the Chesapeake, 1700–1776* (Cambridge: Harvard University Press, 1980).

6. Wright, "Bound and Unbound Labor." Technically, a groat was a small silver coin worth 4 pence.

7. For more about Anglican treatment of Quakers in England, see Craig Horle, *The Quakers and the English Legal System, 1660–1688* (Philadelphia: University of Pennsylvania Press, 1988). For more about the Quaker migration and its impact on the New World, see David Hackett Fischer, *Albion's Seed: Four British Folkways in America* (New York: Oxford University Press, 1989), 419–604.

8. The best economic history of eighteenth-century Philadelphia is Thomas Doerflinger, *A Vigorous Spirit of Enterprise: Merchants and Economic Development in Revolutionary Philadelphia* (Chapel Hill: University of North Carolina Press, 1986).

9. Adam Smith, *An Inquiry into the Nature and Causes of the Wealth of Nations* (London: W. Strahan & T. Cadell, 1776), 538.

10. Robert E. Wright, "Thomas Willing," in *Lawmaking and Legislators in Pennsylvania: A Biographical Dictionary,* vol. 3, ed. Craig Horle and Joseph Foster (Harrisburg: Pennsylvania House of Representatives, 2005); Robert E. Wright, "Thomas Willing (1731–1821): Philadelphia Financier and Forgotten Founding Father," *Pennsylvania History* 63 (1996): 525–60.

11. Except where otherwise noted, this section is based on Robert E. Wright, *Origins of Commercial Banking in America, 1750–1800* (New York: Rowman and Littlefield, 2001), 149–186; Robert E. Wright, "Ground Rents against Populist Historiography: Mid-Atlantic Land Tenure, 1750–1820," *Journal of Interdisciplinary History* 29 (1998): 23–42; and Robert E. Wright, "John Potts, Ground Rents, and the Early Economic Development of Pottstown, 1752–1776," *Bulletin of the Historical Society of Montgomery County* 31 (1999): 5–18.

12. Bruce Mann, *Republic of Debtors: Bankruptcy in the Age of American Independence* (Cambridge: Harvard University Press, 2002), 78–146.

13. William Allen to John Criswell, October 2, 1754, William Allen Letterbook, Burd-Shippen-Hubley Papers, Historical Society of Pennsylvania.

14. For more about colonial Pennsylvania's loan offices, see Mary Schweitzer, *Custom and Contract: Household, Government, and the Economy in Colonial Pennsylvania* (New York: Columbia University Press, 1987).

15. Robert E. Wright, *Hamilton Unbound: Finance and the Creation of the American Republic* (Westport, CT: Praeger, 2002), 19–26.

16. *Pennsylvania Chronicle,* December 28, 1767.

17. For more on the history of ground rents, see Richard Cadwalader, *A Practical Treatise on the Law of Ground Rents in Pennsylvania* (Philadelphia: Kay, 1879). For exchange-rate fluctuations, the best source by far is John J. McCusker, *Money and Exchange in Europe and America, 1600–1775: A Handbook* (Chapel Hill: University of North Carolina

Press, 1978). William Allen to David Barclay and Sons, February 4, May 23, November 16, 1758; June 20, October 18, 1759; February 9, October 20, 1760; September 11, 1761, William Allen Letterbook, Burd-Shippen-Hubley Papers, Historical Society of Pennsylvania.

18. Except where otherwise noted, this section is based on J. A. Fowler, *History of Insurance in Philadelphia for Two Centuries (1683–1882)* (Philadelphia: American Publishing and Engraving Co., 1888).

19. David J. Cowen and Robert E. Wright, *Financial Founding Fathers* (Chicago: University of Chicago Press, forthcoming) contains extensive biographies of both Willing and Morris.

20. Wright, "Thomas Willing," *Pennsylvania History,* 531.

21. David A. Moss, *When All Else Fails: Government as the Ultimate Risk Manager* (Cambridge, MA: Harvard University Press, 2002), 22–52.

22. Except where noted, this section is based on Fowler, *History of Insurance.*

23. Simeon Baldwin, "American Business Corporations Before 1789," *American Historical Association Report* 1 (1903): 253–74.

24. This section is based on Wright and Smith, *Mutually Beneficial,* 15–25, 403–4; and Murphy, "Life Insurance." Unfortunately, this book was completed before Sharon Murphy's excellent dissertation was available. Sharon Murphy, "Security in an Uncertain World: Life Insurance and the Emergence of Modern America" (PhD diss., University of Virginia, 2005).

25. This section is based on Leslie Brock, *The Currency of the American Colonies, 1700–1764: A Study in Colonial Finance and Imperial Relations* (New York: Arno Press, 1975).

26. Wright, "Thomas Willing," *Pennsylvania History,* 529.

27. Hendrick Oudenaarde, *Seven Letters to the Honourable Daniel Horsmanden, Esq.; Concerning the Unnecessary and Cruel Imprisonment of Hendrick Oudenaarde, Late Merchant in the City of New York* (New York: William Weyman, 1766); *New York Journal,* November 12, 1767, September 2, 1768; *Pennsylvania Gazette,* September 27, December 13, 1770; January 3, May 16, December 12, 1771; April 13, 1774.

28. Wright, *Origins of Commercial Banking,* 60.

29. For excellent descriptions of the economy of colonial Pennsylvania, see James Lemon, *The Best Poor Man's Country: A Geographical Study of Early Southeastern Pennsylvania* (Baltimore: Johns Hopkins University Press, 1972); Alice Hanson Jones, *The Wealth of a Nation to Be: The American Colonies of the Eve of the Revolution* (New York: Columbia University Press, 1980); William Pollard Letterbook, Historical Society of Pennsylvania.

CHAPTER THREE

1. This section is based on Wright, *Hamilton Unbound,* 9–56.

2. Johan Christopher Sauer, letter, 1724, Haverford College Library.

3. Algebraically, the price of an asset is equal to $P = C/(1 + i) + C/(1 + i)^2 + \ldots (C + F)/(1 + i)^n$ where C = the yearly income produced by the asset; i = the market interest rate; F = the face, par, or sale value of the asset; and n = year to maturity (principal repayment) or sale. The key feature of the equation to note here is that the interest-rate variable is in the denominator. As it grows larger, therefore, P must grow smaller, holding C and F constant. For further details, see Mishkin, *Economics of Money,* 61–84.

4. John Locke, *Two Treatises on Government* (London: Awnsham Churchill, 1690).

5. This section is based on Richard Buell Jr., *In Irons: Britain's Naval Supremacy and the American Revolutionary Economy* (New Haven, CT: Yale University Press, 1998); and Paul Studenski and Herman Krooss, *Financial History of the United States* (Washington, DC: Beard Books, 2003).

6. Robert E. Wright, "Revolution: Finance," in *Encyclopedia of the New American Nation*, ed. Paul Finkelman et al. (New York: Charles Scribner's Sons, 2005).

7. "Descriptions of Counterfeit Bills" (Philadelphia, 1779); Albert S. Bolles, *Financial History of the United States from 1774 to 1789* (New York: D. Appleton, 1879), 150–57.

8. This section is based on Ron Michener, "Fixed Exchange Rates and the Quantity Theory," *Carnegie-Rochester Conference Series on Public Policy* 27 (1987): 745–53; Ron Michener, "Money in the American Colonies," *EH.Net Encyclopedia,* http://www.eh.net/encyclopedia/contents/michener.american.colonies.money.php.

9. Thomas McKean, "An account of money lost by the depreciation," January 1, 1780, Historical Society of Pennsylvania; Catharine Ray Greene to Benjamin Franklin, May 8, 1782, in William Greene Roelker, *Benjamin Franklin and Catharine Ray Greene: Their Correspondence, 1755–1790* (Philadelphia: American Philosophical Society, 1949), 147.

10. Wright, *Origins of Commercial Banking,* 49–75.

11. The best recent history of the Bank of North America is George Rappaport, *Stability and Change in Revolutionary Pennsylvania: Banks, Politics, and Social Structure* (University Park: Pennsylvania State University Press, 1996).

12. Wright, *Origins of Commercial Banking,* 64, 91. For an excellent overview of counterfeiting, see Stephen Mihm, *Making Money, Creating Confidence: Counterfeiting and Capitalism in the United States, 1789–1877* (Cambridge, MA: Harvard University Press, forthcoming), and Stephen Mihm, "Making Money, Creating Confidence: Counterfeiting and Capitalism in the United States, 1789–1877" (PhD diss., New York University, 2003).

13. This section is based on Ron Michener and Robert E. Wright, "State 'Currencies' and the Transition to the U.S. Dollar: Clarifying Some Confusions," *American Economic Review* (June 2005): 682–703.

14. This is not to say that there were not periods when paper money was the standard. Britain, for example, "went off" specie from 1797 to 1821 to help finance the struggle against Napoléon. The United States, too, occasionally resorted to paper money for brief periods during financial panics. But until the Nixon administration, the United States always returned to a gold (and sometimes silver) anchor.

15. The best source for early U.S. banking statistics is still J. Van Fenstermaker, *The Development of American Commercial Banking: 1782–1837* (Kent, OH: Kent State University, 1965).

16. This section is based on E. J. Ferguson, *Power of the Purse: A History of American Public Finance, 1776–1790* (Chapel Hill: University of North Carolina Press, 1961).

17. Mathew McConnell, *An Essay on the Domestic Debts of the United States of America* (Philadelphia: Robert Aitkin, 1787), iii—iv.

18. Wright, *Wealth of Nations Rediscovered,* 51–74.

19. McConnell, *An Essay on the Domestic Debts,* iv, 49–52.

20. Except where otherwise noted, this section is based on Wright, *Hamilton Unbound,* 59–88.

21. E. James Ferguson et al., eds., *The Papers of Robert Morris, 1781–1784,* 9 vols. (Pittsburgh: University of Pittsburgh Press, 1973–99), 9:691.

22. McConnell, *An Essay on the Domestic Debts,* 52.

CHAPTER FOUR

1. Except where otherwise noted, the first part of this chapter, up to the discussion of the U.S. Mint, is based on Michener and Wright, "State 'Currencies.'"

2. Mishkin, *Economics of Money,* 46.

3. Armen Alchian, *Economic Forces at Work* (Indianapolis: Liberty Fund, 1977), 111–23.

4. The best historical overview of U.S. monetary issues is still Richard Timberlake, *Monetary Policy in the United States: An Intellectual and Institutional History* (Chicago: University of Chicago Press, 1993).

5. For a fuller discussion of the transition from commodity to fiat money, see Thomas Sargent and François Velde, *The Big Problem of Small Change* (Princeton, NJ: Princeton University Press, 2002).

6. *Pennsylvania Chronicle,* January 4, 1768.

7. *Pennsylvania Gazette,* June 4, 1767; *Maryland Journal,* July 28, 1786.

8. "Despite Euro, Buck Rules Russia," www.CNN.com, January 2, 2002.

9. *Pennsylvania Statutes,* March 30, 1723; *Pennsylvania Gazette,* September 16, 1742; February 15, 1775.

10. *Pennsylvania Gazette,* September 16, 1742; June 4, 1767.

11. *Pennsylvania Gazette,* November 17, 1757.

12. *Pennsylvania Gazette,* October 16, 1755; December 6, 1764; April 23, 1772.

13. David T. Flynn, "Credit in the Colonial American Economy," *EH.Net Encyclopedia,* http://www.eh.net/encyclopedia/contents/flynn.colonialcredit.php.

14. Wilbur Plummer, "Consumer Credit in Colonial Philadelphia," *Pennsylvania Magazine of History and Biography* 66 (1942): 385–409.

15. Gary Gorton, "Reputation Formation in Early Bank Note Markets," *Journal of Political Economy* 104 (1996): 346–97.

16. Edward Stevens, "Composition of the Money Stock Prior to the Civil War," *Journal of Money, Credit and Banking* 3 (1971): 84–101.

17. Except where otherwise noted, this section is based on Andrew Smith, *Coins and Coinage: The United States Mint* (Philadelphia: A. M. Smith, 1881); George G. Evans, *Illustrated History of the United States Mint with a Complete Description of American Coinage, from the Earliest Period to the Present Time* (Philadelphia: G. G. Evans, 1888); and Jesse Watson, *The Bureau of the Mint: Its History, Activities and Organization* (Baltimore: Johns Hopkins University Press, 1926).

18. For an overview of Rittenhouse's fascinating life, see Edward Ford, *David Rittenhouse, Astronomer-Patriot* (Philadelphia: University of Pennsylvania Press, 1946); and William Barton, *Memoirs of the Life of David Rittenhouse* (Philadelphia: Edward Parker, 1813). David Rittenhouse to Thomas Jefferson, June 16, 1792, David Rittenhouse Letterbook, Historical Society of Pennsylvania.

19. Committee on the Mint, *Report on the State of the Mint,* U.S. 3rd Congress. House. (Philadelphia: Francis Childs, 1795), 5–8.

20. Samuel Moore to Joseph Anderson, March 21, 1831, Rush Collection, Library Company of Philadelphia.

21. George Washington to Alexander Hamilton, November 29, 1792, Papers of George Washington, Library of Congress.

22. Oliver Wolcott, *Letter from the Secretary, Inclosing Sundry Statements Prepared Under the Direction of the Comptroller of the Treasury* (Philadelphia: Way and Groff, 1799), tables A–E.

23. House of Representatives, *Report of the Committee to Whom Was Referred . . . a Letter from the Secretary of State* (Philadelphia, 1797), 115–20.

24. United States Senate, *Executive Documents of the U.S. Senate,* 32nd Congress, 2nd Session, nos. 21, 39.

25. George Boyd, *Elias Boudinot: Patriot and Statesman, 1740–1821* (Princeton, NJ:

Princeton University Press, 1952), 198, 218; Gordon Wood, *The Creation of the American Republic, 1776–1787* (New York: W. W. Norton, 1969), 46–124; House of Representatives, *Report of the Committee* (1797), 118.

26. Elias Boudinot, *Orders and Directions for Conducting the Mint of the United States* (Philadelphia: John Fenno, 1795), 33–36.

27. Chester Destler, *Joshua Coit: American Federalist, 1758–1798* (Middletown, CT: Wesleyan University Press, 1962), 56, 75–86; Boyd, *Elias Boudinot*, 222–52; Committee on the Mint, *Report on the State of the Mint, Annals,* 3rd Congress, 2nd session, 971; "Report of the Committee Appointed on the Mint with Outlines of Some Laws to Be Passed, January 1795," Society Collection, U.S. Mint, Historical Society of Pennsylvania.

28. James Soltow, *The Economic Role of Williamsburg* (Charlottesville: University Press of Virginia, 1965), 108–76; John Hickcox, *An Historical Account of American Coinage* (Albany, NY: Joel Munsell, 1858); Louis Jordan, *John Hull, the Mint and the Economics of Massachusetts Coinage* (Lebanon, NH: University Press of New England, 2002).

29. Henry William De Saussure, U.S. Government Correspondence, 1795, De Saussure Papers, South Carolina Historical Society; George Selgin, "Steam, Hot Air, and Small Change: Matthew Boulton and the Reform of Britain's Coinage," *Economic History Review* 56 (2003): 478–509.

30. Boudinot, *Orders and Directions*, 3–11; G. Ohrenzeller for Benjamin Rush to the Phoenix Insurance Company, August 25, 1807, McAllister Collection, Library Company of Philadelphia.

31. *Documents Accompanying a Bill, To Repeal so Much of Two Acts of Congress as Relate to the Establishment of a Mint* (Washington, DC: William Duane, 1802), 10.

32. George Washington to Timothy Pickering, September 16, 1795; George Washington to Henry William De Saussure, November 1, 1795, Papers of George Washington, Library of Congress.

33. Boyd, *Elias Boudinot,* 222–52.

34. U.S. Senate, *The Committee to Whom Was Referred* (1800), 2.

35. *Documents Accompanying a Bill,* 5–6; Uriah Tracy to Elias Boudinot, February 17, 1802, Gratz, U.S. Senators, Historical Society of Pennsylvania.

36. For details of the exchange, see 29 Rush Collection 20, 23, 24–32, 40–53, 57, Library Company of Philadelphia.

37. Alexander James Dallas to Elias Boudinot, November 27, 1802, George Green Shackelford Papers, University of Virginia Special Collections.

38. For an overview of the controversy, see Richard McCulloh, *The Proceedings of the Late Director of the Mint, in Relation to the Official Misconduct of Franklin Peale, Esq., Chief Coiner, and Other Abuses in the Mint* (Princeton, NJ, 1853); Register of the Medal Dies of the U.S. with Notes & ca., Chief Coiner's Office Mint of the United States 1841–1849, Historical Society of Pennsylvania; Ebenezer Stevens & Sons to R. Rush, September 28, 1821, 23 Rush Collection 121, Library Company of Philadelphia.

39. Except where otherwise noted, the rest of this chapter is based on the U.S. Mint and the James Snowden sections of the Society Collection, Historical Society of Pennsylvania.

40. Christian Gobrecht Collection, 1795–1844, Historical Society of Pennsylvania.

41. For more about the mint in Georgia, see William R. Cavasher, "The United States Branch Mint at Dahlonega, Georgia" (MA thesis, Southern Illinois University, 1975); Clair Birdsall, *The United States Branch Mint at Dahlonega, Georgia: Its History and Coinage* (Easley, SC: Southern Historical Press, 1984); and Sylvia Head, *The Neighborhood Mint: Dahlonega in the Age of Jackson* (Macon, GA: Mercer University Press, 1986).

CHAPTER FIVE

1. For more on Hamilton, see Ron Chernow, *Alexander Hamilton* (New York: Penguin Press, 2004); Harvey Flaumenhaft, *The Effective Republic: Administration and Constitution in the Thought of Alexander Hamilton* (Raleigh, NC: Duke University Press, 1992); Louis M. Hacker, *Alexander Hamilton in the American Tradition* (New York: McGraw-Hill, 1957); Forrest McDonald, *Alexander Hamilton: A Biography* (New York: W. W. Norton, 1979); John C. Miller, *Alexander Hamilton: Portrait in Paradox* (New York: Harper & Brothers, 1959); Broadus Mitchell, *Alexander Hamilton: The National Adventure, 1788–1804* (New York: Macmillan, 1962); and Willard Randall, *Alexander Hamilton: A Life* (New York: HarperCollins, 2002).

2. Cowen and Wright, *Financial Founding Fathers;* Richard Brookhiser, *Gentleman Revolutionary: Gouverneur Morris—The Rake Who Wrote the Constitution* (New York: Free Press, 2003).

3. William L. Smith, *The Politicks and Views of a Certain Party, Displayed* (Philadelphia, 1792), 4.

4. John Wood, *Monetary Policy in Four Democracies: Four Resumptions and the Great Depression* (Great Barrington, MA: American Institute for Economic Research, 2000), 3.

5. As quoted in Fowler, *History of Insurance,* 36.

6. Except where noted, this section is based on David J. Cowen, *The Origins and Economic Impact of the First Bank of the United States, 1791–1797* (New York: Garland, 2000).

7. William Constable to ?, April 15, 1794, William Constable Letterbook, 1793–1794, New York Historical Society.

8. Albert Gallatin, *Report of the Secretary of the Treasury, to Whom Was Referred the Memorial of the Stockholders of the Bank of the United States* (Washington, DC: R. C. Weightman, 1809), 4.

9. Cowen and Wright, *Financial Founding Fathers.*

10. Gallatin, *Report of the Secretary of the Treasury,* 13.

11. Hammond, *Banks and Politics in America,* 197–226.

12. Cowen and Wright, *Financial Founding Fathers.*

13. For more on Girard's bank, see Donald Adams, *Finance and Enterprise in Early America: A Study of Stephen Girard's Bank, 1812–1831* (Philadelphia: University of Pennsylvania Press, 1978).

14. Except where noted, this section is based on Wright, *Wealth of Nations Rediscovered,* and is informed by Max Edling, *A Revolution in Favor of Government: Origins of the U.S. Constitution and the Making of the American State* (New York: Oxford University Press, 2003).

15. For a wealth of details about the national debt, see Jonathan Elliot, *The Funding System of the United States and Great Britain* (Washington, DC: Blair and Rives, 1845); and Robert E. Wright, ed., *The U.S. National Debt, 1785–1900,* 4 vols. (London: Pickering and Chatto, 2005).

16. James MacDonald, *A Free Nation Deep in Debt: The Financial Roots of Democracy* (New York: Farrar, Straus and Giroux, 2003), 292–306; John Steele Gordon, *Hamilton's Blessing: The Extraordinary Life and Times of Our National Debt* (New York: Penguin, 1997), 11–41.

17. The national debt transfer ledgers survive to this day in the National Archives and Records Administration's vaults in College Park, Maryland. For the newspaper prices, see Richard Sylla, Jack Wilson, and Robert E. Wright, "Database of Early U.S. Securities Prices," Inter-University Consortium for Political and Social Research, Ann Arbor, Michigan.

18. *Pennsylvania Gazette,* October 13, 1784; September 14, 1785; March 15, 1786.

19. Except where otherwise noted, this section is based on Wright, *Wealth of Nations Rediscovered,* 26–166.

20. Robert E. Wright, "Reforming the U.S. IPO Market: Lessons from History and Theory," *Accounting, Business, and Financial History* 12 (2002): 419–37.

21. Harvey Tuckett, *Practical Remarks on the Present State of Life Insurance in the United States* (Philadelphia: Peters and Smith, 1850), 17.

22. Thomas Law, *Considerations Tending to Render the Policy Questionable of Plans for Liquidating, within the Next Four Years, the Six Per Cent. Stocks of the United States* (Washington, DC: S. A. Elliot, 1826), 4.

23. Robert E. Wright, "Banking and Politics in New York, 1784–1829" (PhD diss., SUNY Buffalo, 1997), 951–71.

24. Gallatin, *Report of the Secretary of the Treasury,* 10.

25. Except where otherwise noted, this section is based on Wright, *Origins of Commercial Banking;* Howard Bodenhorn, *A History of Banking in Antebellum America: Financial Markets and Economic Development in an Era of Nation-Building* (Cambridge: Cambridge University Press); Naomi Lamoreaux, *Insider Lending: Banks, Personal Connections, and Economic Development in Industrial New England* (Cambridge: Cambridge University Press, 1994); and Paul Lockard, "Banks, Insider Lending, and Industries of the Connecticut River Valley of Massachusetts, 1813–1860" (PhD diss., University of Massachusetts, 2000).

26. *Speech of Mr. Keating in the House of Representatives of Pennsylvania* (Harrisburg, PA: Henry Welsh, 1834), 31; Adams, *Finance and Enterprise,* 126–27.

27. *Freeman's Journal,* December 13, 1786.

28. Wilkins and Atkinson, Daybook, 1808, Historical Society of Pennsylvania.

29. Patrick O'Bannon, "Inconsiderable Progress: Commercial Brewing in Philadelphia Before 1840," in *Early American Technology: Making and Doing Things from the Colonial Era to 1850,* ed. Judith McGaw (Chapel Hill: University of North Carolina Press, 1994), 148–63.

30. Bank of North America, Individual Ledgers, 1792, Historical Society of Pennsylvania.

31. *Speech of Mr. Keating,* 27. *Origins, Provisions, and Effect of the Safety Fund Law* (New York, 1834), in *History of Corporate Governance: The Importance of Stakeholder Activism,* ed. Robert E. Wright, Wray Barber, Matthew Crafton, and Anand Jain, 6 vols. (London: Pickering and Chatto, 2004), 2:197.

32. Margaret Moulder Account Book, Historical Society of Pennsylvania.

33. William Constable to ?, April 15, 1794, William Constable Letterbook, 1793–1794, New York Historical Society.

34. Thomas Fortune, *An Epitome of the Stocks and Public Funds* (1796), in *The History of Corporate Finance: Development of Anglo-American Securities Markets, Financial Practices, Theories and Laws,* 6 vols., ed. Robert E. Wright (London: Pickering and Chatto, 2003), 1:17–91. Except where otherwise noted, this section is based on Mira Wilkins, *The History of Foreign Investment in the United States to 1914* (Cambridge, MA: Harvard University Press, 1989).

35. Fowler, *History of Insurance,* 324; Joshua Gilpin, "Journal of a Tour from Philadelphia," Historical Society of Pennsylvania.

36. This section is based on Wright, "Early U.S. Financial Development."

37. See, for instance, Alexis de Tocqueville, *Democracy in America* (Chicago: University of Chicago Press, 2000), 293, 433–39, 594; and Michael Chevalier, *Society, Manners and*

Politics in the United States, Being a Series of Letters on North America (Gloucester, MA: Peter Smith, 1967), 292–302, 308, 345, 348–49, 351, 354, 447, 453, 466.

CHAPTER SIX

1. For women in business, see Wright, *Hamilton Unbound*, 173–94; and Robert E. Wright, "Women and Finance in the Early National U.S.," *Essays in History* 42 (2000), http:// etext.lib.virginia.edu / journals / EH / EH42 / Wright42.html.

2. These stories are amalgams of several incidents related in early newspapers and letters. They are, in short, fictional but informed by the realities of life in early America.

3. Israel Whelen Papers, William L. Clements Library, University of Michigan.

4. Except where otherwise noted, this section is based on Wright and Smith, *Mutually Beneficial,* and Fowler, *History of Insurance.*

5. A tontine is any investment pool where the profits fall to a surviving member or members. In its more extreme forms, it is a form of gambling on one's longevity. Less extreme forms, however, like deferred dividend life insurance policies, were legitimate investment vehicles. See Roger Ransom and Richard Sutch, "Tontine Insurance and the Armstrong Investigation: A Case of Stifled Innovation, 1868–1905," *Journal of Economic History* 47 (1987): 379–90.

6. *Proposals of the Pennsylvania Company for Insurances on Lives and Granting Annuities* (Philadelphia: James Key, Jr., and Brother, 1837).

7. Tuckett, *Practical Remarks on the Present State of Life Insurance,* 5, 17, 28–32.

8. Mann, *Republic of Debtors,* 87, 78–108.

9. This section is based on Fowler, *History of Insurance.*

10. Except where otherwise noted, this section is based on Fowler, *History of Insurance,* and Mary Ruwell, *Eighteenth-Century Capitalism: The Formation of American Marine Insurance Companies* (New York: Garland, 1993).

11. David and Philip Grim to Watson and Paul, February 4, 1799, Library Company of Philadelphia.

12. Sylla, Wilson, and Wright, "Database of Early U.S. Securities Prices."

CHAPTER SEVEN

1. The best study of early Philadelphia buildings to date is Donna Rilling, *Making Houses, Crafting Capitalism: Builders in Philadelphia, 1790–1850* (Philadelphia: University of Pennsylvania Press, 2001).

2. Except where otherwise noted, this section is based on Rilling, *Making Houses, Crafting Capitalism.*

3. Michener and Wright, "State 'Currencies.'"

4. For more on early New York savings banks, see Charles Knowles, *History of the Bank for Savings in the City of New York, 1819–1929* (New York: The Bank for Savings, 1929).

5. This section is based on Wright, "New Financial Services."

6. This section is based on Robert E. Wright, "Mordecai Noah's *Essays of Howard* and the Transition of American Political Rhetoric," American Literature Association Annual Conference, Baltimore, Maryland, May 29, 1999.

7. For more on Noah, see Jonathan Sarna, *Jacksonian Jew: The Two Worlds of Mordecai Noah* (New York: Holmes & Meier, 1981); Michael Schuldiner and Daniel Kleinfeld, eds., *The Selected Writings of Mordecai Noah* (Westport, CT: Greenwood Press, 1999).

8. For more about the history of savings banks, see Knowles, *History of the Bank for Savings;* Oliver Horne, *A History of Savings Banks* (London: Oxford University Press,

1947); Emerson Keyes, *A History of Savings Banks in the United States* (New York: B. Rhodes, 1876); and Alan Olmstead, *New York City Mutual Savings Banks, 1819–1861* (Chapel Hill: University of North Carolina Press, 1976).

9. This section is based on James Willcox, *A History of the Philadelphia Savings Fund Society, 1816–1916* (Philadelphia: J. B. Lippincott, 1916).

10. The best study of how early savings banks actually functioned is Peter Payne and Lance Davis, *The Savings Bank of Baltimore, 1816–1866: A Historical and Analytical Study* (Baltimore, MD: Johns Hopkins University Press, 1956).

11. Wright, "New Financial Services."

12. This section is based on Henry Bodfish, *History of Building and Loan in the United States* (Chicago: United States Building and Loan League, 1931).

13. Readers interested in that story should consult David Mason, *From Building and Loans to Bail-Outs: A History of the American Savings and Loan Industry, 1831–1995* (New York: Cambridge University Press, 2004).

14. *An Ordinance for Raising Supplies, and Making Appropriations, for the Services and Exigencies of the City of Philadelphia, for the Year 1799* (Philadelphia: Zacharian Poulson, 1799); *Ordinances of the Corporation of the City of Philadelphia* (Philadelphia: Moses Thomas, 1812); *Accounts of the Corporation of the City of Philadelphia from the First of April, 1819* (Philadelphia, 1823).

15. James Stuart, *Three Years in North America* (New York: J & J Harper, 1833), 237. For more on the early Manhattan Company's operations, see Gregory Hunter, *The Manhattan Company: Managing a Multi-Unit Corporation in New York, 1799–1842* (New York: Garland, 1989).

CHAPTER EIGHT

1. Henry Fearon, *Sketches of America: A Narrative of a Journey of Five Thousand Miles through the Eastern and Western States of America* (London: Longman, Hurst, Rees, Orme, and Brown, 1818), 340–42; Basil Hall, *Travels in North America* (Edinburgh: Cadell and Co., 1829), 394.

2. This section is based on James Livingood, *The Philadelphia-Baltimore Trade Rivalry, 1780–1860* (Harrisburg: Pennsylvania Historical and Museum Commission, 1947).

3. Jean-Pierre Brissot de Warville, *New Travels in the United States, Performed in 1788* (London: J. S. Jordan, 1792), 260–61, 339–41.

4. Except where noted otherwise, this section is based on Donald Jackson, "Roads Most Traveled: Turnpikes in Southeastern Pennsylvania in the Early Republic," in *Early American Technology: Making and Doing Things from the Colonial Era to 1850*, ed. Judith McGaw (Chapel Hill: University of North Carolina Press, 1994), 197–239.

5. *An Act to Incorporate the Union Canal Company of Pennsylvania, with the Bye-Laws, Rules, Orders and Regulations Enacted at a Meeting of the Stockholders, on the 24th July, 1811* (Philadelphia: John Binns, 1811), 25–34.

6. Gilpin, "Journal of a Tour from Philadelphia."

7. J. David Lehman, "Explaining Hard Times: Political Economy and the Panic of 1819 in Philadelphia" (PhD diss., University of California at Los Angeles, 1992), 1–9.

8. Except where noted, this section is based on Livingood, *Philadelphia-Baltimore Trade Rivalry.*

9. This section is based on F. H. Stow, *The Capitalist's Guide and Railway Annual for 1859* (New York: Samuel Callahan, 1859), 7–20, 526–28, 536.

10. For more on New York State's development, see Nathan Miller, *Enterprise of a*

Free People: Aspects of Economic Development in New York State during the Canal Period, 1792–1838 (Ithaca, NY: Cornell University Press, 1962); and Beatrice Reubens, "State Financing of Private Enterprise in Early New York" (PhD diss., Columbia University, 1960).

11. The section on lotteries is based on *An Act to Incorporate the Union Canal Company;* Harrold Gillingham, "Lotteries in Philadelphia Prior to 1776," *Pennsylvania History* (1938): 77–100; Asa Martin, "Lotteries in Pennsylvania Prior to 1833," *Pennsylvania Magazine of History and Biography* (1923–24): 159–78, 66–96, 307–27; and Henrietta Larson, "S. & M. Allen—Lottery, Exchange, and Stock Brokerage," *Journal of Economic and Business History* 4 (1931): 424–45.

12. Cowen and Wright, *Financial Founding Fathers.*

13. *Public Works of Pennsylvania: Cost, Revenue and Expenditure Up to November 30, 1853* (Harrisburg, PA: A. Boyd Hamilton, 1853); "A Brief Review of the Financial History of Pennsylvania," in *Report of the Auditor General on the Finances of the Commonwealth of Pennsylvania* (Harrisburg, PA: Lane S. Hart, 1881), 266–316.

14. Majewski, *A House Dividing;* John Melish, *Travels in the United States of America,* 2 vols. (Philadelphia: For the Author, 1812), 1:153. For other vivid descriptions of Philadelphia and its denizens, see 1:150–56, 168–76, 371–74.

CHAPTER NINE

1. For more on these and other Chestnut Street financiers, see Wright, "Thomas Willing"; Eugene Slaski, "Thomas Willing: Moderation during the American Revolution" (PhD diss., Florida State University, 1971); Clarence Ver Steeg, *Robert Morris: Revolutionary Financier* (Philadelphia: University of Pennsylvania Press, 1954); Eleanor Young, *Forgotten Patriot: Robert Morris* (New York: Macmillan, 1950); Barbara Chernow, "Robert Morris and Alexander Hamilton: Two Financiers in New York," in *Business Enterprise in Early New York,* ed. Joseph Frese and Jacob Judd (Tarrytown, NY: Sleepy Hollow Press, 1979), 77–98; Robert C. Alberts, *The Golden Voyage: The Life and Times of William Bingham, 1752–1804* (Boston: Houghton Mifflin, 1969); Harry Emerson Wildes, *Lonely Midas: The Story of Stephen Girard* (New York: J. J. Little and Ives, 1943); Adams, *Finance and Enterprise.*

2. This chapter is based on Robert E. Wright, "Michael Hillegas," in *Lawmaking and Legislators in Pennsylvania,* vol. 3, ed. Craig Horle and Joseph Foster (Harrisburg: Pennsylvania House of Representatives, 2005). That essay contains copious primary source documentation of all of the points made here about Hillegas.

3. For more on the early coal industry, see Sean Patrick Adams, *Old Dominion, Industrial Commonwealth: Coal, Politics, and Economy in Antebellum America* (Baltimore, MD: Johns Hopkins University Press, 2004).

4. Joseph John Gurney, *A Journey in North America* (Norwich, Eng.: Josiah Fletcher, 1841), 89.

CHAPTER TEN

1. Gurney, *Journey in North America,* 134.

2. Except where otherwise noted, this section is based on Walter Buckingham Smith, *Economic Aspects of the Second Bank of the United States* (Cambridge, MA: Harvard University Press, 1953); Thomas Govan, *Nicholas Biddle: Nationalist and Public Banker, 1786–1844* (Chicago: University of Chicago Press, 1959); and Jean Wilburn, *Biddle's Bank: The Crucial Years* (New York: Columbia University Press, 1967).

3. Joseph Saltar, "Among the Causes that Contributed to the Growth and Prosperity of Buffalo," July 1862, William Beatty Rochester Papers, University of Rochester, New York.

4. This section is based on Donald Cole, *Martin Van Buren and the American Political System* (Princeton, NJ: Princeton University Press, 1984); and John Niven, *Martin Van Buren: The Romantic Age of American Politics* (New York: Oxford University Press, 1983).

5. For more on the nullification crisis, see Richard E. Ellis, *The Union at Risk: Jacksonian Democracy, States' Rights and the Nullification Crisis* (New York: Oxford University Press, 1987).

6. This section is based on Wright, "Banking and Politics," 1018–47.

7. For more on the Safety Fund, see Robert Chaddock, *The Safety Fund System in New York State, 1829–1866* (Washington, DC: Government Printing Office, 1910).

8. This section is based on Cowen and Wright, *Financial Founding Fathers;* and Hammond, *Banks and Politics in America,* 286–48.

9. Except where noted, this section is based on Robert Remini, *Andrew Jackson and the Bank War* (New York: W. W. Norton, 1967); and Robert Remini, *The Life of Andrew Jackson* (New York: Harper and Row, 1988).

10. *Speech of Mr. Keating,* 20–24; Adams, *Finance and Enterprise,* 139–41.

11. For more on the Independent Treasury, see David Kinley, *The Independent Treasury of the United States and Its Relations to the Banks of the Country* (Washington, DC: Government Printing Office, 1910).

12. This section is based on Bray Hammond, "The Chestnut Raid on Wall Street, 1839," *Quarterly Journal of Economics* 61 (1947): 605–18.

13. Ranald Michie, *The London and New York Stock Exchanges, 1750–1914* (London: Allen & Unwin, 1987), 170.

14. Eliza Cope Harrison, ed., *Philadelphia Merchant: The Diary of Thomas P. Cope, 1800–1851* (South Bend, IN: Gateway Editions, 1978), 428–29.

CHAPTER ELEVEN

1. The best overview of Philadelphia's trade rivalries remains Livingood, *Philadelphia-Baltimore Trade Rivalry.*

2. Fearon, *Sketches of America,* 340–47.

3. Except where otherwise noted, this chapter is based on Wright, *Wealth of Nations Rediscovered;* Robert E. Wright, ed., *The History of Corporate Finance: Development of Anglo-American Securities Markets, Financial Practices, Theories and Laws,* 6 vols. (London: Pickering and Chatto, 2003); and Robert E. Wright, Wray Barber, Matthew Crafton, and Anand Jain, eds., *History of Corporate Governance: The Importance of Stakeholder Activism,* 6 vols. (London: Pickering and Chatto, 2004).

4. According to the Census Bureau, in 2000, out of a total of 25 million American businesses of all types, 5 million, or 20 percent, were corporations. However, business corporations account for more than 65 percent of all net business income and more than 85 percent of all business receipts. U.S. Census Bureau, "Business Enterprise," *Statistical Abstract of the United States: 2003,* section 15, no. 731, 495, http://www.census.gov/prod/2004pubs/03statab/business.pdf.

5. Donald Adams, "The Beginning of Investment Banking in America," *Pennsylvania History* 45 (1978): 99–116.

6. Wilkins and Atkinson, Daybook, 1808, Historical Society of Pennsylvania.

7. George Taylor, *Effect of Incorporated Coal Companies upon the Anthracite Coal Trade of Pennsylvania* (Pottsville, PA: Benjamin Bannan, 1833), in Wright et al., *History of Corporate Governance,* 2:31–66.

8. Tuckett, *Practical Remarks on the Present State of Life Insurance,* 3.

9. William Tilghman to Edward Tilghman, March 4, 1790, William Tilghman Letterbook, Historical Society of Pennsylvania.

10. Carolyn Cooper, "A Patent Transformation: Woodworking Mechanization in Philadelphia, 1830–1856," in *Early American Technology: Making and Doing Things from the Colonial Era to 1850,* ed. Judith McGaw (Chapel Hill: University of North Carolina Press, 1994).

11. Fowler, *History of Insurance,* 320.

12. Taylor, *Effect of Incorporated Coal Companies,* 36–37, 43–44.

13. James Sullivan, *The Path to Riches: An Inquiry into the Origin and Use of Money; and into the Principles of Stocks and Banks* (Boston: P. Edes, 1792), 48; Fowler, *History of Insurance,* 47–50.

14. Moss, *When All Else Fails,* 25–26, 40, 74.

15. Taylor, *Effect of Incorporated Coal Companies,* 40.

16. Wright et al., *History of Corporate Governance,* 1:297–332.

17. Stow, *The Capitalist's Guide,* 7–20.

18. *An Act to Incorporate the Stockholders of the Bank of the United States of Pennsylvania* (Philadelphia: Joseph and William Kite, 1836).

19. This section is based on Taylor, *Effect of Incorporated Coal Companies,* 51–64.

20. Cooper, "A Patent Transformation," in *Early American Technology: Making and Doing Things from the Colonial Era to 1850,* ed. Judith McGaw (Chapel Hill: University of North Carolina Press, 1994), 278–327.

21. This section is based on Diane Lindstrom, *Economic Development in the Philadelphia Region, 1810–1850* (New York: Columbia University Press, 1978).

22. Eli Bowen, *The Pictorial Sketch-Book of Pennsylvania* (Philadelphia: Willis P. Hazard, 1852), 72–119.

23. For more on Philadelphia's early publishing industry, see Rosalind Remer, *Printers and Men of Capital: Philadelphia Book Publishers in the New Republic* (Philadelphia: University of Pennsylvania Press, 1996).

24. Ibid., 59.

25. Moreover, according to European financial historian Charles Kindleberger, "financial distinction appears to have followed temporally after supremacy in trade and to have been causally connected with the decline in trade." So if Philadelphia followed the European pattern, the loss of its trade should have enhanced its role as a financial center. Of course, America was not Europe. Charles Kindleberger, *Keynesianism vs. Monetarism and Other Essays in Financial History* (London: George Allen and Unwin, 1985), 158–59.

26. On the Philadelphia Stock Exchange, see John C. Caskey, "The Philadelphia Stock Exchange: Adapting to Survive in Changing Markets," *Business History Review* 78 (Autumn 2004): 451–87.

INDEX

Adams, John Quincy, 151–52
adverse selection, 5; in marine insurance, 21, 98. *See also* agency theory; asymmetric information
agency theory, 41–42. *See also* asymmetric information; principal-agent problem
Allen, William, 18, 20
Alsop, Richard, 162
American Fire Insurance Company of Philadelphia, 95–96, 108
American Insurance Company of Philadelphia, 100
American Revolution: book accounts during, 52; borrowing by governments during, 32–33, 39; causes of, 28, 31, 67; financial causes of, 29; financial innovation spurred by, 13; financing of, 32–33; inflation during, 33, 35; internecine struggles during, 32; lotteries during, 125; marine insurance markets disrupted by, 96; monetary causes of, 31; monetary chaos during, 32; prices of debt instruments issued by governments during, 37; seminal event in U.S. financial development, 131; support for among colonists, 32; taxation during, 32
amortized installment loans, 7
Amsterdam, 25, 82
Anti-Federalists, 42
Appleton, Nathaniel, 145
artisans: and banking, 78–79; financing options available to, 17. *See also* businesses
assets, 5
asymmetric information, 5, 6; conflicts between bondholders, stockholders, and managers and, 123; in life insurance, 91. *See also* adverse selection; agency theory; moral hazard; principal-agent problem
Atherton, Nathan, 79

Babbage, Charles, 76
balance sheets, 5
balloon loans, 7
Baltimore, 69, 118, 149; as early financial center, 11; economic hinterland of, 123, 129; ground rents in, 109; growth of, 15, 100; investors from, 161; as an ocean port, 15; savings banks of, 112; trade rivalry with Philadelphia of, 13, 119, 149
bank checks, 53
bank deposits, 35, 52
Bank for Savings (New York City), 109, 148
bank liabilities, 44, 52
bank loans, 166
bank money, vs. bills of credit, 37
banknotes, 6, 36, 53. *See also* bills of credit; commodity money; medium of exchange; money; paper money
Bank of England: as central bank, 68; as model for the Bank of North America, 36; refuses to aid the United States Bank of Pennsylvania, 161
Bank of New York: default rates of borrowers of, 77; formation of, 148
Bank of North America, 3, 36, 143; advice of to other banks, 36; anti-counterfeiting devices used by, 36–37; charter of, 68, 69; default rates of, 77; demand for the liabilities of, 36; deposits and checks of, 53; early operations of, 36; as early U.S. central bank, 68; economic functions of, 38; expansion of, 39; foreign investment in, 83; profitability of, 5–6
Bank of Pennsylvania, 3, 39
Bank of the United States (BUS) (1791–1811), 12, 71, 87; Alexander Hamilton's brainchild, 67–68, 148; branches of, 69; building of, 71; capital of, 69; central bank characteristics